MW00877946

Finding Fab-YOU-lous

A *Self-Help with Sass* Guide to
Finding, Celebrating and Capitalizing on
the Fab**YOU**lousness That Makes You,
YOU

by

Melissa Venable

Finding Fab-YOU-lous

Happy reading!
♡ Melissa
Venable

Finding Fab**YOU**lous   Melissa Venable

Version 1.0 – 2017

Published by *FabYOUlous Life Publishing*

ISBN: 978-1547233823

Copyright © 2017 by Melissa Venable

Discover other titles by Melissa Venable at
www.FabYOUlousLife.com

Cover design by Danielle Raine

This book is a work of non-fiction; however, names,
places and incidents may have been changed to protect
anonymity.

Any Internet references contained in this book are current
at publication time, but the publisher cannot guarantee
that a specific location will continue to be maintained.

All rights reserved, including the right of reproduction in
whole or in part in any form.

**For bulk ordering inquiries, please visit the contact
tab at *www.FabYOUlousLife.com***

In Gratitude

To my Superman, Dave. Thank you for helping me to see the best in myself and in others. Your encouragement has given me wings to soar, but your love is the nest to which I will ALWAYS return. I love you. Thank you for loving me.

To my boys, Walker and Creighton. Everything I do in this life is for you. You are my pride and joy, my hope and happiness, my sunshine and my laughter. Being your mom has been the greatest blessing of my life. No matter how old you are, your mama will ALWAYS love you more than all the stars in the sky.

To Becca. I didn't give you the gift of life but life gave me the gift of you, and for that I will be forever grateful. I love you sweet girl.

To my parents. "Well…did you learn anything?" Yes dad—I did. I learned that life is FabYOUlous if you make it so. I owe absolutely everything to you and mom. You've picked me up when I've fallen down, tough loved me when I needed it and always had my back. I love you both and am so grateful for the lessons that you both continue to teach me.

To my *broad squad*, Mia, Amy, Melisa, Kathy and Angela. Without you girls, I'd be drooling on myself in a padded room somewhere. Thank you for loving me, crying with me, cheering for me, and saving me TONS of money on therapy bills.

Table of Contents

Feeling Fab

FabYOUlously Connected

Fab Purpose

Be Sure to Visit
www.FabYOUlousLife.com/FindingFabYOUlousbookbonuses
for bonus material to guide you on your quest of Finding
FabYOUlous

Follow the Fab...

www.Facebook.com/FabYOUlousLife

www.Instagram.com/FabYOUlous_Life

www.Pinterest.com/FabYOUlousLife

www.Twitter.com/FabYOUlousLife

#FindingFabYOUlous #FabYOUlousLife #SelfHelpwithSass

INTRODUCTION

Hey you—yes, YOU. The one with your hair in a ponytail, wearing the same sweatpants that you wore yesterday…and the day before. Or, maybe it's *you*…the one in the business suit with the perfectly manicured nails, designer handbag and *not-so-designer* bags under your eyes from too many weeks of burning the candle at both ends. Or, perhaps it's *you*…the one who has the pretty good life with the pretty good job, pretty good family and pretty good headache from all of the stress of trying to keep up your pretty good façade. This book is for YOU.

This book is also for all of the *yous* out there who are going to work, raising families, burning the dinner, watching the Real Housewives (but denying it of course), taking night classes, trying to bring the sizzle back to your marriage and wondering to yourself just how in the world you got yourself into this exhausting hamster wheel of an existence. Please keep reading because this book is for YOU.

Okay—so maybe your circumstances aren't quite *that* dire. Maybe your life really is pretty decent. Maybe you're comfortable where you're at, and yet still can't deny the fact that there is a longing in your soul that craves something more. This book is *definitely* for YOU.

How do I know that this book is for you? Because I've been you. I *am* you. I know what it is like to feel as though you are stuck in a desperate, soul-sucking existence where just dragging your sorry self out of bed in the morning takes more energy than it's worth. On the flip-side, I also know what it is like to have a pretty good life and yet still feel like something huge is missing. I've been through hell and back (you'll read more about that later) but thankfully, I've learned a few lessons along the way—the most important of which, is that if your life is anything less than what you long for it to be, something is missing; and until you discover that crucial missing ingredient, your life will continue to be a struggle.

Thankfully, you don't have to search for that mystery ingredient any longer. I'm here to tell you that the one and ONLY thing that can transport your life from drab to FAB is...(drumroll please)...YOU. That is why this book is called Finding Fab**YOU**lous. Once you learn how to rediscover the person that you were created to be, and bring that incredible being back to life *in* your life, you will discover just how Fab**YOU**lous life can be.

This quest to rediscover, recharge and reinvigorate won't necessarily be easy—but I promise that it *will* be worth it. Life is a laboratory and it often requires lots of experimentation; so, consider this book to be your lab book. I will be here to guide you on your journey; however not so much in the role of teacher (though certainly you will learn) as in the role of "awakener", because much of what you will encounter on this journey already lies dormant within you. Your Fab**YOU**lousness just needs someone to find it, grab hold of it, shake some life into it and release it to do its work in your life, and in the world. I'm here to help facilitate that finding, grabbing, shaking and releasing. Don't worry though—unlike your high school or college lab classes, I can promise you that we are going to have a lot of fun along the way as we undertake this adventure together; because let's face it—how truly Fab**YOU**lous can something be if it's no fun, right? So, turn the page and let's set the wheels in motion to *ditch the drab and find your FAB*. Let's get busy finding Fab**YOU**lous.

Chapter 1

COME OUT, COME OUT, WHOEVER YOU ARE

Remember what it was like when you were seven years old playing Hide & Seek with your friends? You'd hear the "seeker" counting while you scurried around trying to find the perfect, undiscoverable hiding spot, and then, once you'd found it, you'd try so hard not to reveal your location by giggling when the seeker started to get "warm"?

Well, today we are going to embark upon a little game of Hide & Seek of the grown-up variety. We are going to go searching for all of the Fab**YOU**lousness inside of you that—for whatever reason—seems to have gone into hiding. Now, before you open your mouth and start to argue that there *is no* Fab**YOU**lousness inside of you, let me stop you right now and tell you that YES THERE IS! Every single person on this planet has gifts, talents, passions and purposes that (if utilized and allowed to grow and breathe) would flat-out astound anyone privileged enough to witness the transformation. These inner nuggets of Fab**YOU**lousness *are* there. Maybe you've felt them before. Maybe you've even had moments when they were the guiding force in your life before they became lost among the deadlines, to-do lists and drudgery of the modern existence. Maybe, on the other hand, you have no clue what I'm talking about. Maybe you feel like you are lost among the masses and that there can't possibly be anything special or unique, much less, *FabYOUlous* about you. Regardless of where you fall in this Fab**YOU**lous spectrum; keep reading because this game of Hide & Seek for your Fab**YOU**lous self is about to get interesting.

In the children's game of Hide & Seek, you crouch behind a bush in the backyard or skinny your way into the back of a closet in the house. You are hiding but you're not *lost*. You're not lost because you know exactly where you are, even if no one else does. Unfortunately, in the grown-up version of this Hide & Seek game, things are a bit more complicated because we often discover that we have gone beyond simply *hiding* our FabYOUlousness from the world and instead seem to have genuinely *lost* it…or maybe we wonder if we ever really had it in the first place.

Well, just like in childhood Hide & Seek, the true fun of the game begins once we are found. I mean, let's face it—hiding is fun for a while, but before long, crouching behind that bush starts to make our back ache and hiding in the back of that closet next to dad's smelly gym sneakers gets old in a hurry. It is when our friend joyfully *finds* us that we start to laugh and the game is able to continue on with us taking on the role of the seeker. Things are no different in this grown-up game of Finding FabYOUlous in that, once again, the fun is in the *finding*. The part that gets a little sticky in our grown-up version, is that in *this* game, you play the role of *both*, the seeker *and* the one being sought.

As I mentioned in the introduction, I know all too well what it is like to feel lost. I've been that desperate, sad woman who has lost all sense of self. In trying to be too many different things to too many different people, I managed to completely lose myself and my FabYOUlousness behind masks and facades that I had erected in an attempt to be the woman/wife/daughter/mother/friend/employee that I thought other people wanted and expected me to be. It wasn't until my life spiraled completely out of control (you'll read all of the juicy, horrible details in later chapters) that I was faced with the realization that we can only hold the fantasy together for so long before we start to crack. Our true essence—our FabYOUlousness—is beautiful, creative and daring and it *begs* to be set free to work miracles in our lives. When we stifle that inner creature out of fear, or in an attempt to appease others, we are only putting off the inevitable breakdown that will come as a result of our unrest, depression and lack of fulfillment. Thank goodness, it is entirely possible to avoid the breakdown by getting back in touch with your Fab**YOU**lous self, or *use* the breakdown as a springboard to a *breakthrough* if the bottom has already dropped out on your situation.

While working through my own issues and later, coaching others, I discovered that one of the easiest ways to rediscover (or discover for the first time) your Fab**YOU**lousness is to start by asking questions. I tend to agree with good ol' Socrates in that "an unexamined life is not worth living". I believe that we all really do, deep down (sometimes **WAY** deep down) know what is best for us and for what purpose we were put upon this earth. The problem is that too often, our soul's purpose and thus our Fab**YOU**lousness gets buried beneath the traumas, trials and responsibilities of life, and throttled by our failed attempts to live up to the (real or perceived) expectations of others.

How then do we go about getting back to the person that we were created to be? How can we continue our game of Hide & Seek and find our Fab**YOU**lous when it has been hidden in some deep, dark corner of our psyche for years…maybe even decades? Well, we start the treasure hunt (because it truly *is* a hunt for the greatest treasure that one can ever possess) by asking questions.

These questions are going to sound familiar to you because they are the same questions that you were taught to answer back in school when writing an expository essay. In the next couple of chapters, we will begin our quest of Finding Fab**YOU**lous by exploring the answers to the questions: Who? What? When? Where? and Why? (though in a slightly different order). Then, we'll use the *rest* of the book to piece together the "How?"

As I mentioned in the introduction, we will be doing a lot of experimentation as we work our way through this Finding FabYOUlous journey; and this book is meant to serve as a lab book in which you can record various observations and discoveries that are made along the way. In keeping with the "life is a laboratory" theme, you'll discover that each chapter in the first section of the book wraps up with opportunities to observe, test, record and think. The exercises that are included in each chapter's FAB LAB section are not required work and you won't be receiving a grade. They *are* however, valuable; and just like those college lab classes—the more effort that you put into this process of finding FabYOUlous, the more benefit you will receive. So, let's take our first step inside the FAB LAB and get to work.

FAB LAB

Observe it...

- Take some time to think about the people in your life that you feel embody and live out their FabYOUlousness. If you don't know any people like that, think of celebrities who seem confident in their FabYOUlousness. What qualities do these individuals possess that you admire? What qualities do they have in common? Do you notice any themes in the similarities? Are they all confident, smart or witty? Do they have solid relationships? Do they possess self-discipline or spirituality? If you discover that the people on your list seem to have many of the same, overlapping qualities, there is a good chance that these qualities are ones that you long to manifest in your life as well. These qualities are likely to be ones that will be key indicators of your own FabYOUlousness.

Test it…

- Do a quick google search of someone famous whom you feel is a good representation of Fab**YOU**lousness and read a bit about their background. Was this person's life *always* Fab**YOU**lous? My hunch is that the answer to that question is probably no. Most people who have truly found their Fab**YOU**lousness are people who are Fab**YOU**lous *thanks in part* to the hardships and trials that they've been through. Let this give you hope! No matter where you are starting the journey—you CAN find your Fab**YOU**lous!

Record it…

- In your journal, write about your feelings regarding your Fab**YOU**lousness. Do you know it well enough to recognize it? Have you felt it before? Do you feel like you were born without it? What do you think a Fab**YOU**lous life looks and feels like? Write about any apprehension that you might have as you begin this quest to find your Fab**YOU**lous.

Think about it…

"Knowing yourself is the beginning of all wisdom"   ~Aristotle

"What you are looking for is who is looking"
~St. Francis of Assisi

"The big question is whether you are going to be able to say a hearty yes to your adventure"   ~Joseph Campbell

"No question is so difficult to answer as that to which the answer is obvious"   ~George Bernard Shaw

"Judge a man by his questions rather than by his answers"
~Voltaire

"There is only one great adventure and that is inwards toward the self" ~Henry Miller

DON'T FORGET TO VISIT
WWW.FABYOULOUSLIFE.COM/FINDINGFABYOULOUSBOOKBONUSES
FOR ADDITIONAL SUPPLEMENTAL GOODIES!

Chapter 2

WHO ARE YOU?
WHO? WHO? WHO? WHO?

(To be sung as in the way of Roger Daltrey of *The Who*)

Ahhh…I wonder if Roger Daltrey, Pete Townsend and the boys knew just how powerful that seemingly simple question could be and yet, just how incredibly difficult it could be to answer. Now, before we go any further—if you don't know who Roger and Pete are, *please* put down this book and go download the album *Who Are You?* By *The Who* from iTunes right now. Seriously…do it. You'll thank me. You'll thank me even more if you watch the video on YouTube—Roger Daltrey was a hottie back in the day—those curls!

For the rest of us who grew up listening to rock & roll, we are very familiar with that famous chorus, but have we ever given any real thought as to the answer to that question?

Often, when asked who we are, we'll answer either with our name, our job title or some other role that we play (Bill's wife, Sally's mom, Vice-President of Sales, Girl Scout troop leader etc.) and though these labels are usually sufficient for the purposes of making introductions, they are nowhere near expansive enough to encompass the true WHO behind the YOU. I mean think about it—even something as personal as our name is a label that (for most of us) was assigned to us by someone else.

Now, I'm not suggesting that we all run out and change our names (though I have always thought that I seemed more like a Jennifer

7

than a Melissa—oh well) but I *am* suggesting that we start to dig beyond the surface level labels that merely describe various roles that we fill and instead start to uncover the truth as to who we really are and were created to be. In my own explorations, I've learned that one of the quickest and easiest ways to do this is to start thinking like a child.

I saw a bumper sticker the other day that read "Don't Grow Up—It's a Trap!" and I just had to laugh. It is so true though isn't it? We spend our childhoods playing, dreaming, imagining and creating without the overlying worry of bills, jobs, mortgage payments or jury duty. That's what is so great about little kids—they just naturally do what they love. No one tells a four year old to stop playing with her finger paints because finger painting isn't a lucrative career choice and that she needs to be more practical if she ever expects to be able to support herself (at least I would *hope* that no one would ever tell that to a four year old!) Why then are we so quick to stifle our adult selves when it comes to the things that bring us joy?

Look back in your own life and think about the things that you enjoyed doing as a child. Maybe you loved to play house and take care of your baby dolls. Maybe you spent hours outside with a ball glove and baseball bat. Maybe you used masking tape to make casts for your stuffed animal's broken legs. Maybe you sang, danced, drew pictures, played superhero, dug up pretend dinosaur bones, acted out stories or played grocery store in your mom's kitchen pantry. Maybe you did all of this before 10:00 a.m. and your mom made you take a nap so that she could preserve her sanity.

That's the magic of childhood—we were able to just play and do the things that we loved. For me, those things included playing "school" with my stuffed animals and dolls as the students (I even made my own handouts and worksheets for them), playing LOTS of baseball in the front yard with my dad, and writing stories on little pieces of paper that I would then staple together to make into books. Interestingly enough, as I look back on my child's "play" I realize that those things that I loved back then are the very things that I still love to this day. I love teaching others the valuable wisdom that I've gained regarding Finding Fab**YOU**lous *and* I enjoy creating the curriculums to go along with my coaching programs. I also still love baseball and even though I no longer aspire to be the shortstop for the New York Yankees, I *am* still an ardent Yankee fan and enjoy playing on a rec. league softball team called the *Sons of Pitches* (we take our softball very seriously…*not!*) Additionally, the fact that you are holding this book in your hands and reading it, is proof that I still enjoy writing, though my books now require more than just a few staples to hold them together.

I wholeheartedly believe that even as small children, we all had an inkling as to what our Fab**YOU**lous life should look like and I'm in good company when it comes to believing this theory. The ancient philosopher Aristotle, first voiced the notion that we all have a deeply ingrained inner Fab**YOU**lousness (okay, maybe he didn't use that actual word—the word he used was *entelechy* which was a Greek word meaning "having its end within itself") and that this Fab**YOU**lousness inside of us is what (if nurtured and allowed to germinate), propels us forward into a life of purpose, passion and joy.

This theory of entelechy can be easily demonstrated in the example of an acorn. Under the right conditions, an acorn will eventually grow up and become a mighty oak tree. It *must* become an oak tree. It can't become a pine tree or a giraffe. Its sole purpose or ultimate entelechy is to become an oak tree. All of the potential to become a mighty oak is ever present even in the tiny acorn. So too is all of the potential to live a Fab**YOU**lous life present in the young child at play. Yet, despite our natural inclinations towards the things that once brought us joy; how many of us have given up on our childhood dreams in exchange for a paycheck? How many of us spend our days, weeks, months and years doing something that we don't love in the hopes that one day we might be able to retire and find some time to play again? How many of us are trying to fill the role of a giraffe despite the fact that we were created to be an oak tree? Desperately trying to be something that we are not is *not* Fab**YOU**lous; and yet, so many of us find ourselves in that very situation, despite the fact that our inner essence and core desires are screaming to be set free.

Now, as a disclaimer—*please* don't think that I am encouraging you to run around the city in your underwear with a dishtowel tied around your neck because that's what you did as a child while playing superhero. That will likely get you arrested and no, I will not post your bail. What I *am* encouraging you to do however, is take a little time to think about, or better yet, journal about some of the things that you loved doing as a child because there is a good chance that exploring those favorite, early activities will help you to gain some clarity on the matter of who you were truly created to be. I also encourage you to explore ways in which you might begin to incorporate that *play* back into your life again. Running around in your underwear won't really make you a superhero— volunteering your time as a mentor in a youth program however; absolutely *will*.

By looking back to our youths and our first loves, we can catch a glimpse of the things that delighted our souls before we became jaded by adulthood and felt forced to conform to what society thought we should be doing instead. Rediscovering those things that brought us joy can be a huge clue as we progress on our search toward finding Fab**YOU**lous. Incorporating aspects of that play back into our adult lives (whether it's volunteering at an animal shelter because you used to love playing pet store with your stuffed animals, or starting a cake decorating business on the side because you went through four Easy Bake Ovens when you were eight) can help to point you in the right direction on your Finding Fab**YOU**lous quest.

FAB LAB

Observe it...

- Spend some time (in a NON-CREEPY way) observing young children at play. Does their play give any indication as to what their entelechy (Fab**YOU**lousness) might be? Do you notice any budding artists, ballerinas, architects or doctors? Do the children seem concerned that their play might not be *practical* or are they simply engrossed in having fun? Now, imagine these same kids twenty years later in "grown up" versions of these pretend roles. Do the images of the now-grown-up kids in your mind seem happy? Do you think that it might just be possible that these children are *meant* to carry their "play" on into their adult lives? Do you think that it might be possible that the same is true for all of us?

Test it...

- Carve out a couple of hours to play. Yes, I know that you're busy. Yes, I know that you are a mature adult. Yes, I know that you have obligations. I don't care. Even the busiest, most mature adult with a boatload of obligations can manage to carve out a few hours of time if something is important enough. Spend this time doing something for the sheer pleasure of it. Ride a bike, toss a football, paint, jump rope, play with an animal...whatever sounds fun to you—do it. How does this playtime feel to you? Are you able to truly cut loose and enjoy yourself or are you dogged by feelings of guilt because you really *should* be at the office crunching those numbers? If your feelings tend more towards the latter, don't panic; this exercise is just a chance for us to explore the joys *and* hang-ups that we have when it comes to play. As we progress on our

Finding Fab**YOU**lous quest, we'll learn more strategies to help us ditch the hang-ups and embrace the joy as we move closer to our unique, authentic and Fab**YOU**lous selves.

Record it...

- Use your journal to go back to your childhood days and explore some of the activities that brought you the most joy. What could you (as a child) spend hours doing? How did you feel while you were doing it? Is there a "grown up" version of this activity that you could incorporate into your life now? How connected do you currently feel to your inner child? What can you do to bridge any gaps in that connection?

Think about it...

"In every real man a child is hidden that wants to play"
~Friedrich Nietzsche

"It takes courage to grow up and become who you really are"
~E.E. Cummings

"I love asking little kids what they want to be when they grow up because I'm still taking suggestions"   ~Melissa Venable

"When they tell you to grow up, they mean stop growing"
~Tom Robbins

"But mother, I don't want to grow up"
~Wendy from *Peter Pan*

"If you don't grow up by age 35, you don't have to"
~James Gurney

"When I grow up, I want to be a little boy"   ~Joseph Heller

"Growing old is mandatory, growing UP is optional"
~Chili Davis

"The greatest oak was once a little nut that held its ground"
~Anonymous

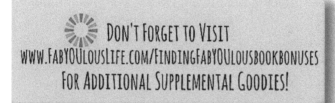

Chapter 3

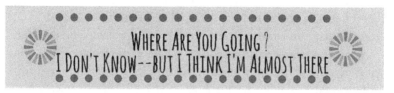

WHERE ARE YOU GOING ?
I DON'T KNOW--BUT I THINK I'M ALMOST THERE

That was an actual exchange that I recently had with my husband. I was driving to a meeting that was to be held at a beautiful country club in the mountains just west of Denver, Colorado. I knew that I had to be getting close to my destination but the more I drove around on the winding, mountain roads, the more confused I got. Even Siri was confused—she kept telling me that I had arrived at my destination but the only thing that I had arrived at was a house on the side of a mountain. The house was nice and all but it clearly was not a country club.

After making a call to the meeting's organizer, I discovered the reason for my (and Siri's) confusion. I had mistakenly entered the final destination as River Ranch Rd. instead of River *Valley* Ranch Rd. into my GPS. I left out one small detail but it was enough to send me (and Siri) on a wild goose chase. Fortunately, the meeting's organizer was able to give me better directions and I didn't end up being *too* late for the meeting.

"If you don't know where you're going, you might wind up someplace else"

~Yogi Berra~

Now, as I look back on that experience, it occurs to me that (just like I spent too much time driving around lost in the mountains) so many of us spend our days, weeks and years driving around on our own figurative mountains looking for *something* but not knowing exactly what it is or how to get to it. We have a vague idea as to what we *might* be looking for in life, but our destination is fuzzy which causes our tracking system to be useless.

Not having a crystal-clear understanding of our final desired destination, can cause us to waste all kinds of valuable time, energy and effort without ever arriving anywhere in particular. This is why it is crucial that the next question that we answer on our quest for finding Fab**YOU**lous is *where do you want to go?* This is a question that I'm sure you've thought about from time to time; I mean, we *all* have things that we'd like to do someday, places we'd like to go and goals that we hope to accomplish. We all have some sort of notion of what we'd like our future life to look like. The thing that we need to consider as we ponder this question is, how *clear* are we on our intended destination? Are the visions in our mind nothing more than fuzzy, out of focus musings that we *hope* might come to pass one day, or are they clearly defined images of concrete goals that we have strategized, mapped out and are taking daily action to achieve? One will leave us (and Siri) driving around in circles, lost and confused on the side of a mountain, while the other will move us ever closer to our desired destination.

If you aren't exactly sure where you'd like to eventually end up in life, it's time for you to start exploring what your life will look and *feel* like when you are truly living within the fullest expression of your Fab**YOU**lousness. This destination can almost always be found at the intersection of your talents/gifts, your passions and your contribution to the world at large. When you are successfully able to integrate your natural gifts and abilities with your ingrained passions in a way that serves others, you will know that you have arrived at your Fab**YOU**lous sweet spot.

This Venn diagram shows a visual representation of what this looks like in real life. The place where all components of fulfillment intersect, is the sweet spot—the bullseye where the fullest expression of our Fab**YOU**lousness is lived.

 Your FabYOUlous Purpose

Sometimes though, it can take a little work to sharpen the focus of this vision and move it from some vague and fuzzy notion to a fine-tuned and actionable goal. One of my favorite ways to get the ball rolling and creative juices flowing in regard to creating a vision of where I want my life to go, is to create a vision board.

Now, before you roll your eyes and decide that I'm some new age whack job, let me assure you that I am not. I understand that there are two different camps when it comes to creating vision boards—those who have watched *The Secret* seventeen times and have vision boards in every room of their house, and those who think that vision boards, while fun to create, have very little real impact upon a person's life. I happen to fall somewhere in the middle. Yes—I've watched *The Secret* (once) and I have a vision board (one). I do not however, buy into the notion that just cutting out pictures and gluing them to a piece of poster board is all that is required in order

17

for all of those beautiful images to magically become manifested in our lives. This does not, however, mean that I don't find *any* value in vision boards. Quite the contrary—I find vision boards to be incredibly valuable *and* effective. I simply believe that the true power behind a vision board comes from its ability to inspire you, excite you and propel you toward *action*. As I mentioned earlier, I have a vision board of my own and it is hanging front and center in my office where I see it every single day. I also have a photo of it on my phone and it is the backdrop on my laptop computer. Having my vision board in my face (literally) every day is a great motivator and not-so-subtle reminder for me to take strategic action towards my goals. Every. Single. Day.

For you hard core cynics out there (it's okay—I get it; I was one too before I started to experience the magic of my vision board) there is legitimate science behind the power of visualization. It involves using images to program our Reticular Activating System (the part of our brain that acts as a filter between our conscious and subconscious minds) to work on our behalf. When we regularly visualize our desired outcomes, our Reticular Activating System will spring into action and begin to filter information accordingly. Your Reticular Activating System will begin paying attention to information and details that will help you to reach your desired destination. This information would have previously been filtered out, but now is made accessible to you.

There is plenty more scientific data to back up the validity of vision boards, but though I refer to *Finding FabYOUlous* as a lab book for life, it is not, in fact, an actual scientific text. Therefore, I will leave you to do your own additional research on this subject (you can start by Googling 'Law of Attraction' or 'Quantum Physics') if it interests you. Instead, I want to provide you with the inspiration and direction to create your own powerful vision board. If however; you still think that vision boards are a bunch of new age hooey, that's fine—just create your board as an *experiment* and see where it takes you...I bet that you'll be pleasantly surprised.

Creating Your Own Vision Board

The first step for creating a vision board is to determine a theme for your board. My board is fairly general, so I just call it my Fab**YOU**lous Life board. You might want to narrow the focus a bit more by choosing a specific theme such as career, fitness or relationships. Choose whatever theme (however general or specific) feels right to you.

The next step to creating an effective vision board is to begin collecting images. You can print images that you find online or cut images out of magazines, catalogs etc. These images should be images that get you excited and that make you feel inspired to take action. I also happen to be someone who is motivated by words and phrases so I include those on my vision board as well. This use of words and phrases has scientific validity as is discussed in the book *Blink* by Malcom Gladwell. In his book, Gladwell gives numerous examples of how simply reading lists of words designed to evoke certain feelings, can indeed bring about those emotions within us, without our conscious awareness. Since this is a scientifically proven strategy for altering one's emotional state, we might as well put the science to good use by including powerful and positive words and phrases on our boards, along with the inspiring images.

Once you have a pile of images and words/phrases, it is time to find something to anchor them to. I've seen some vision boards created on bulletin boards and others on large pieces of poster board. My personal vision board is created on a piece of foam core board. I like that the foam core board feels a bit heftier than a regular piece of poster board but is still light enough that it doesn't require anything heavy duty to hang it. I've also seen vision boards that were nothing more than photos stuck to the front of a refrigerator. There really is no *wrong* way to create your board—as long as it works for *you*.

Now it is time to really start having some fun. Grab your pile of images and start arranging them onto your board. Don't glue anything down just yet because you'll probably need to move things around a few times before you settle on an arrangement that you like. Once you have your board arranged, I would suggest taking a picture of it with your phone. This will serve two purposes 1.) it will enable you to always have a photo of your vision board with you so that you can look at it whenever you are needing a shot of inspiration and 2.) if you get up to use the restroom and come back to find that your cat has sprawled out in the middle of your board and has stretched and rolled around enough to totally rearrange your images, you'll have a cheat sheet to show you where everything was. Yes—this happened to me. If you look closely enough at my vision board, you will probably see that it still has cat hair on it.

Once you have your images/phrases arranged in a way that you like, it is time to stick them down. For this step, I like to use good ol' Elmer's glue sticks but I have some friends who insist on using fancy scrapbooking adhesive that comes with its own dispenser. Seriously though—cheap glue sticks work just fine. Stick your images down and allow the glue (if that's what you're using) to dry. Obviously, if you are choosing to create your vision board on a bulletin board or the front of your fridge, you'll want to use thumbtacks or magnets instead of glue (duh!).

The final step in vision board creation is the most important step, and that is to find a special place for your board where you will see it EVERY day.

It might sound crazy, but there truly is power in keeping your vision board in front of you and looking at it EVERY. SINGLE. DAY. I won't pretend to understand all of the magic behind it—oh sure, I've read about the law of attraction and raising one's vibration to match the frequency of the things that you desire and I absolutely believe that there is a lot truth in all of this—even though I'll admit that I don't completely understand it. What I *do* know from personal experience is that focusing on your vision board every single day WORKS. Maybe it has to do with vibrations and frequencies etc., but I suspect that it also has something to do with what I call the *Racecar Effect*.

The *Racecar Effect* is something that I came up with a few summers ago while chatting with a good friend of mine who also happens to be a racecar driver. After one of his races, I mentioned how frightening I thought it must be to go around a track at such a high rate of speed because the slightest mistake could spell disaster. I could just imagine myself careening into the wall or another car if one of my tires accidently slipped or I hit a slick spot on the track. That's when my friend told me something that I will never forget. He said that no matter what happens, you *must* keep your eyes focused in the direction that you want your car to go. Do not look at the wall on your right, do not look at the car that you're about to hit—keep your attention focused in the direction that you want to go—it is the only hope that you have of being able to pull yourself out of the impending disaster. If you lose your focus and look at the wall for even a split second, you're toast.

I don't ever intend to put his advice to the test out on a racetrack (though with the number of speeding tickets that I've had on *normal* streets, maybe I *should* give racing a try) but I can absolutely see how his advice can be applied to everyday life. As human beings, we tend to gravitate towards the things upon which we focus. If we are focusing on all of the crappy and unfortunate circumstances in our life, we will slam into that brick wall and break apart. On the other hand, if we focus on the positive aspects of our lives and the FabYOUlously exciting goals that we have created for ourselves, we will naturally move towards *those* things and bring more of those positive experiences into our lives. *This* is where a vision board comes into play. By creating a vision board and keeping it front and center in your life, you will force yourself to focus upon those inspiring and energizing images *instead of* the brick wall that threatens to smash you to pieces. Focusing daily on your vision board will cause those Fab**YOU**lous images to remain in your top of mind awareness, therefore powerfully charging your Reticular Activating System, *and* focusing on your vision board will generate enthusiasm and excitement which will raise your vibration and align you with the frequency of your desired outcomes.

I hope that this has been enough to convince you to get your vision board put together since doing so is such a valuable exercise for helping to determine where you want to end up in your life; but now that you've got your board put together—what's next? I like to think of my vision board as the treasure on a treasure map. It's the X that marks the sweet spot of my full Fab**YOU**lousness. Just like any good treasure map however; there are twists, turns and obstacles along the way, and just like any good treasure hunter, you are going to need a few tools in your backpack as you head out on your quest for your treasure.

The first tool that you'll want to make sure that you have in your possession is a trustworthy compass. This compass is comprised of your personal *values* because just as a compass guides our direction as we stumble through a rain forest in search of a magnificent waterfall, it is our *values* that will ultimately keep us on track as we trek our way through the wilderness towards our most Fab**YOU**lous life.

This begs the question then—do you know what your values are? Often, when I ask clients this question, I'll get responses like "family, marriage, faith, money, etc." While all of these things sound great, they are not really *values*; instead, they are simply means to an end. For example, let's take family since that is something that most of us consider to be important. What exactly does your family contribute to your life that you place great value in? Connection? Love? Loyalty? Safety? Acceptance? *These* things are your values and your family is one of the means by which you trigger the emotions associated with these particular values. You don't really value money in and of itself; you value the security, freedom, generosity or power that it allows you to have. Your faith isn't a value but the connection, purpose or serenity that it provides to you *is*.

By looking beyond the different vehicles through which we experience our values and becoming clear on what our values are, we will be able to determine the "true north" on our compass. Knowing exactly what our values are will enable us to navigate our course more confidently because we'll always have a steadfast marker by which to gauge our steps. For example, if you come to a fork in the road and have to make a difficult decision regarding which path to take, checking in with yourself and seeing how each choice aligns with your values can give you a good indication as to which direction is the right one for you. Additionally, if you come to a difficult spot and feel as though you've lost your way, checking in with your values can help you to gain clarity as to how you got off track and guide you back to the correct course.

Understanding exactly what our core values are can be a bit tricky because there are so many worthy values to choose from. If you are having a difficult time deciding upon your most sacred values, let the following list serve to help you. Though it certainly isn't exhaustive, this list *does* contain a number of values and will help you to become clearer on those that are important to you. Start off by putting a star next to 20 values that resonate with you and then, of those 20, circle the 5 to 7 that are absolute non-negotiable "must-haves" for you. Once you've done this exercise, you'll have your compass in place and will be more prepared to confidently set off toward your treasure.

Create Your Values Compass

Accomplishment	Accuracy	Acknowledgement	Adventure	Authenticity
Balance	Beauty	Boldness	Calm	Challenge
Collaboration	Community	Comfort	Compassion	Comradery
Confidence	Connection	Contentment	Contribution	Cooperation
Courage	Creativity	Curiosity	Determination	Directness
Discovery	Duty	Ease	Effortlessness	Empowerment
Enthusiasm	Environment	Excellence	Fairness	Flexibility
Focus	Forgiveness	Freedom	Friendship	Fun
Generosity	Gentleness	Gratefulness	Growth	Happiness
Harmony	Health	Helpfulness	Honesty	Honor
Humor	Idealism	Independence	Innovation	Integrity
Intelligence	Intimacy	Intuition	Joy	Kindness
Learning	Listening	Love	Loyalty	Openness
Optimism	Orderliness	Participation	Passion	Patience
Peace	Power	Presence	Productivity	Purpose
Recognition	Relaxation	Respect	Resourcefulness	Romance
Safety	Security	Self-Esteem	Serenity	Service
Simplicity	Spirituality	Spontaneity	Strength	Success
Tact	Tolerance	Tradition	Trust	Understanding
Unity	Vitality	Wisdom	Wonder	Youthfulness
Zest				

Having your values compass in place is an important first step in your journey toward Fab**YOU**lousness because it will keep you heading in the right direction while providing you with true coordinates that (if followed) will prevent you from veering too far off course. However, a compass by itself won't get you very far on your journey—you're also going to need a sturdy pair of hiking boots.

A true adventurer would never set out on a quest without adequate footwear just as a serious runner would never attempt to complete a marathon in stiletto heels. Proper footwear is often the most fundamental and valuable piece of equipment when undertaking a journey. Our feet are what will carry us forward day after day, uphill and down, through soft, grassy meadows and over jagged, rocky terrain. Therefore, our footwear is of paramount importance and the one piece of equipment that can keep us going even when things are difficult and uncertain. Our footwear then, is an excellent representation of one of our most valuable personal attributes—self-discipline.

Wow—I can almost hear the groans already. *No one* likes to talk about discipline; but like it or not, without discipline, your Fab**YOU**lous life will never be anything more than a fantasy. As kids, none of us enjoyed being disciplined when we misbehaved, but it was that very discipline that helped us learn how to behave appropriately *and* that helped to mold us into good, conscientious and responsible adults. When we were children, our discipline usually came at the hand of grown-ups (parents, teachers, etc.) but now that *we* are the adults, we must learn to rely upon *ourselves* for focused and intentional discipline.

Having self-discipline simply means that you possess *and apply* the ability to put off instant, short-term gratification in order to achieve a greater payoff down the road. In my own life, discipline means sitting down at my computer to type because I want the later reward of holding my published book in my hands; even though, *at the moment,* I'd rather be flopped on the couch, eating ice cream straight from the carton and watching *Magic Mike* on DVD.

I'm not going to lie, exhibiting self-discipline can sometimes be painful because it means putting in effort while foregoing pleasure. However; as the late professional development expert Jim Rohn put it, "we must all suffer from one of two pains: the pain of discipline or the pain of regret. The difference is, discipline weighs ounces while regret weighs tons". We must all understand and accept the fact that without discipline (our trusty hiking boots) we aren't going anywhere in life and certainly won't be able to revel in the full Fab**YOU**lousness that is waiting for us at our desired destination. Like it or not—discipline is the very thing that will bridge the gap between your goals and their eventual accomplishment.

If self-discipline isn't your strong suit and you feel more like you are wearing flimsy flip-flops as opposed to sturdy hiking boots, you are not alone—not by a long shot. Fortunately, there are some strategies that you can implement to help you strengthen your self-discipline muscle, and just like any muscle, the more you use it, the stronger it will become. To develop your self-discipline, give these three suggestions a try...

- **Understand that you're not always going to "feel like it".** I can assure you that I pretty much *never* feel like running. What I *feel* like doing is stuffing my face with Cheetos while Netflix bingeing *Game of Thrones.* Unfortunately, those two activities (while undoubtedly easier) will never get me to my goal of running a half marathon. The bottom line is that in order to accomplish something truly meaningful, we are going to have to do things that we don't *feel* like doing. When I am faced with a task that is imperative to my overall goal, and yet is something that I really don't *feel* like doing (this happened just yesterday as I was preparing for my weekly "long" run), I have discovered that the most effective way for me to exercise self-discipline is to use visualization to motivate myself. Yes—woofing down Cheetos might feel better to me in the present moment, but will that fleeting moment of indulgence compare to the immense sense of joy and accomplishment that I experience when I cross the finish line of my first half marathon and see my husband and sons on the side of the road cheering for me? Nope. Not even close.

Understanding and accepting the fact that you're not always going to "feel like it" is an important step towards reaching any major goal. Acting on your goal (despite your feelings to the contrary) is the *only* way to turn your Fab**YOU**lous goal into an even more Fab**YOU**lous reality.

- **Run through the sprinklers, stay away from the drains.** Okay—I'm not really saying that the way to increase your self-discipline is to strip down to your underpants and run through the sprinklers in your back yard (though some of my fondest childhood memories involve doing that very thing at my Grandma & Grandpa Brown's house). Instead, I am using the sprinklers as an analogy to describe the types of people that we need to associate with if we are to develop our self-discipline muscle.

People generally fall into two different categories— sprinklers and drains. Sprinklers are those folks who believe in you and your dreams and who are excited to see you succeed. Their enthusiasm is contagious and their encouragement might just be the added oomph that you need in order to keep going when you want to quit. Drains on the other hand are (just as the name implies) people who literally drain you of energy through their own negativity and pessimism. They are the ones who will give

27

you a thousand reasons why your dream can never happen and who will call you crazy if you decide to persevere. Or...they are the "friend" who, knowing that you are training for a half marathon, will try to goad you into skipping your training so that you can party with them instead. Needless to say, your self-discipline muscle will deflate almost instantly when you come into contact with a drain. Conversely, hanging around with sprinklers can do a great deal to boost your levels of self-discipline. Their encouragement and support can help you to stay focused upon your big-picture goal and recommit to it when you feel your will power flagging.

As difficult as it can be to set boundaries with the drains in your life—doing so is an absolutely crucial step when it comes to developing your self-discipline and pursuing your most FabYOUlous life. As I was going through my eating disorder treatment (you'll read more about this later—I promise), this was probably one of the most challenging aspects of my recovery and yet; had I not done the work to erect some rock-solid boundaries, I know that I'd still be struggling with the same issues that were dragging me down way back then. Each one of us only has a limited amount of emotional and physical energy—it is crucial that we protect that energy by creating boundaries to keep out those who can't be supportive of our dreams. Run in the sprinklers but stay away from those drains.

- **Eliminate distractions.** I am the worst when it comes to being easily distracted. I get distracted by social media (why yes Facebook, I *do* want to take a quiz to find out which Disney princess I would be), text messages, TV commercials and even music (but c'mon—who doesn't have to stop everything and sing along when Bruno Mars' *Uptown Funk* comes on?) In fact, I think that it is these small, seemingly innocent distractions that cause me the most problems when it comes to managing my self-discipline levels. Fortunately, I have learned the value of creating structures to help me maintain my focus. Now, when I really want to get a lot accomplished, I use an online tool that blocks out all social media distractions for a determined amount of time that I have pre-set (my favorite app for this purpose is StayFocusd but Cold Turkey and SelfControl are other good apps worth looking into). I also have a few albums downloaded on my iTunes that provide nice, background music but that *do not* have any lyrics so I am not tempted to sing along. These simple hacks have helped me to increase my productivity levels and make great strides toward reaching my goals. I might not know which Disney princess I am, but I *have* completed two more chapters on my book manuscript.

As I mentioned earlier—just like any muscle that gets regular use, your self-discipline muscle *will* become stronger the more you engage it. Without your trusty hiking boots, you won't get far, but *with* them, there is virtually no limit to where your dreams can take you.

So…now that we have our compass and hiking boots ready to go, we are off to a great start. There are however; still a few crucial pieces of equipment that we'll need if we are to reach our FabYOUlous destination. We still need to pack our water bottle and our knapsack. Without plenty of H2O and vittles to keep our energy levels up, we aren't going to get very far on our trek to our FabYOUlous life; and, just as water and food can nourish and energize our physical bodies; inspiration and motivation can provide energy to our dreams and give us the burst of enthusiasm that we need in order to keep going when things get difficult.

We all know how awesome it feels to be highly motivated about something—think January 1st, all decked out in your cute new workout clothes and ready to put that brand-new gym membership to good use. How does that motivation feel on about January 23rd though? See...that's the problem with motivation—it is impossible to sustain at a consistently high level 24/7. That is precisely why *self-discipline* (our trusty hiking boots) is so, so important. Still, motivation does serve a valuable purpose because let's face it—moving forward on our goals is a heck of a lot more fun *if* we are energized, inspired and motivated to do so.

So...as we take the necessary steps toward our destination, we will feel much more refreshed and energized if we can partake of the nourishment of motivation. There are several ways for us to max our motivation but here are four strategies that I have found to work particularly well—especially at times when the goal seems *so* far off and it is difficult to keep plodding forward...

1) **Dream BIG but start small.** I have big dreams for my life—dreams that are *so* big that when I look at them on the large scale, I easily get overwhelmed and begin to question my sanity. Don't get me wrong—these dreams excite me and I feel compelled to continue striving for them, but they are BIG and I know that there is no chance in heck that I will ever accomplish these dreams *if* I continue to focus on their enormity.

   Big dreams that lie outside of our comfort zones are valuable because they energize us and get us excited about what the future might hold (just look at your vision board for example). However; breaking our big goals down into smaller, bite-size pieces is what will actually help us to inch our way closer and closer to the goalposts. Starting small is what gets the ball rolling and allows us to gain momentum, thereby creating flow. Starting small will also help to keep you focused upon the immediate task at hand, rather than becoming overwhelmed and discouraged by the enormity of your dream

If you aren't sure what small step to take toward your big dream first, try starting with some research. By doing your homework and studying the ins and outs of your dream, you will be better able to manage your expectations and anticipate what setbacks might be encountered along the way.

In order to best make this approach work for me, I have my vision board as well as a printed mind map hanging up in my office. These two pieces serve as daily reminders of the BIG vision that I have for my life. On the other end of the spectrum, I also have weekly and daily to-do lists that help me to take one small, do-able step every single day towards my goals. This dual vision approach helps me to maintain the enthusiasm and energy around my *big* dream while also keeping me on-task and focused on the immediate steps that need to be taken *today*.

2) **Keep inspiration accessible.** Even with FabYOUlously exciting goals and dreams to fuel us, there will still be days (and sometimes weeks & months) when things just seem hard. This "meantime" is when so many people give up.

In order to ensure that you are not one of the zillions who call it quits during this "messy middle" phase, it is vital that you learn to keep yourself motivated to move forward... even when it is difficult to do so. One of the most effective ways to do this is to get crystal clear on your "why". That is, make sure that you have a very firm grasp on the underlying motivation that compels you to follow your dream. For example, while I love creating content and programs for FabYOUlous Life, it is my underlying *why* of wanting to help women "ditch the drab and find their FAB" that keeps me going when I face challenges that make me want to give up. It is remembering where I came from and understanding the struggles that I faced

31

while rebuilding my life from rock bottom that compels me to want to help empower others to do the same. This *why* is a far greater motivating force than any hindrance that I could possibly encounter.

Another way that I stay inspired is by surrounding myself with uplifting messages. I have motivational quotes on my walls (and on my computer & iPhone backgrounds) and I have my Kindle filled with great personal development books. I also have several motivational podcasts that I subscribe to so that I can listen to them on the go. Rarely am I ever in a situation where I can't easily connect myself to some form of inspiring content. This ability to get a mini motivational jump-start whenever I need one, is one of the most valuable weapons in my arsenal when it comes to maintaining forward momentum towards my big dreams.

Finally, I think that we can be our own best sources of inspiration. You are Fab**YOU**lous! You have done some pretty incredible things in your life and you have overcome so much to get where you are right now. Sure—you may have a ways to go when it comes to reaching your big goals but you've also *come* a long way. I have big plans for Fab**YOU**lous Life and I have a loooong way to go before many of those plans come to fruition. However; when I look back to where I was a year ago, I am astounded at the difference that just one year has made. Keep track of your successes on a "Ta-Da! List" (we all have To-Do Lists, right? Isn't it high time we also had Ta-Da! Lists?) and celebrate them. When things start to get hard and you begin to wonder if you'll ever meet your goals, pull out your Ta-Da list and be reminded of just how amazing you are and how far you've already come. It is also important to remember that *you* are your only competition. Don't let yourself get sucked into games of comparison. Yes—there are people who are ahead of you; there will *always* be people ahead of you. Let them serve as an inspiration but *do not* let their success be a discouragement to you. There is plenty of opportunity available for *all* of us, so don't waste your time wishing that you could be like someone else. Instead, just work hard to be better than the person that you were yesterday.

3) **Renew your focus EVERY. SINGLE. DAY.** One of the biggest keys to reaching any goal is to keep that goal at the top of your mind. Write down your goals (or print them out in a pretty font on pretty paper) and the reasons that your goals are important to you. Post this list on your bathroom mirror, your office bulletin board or on your fridge…anywhere where you'll see it every day. This constant reminder of your goals will help to renew your focus, max your motivation and reconfirm your commitment every time you see it.

While you take these steps to focus your attention on your goals, it is also important that you eliminate negative distractions that would seek to siphon your time, energy and attention *away* from your goals. This means spending less time with negative, gossipy people (drains) and more time with positive, uplifting individuals (sprinklers) who will help to support you as you pursue your dreams. It might also mean cutting down on your intake of negative news via the television, newspaper or internet; after all, why fill your mind with depressing, over sensationalized junk when there is so much positive and inspiring content out there waiting to be devoured?

4) **Act as if.** As you renew your focus and recommit to your dream on a daily basis, your motivation level will be supercharged if you also incorporate the practice of "acting as if". Now, I'll admit, when I first started

practicing this, I felt a little silly and like I was being a fraud. However; the more I've begun "acting as if" in my life, the more I've discovered that it doesn't take long before I'm no longer having to "act". For example, as I pointed out earlier in the chapter, I do not, by nature, tend to be a very disciplined individual. I'm fun and creative and outgoing…but NOT very disciplined. However; we've already talked about the importance of our hiking boots and have established that becoming a success in any endeavor requires a good dose of self-discipline. So, that being the case, I decided that even though I'm not a *naturally* self-disciplined individual, I am going to *act* like one. Rather than blowing all my money on yarn and office supplies (what? those are the things I like okay?), I am going to put some into savings and reap the benefit of compound interest. Rather than staying up all night long (which is my natural night-owl tendency) I am going to try to be asleep before midnight so that getting up for work the next morning doesn't totally suck. Rather than frittering away my evenings playing Trivia Crack on my phone while watching *Pretty Little Liars*, I am going to sit at my computer and put together a blog post or type a chapter in my book. None of these things came naturally to me at first, but the more I started to "act as if", the easier they became. Now; when it comes to doing these things, I find that I no longer need to "act" because these disciplines have become second nature to me (well okay…I still tend to stay up too late but I'll keep working on that one!)

5) **Reap the rewards.** Turning your dream into reality will be its own reward, but another key motivation booster is to reward yourself along the way as you move ever closer to your goals. Just as a swig of water from your bottle or a nibble of food from your knapsack can give you a needed energy boost on the way to your destination, mini rewards

can also help to sustain your motivation levels as you strive to remain focused on your goal.

Maybe your desire is to write a book. If this is the case, you could make a deal with yourself and say, "when I finish this chapter, I am going to treat myself to a pedicure". Breaking your big goal down into manageable chunks and then rewarding yourself with special treats at various milestones is a very effective way to maintain motivation for the long haul. Or, perhaps there are ways that you can reward yourself *as* you are working toward your goal. For example, I have a book series that I just LOVE, but I can't lay around reading it every evening if I ever want to complete a half marathon, so instead, I have downloaded the books to my Audible app and now I *only* let myself listen to the books *while* I am running. This tactic has worked so well for me that I have actually found myself adding extra distance to my runs just so I could finish a chapter.

In my own life, I also find it helpful to attack my projects with a "do the worst first" mindset. I tackle my most challenging tasks *first* and then give myself a little treat when these hardest tasks are completed. This works well for me because 1.) I like treats—duh, and 2.) I like the freeing feeling of having my most difficult tasks *behind* me. I've also found that doing the toughest chores *first* gives me a boost of self-confidence that carries me through the rest of my tasks. It's a win-win-win scenario.

As wonderful as rewards can be though, it is important that we understand that things are not always going to turn out the way that we had planned. We will break our goal down into manageable chunks, set milestones and establish rewards—but then something will go haywire. Maybe we fall short on a monthly sales goal or our latest product launch turns out to be a dud. In these instances, it can be very difficult for us to feel like celebrating with a reward. Despite our disappointment however; it is absolutely *crucial* that we maintain a proper perspective on failure. Rather than viewing failure as a fatal blow to our dreams, it is vital that we learn to view failure for what it really is—*feedback*. Whenever I feel as though I've failed at something, I like to recall this quote from Michael Jordan:

"I've missed more than 9000 shots in my career. I've lost almost 300 games. Twenty-six times, I've been trusted to take the game winning shot and missed. I've failed over and over and over again in my life— and that is why I succeed"

Failure is *never* final. It is simply an opportunity for us to reassess, make adjustments and move forward with more data than we had before—and that is *definitely* something worth celebrating.

Okay—now that we have our values determined, our self-discipline strengthened and our motivation levels kicked up a notch, it is time to add our final piece of equipment. We would be in a lot of trouble if we headed out on our adventure without first packing a flashlight, and to be safe, it should be a flashlight with long-life batteries.

I'm always hesitant to bring up the need for a flashlight on our journey to Fab**YOU**lousness because the need for a flashlight automatically insinuates that we are going to run into dark, scary places along our journey, but guess what—we're going to run into dark, scary places along our journey. No matter how well we prepare or how brave we think that we are, there *are* going to be times on our quest when the night is dark and full of terrors (okay—obviously I watch too much *Game of Thrones*). Still; television quotes aside—there *are* going to be times when we feel lost, and our bright, shiny Fab**YOU**lous vision seems hidden somewhere in the dark; somewhere where we are too scared to venture because we can't see our hand in front of our face. It is in these times that we must call upon our flashlight of courage so that we can shine a light in the dark places and illuminate our path.

Fear is such a huge deterrent when it comes to realizing our Fab**YOU**lous life vision that I have dedicated nearly an entire chapter to it later in the book. For now though, understand that fear is often the result of not having an accurate assessment of the situation at hand. We worry about symptoms that we are convinced must be cancer only to discover that we have a simple sinus infection that is causing our lymph glands to swell, or we fear that our spouse is plotting to leave us, when instead he's working late because he is trying to make extra money to take the family on a cruise. When we start to feel overwhelmed by feelings of fear or uncertainty, it is crucial that we use the flashlight of courage to face our fears and shine a light on the situation in order to obtain an accurate assessment of what is truly going on. More techniques for battling fear will be covered later in this book and each technique is one more super-powered, long life battery for your courage flashlight.

Trekking your way through the wilds and toward your Fab**YOU**lous destination won't be easy, but now that you have your gear in place, it *will* be possible. Just make sure that as you plod your way toward your goal, you make time to regularly check your tools. Are you still holding true to your compass coordinates? How is the tread on your hiking boots? Do you need to refill your water bottle and knapsack? Does your flashlight still shine bright? By keeping your equipment (your values, self-discipline, motivation/inspiration and courage) in tip-top shape, your journey will be much easier to navigate and your goal quicker to achieve.

FAB LAB

Observe it...

- When was the last time you were lost? I mean *really, truly* lost? What caused you to lose your way? Incorrect address? Faulty directions? Unfamiliar neighborhood? How did you eventually find your way? Now think of a location that you go to on a regular basis—someplace that you could find even if you were blindfolded. The difference between the two is that the latter is a location that you see every day. You are familiar with it and therefore know exactly what steps to take in order to reach the destination. Make it your goal to become *that* familiar with the Fab**YOU**lous vision that you hold for your life. Look at your vision board EVERY day. Take a small step toward your goals EVERY day. The more familiar you become with your desires, goals and the things that set your soul on fire, the less lost you'll get as you work your way toward them.

Test it...

- If you read through the parts of this chapter about making a vision board but didn't actually take the time to *make* one, stop what you are doing RIGHT NOW (seriously, just stop already) and MAKE ONE. Even if you think it's nothing but a bunch of hippie dippie malarkey, make one as an *experiment* and look at it every day. As you look, spend a few minutes thinking about what your life will be like when you start to manifest the things on the board. Then...let the experiment play out as you continue to look at your board every day. I will be shocked if you don't start to see results, and before long, my guess is that you'll be committed to making a new hippie dippie malarkey board every year.

38

Record it...

- Write out a paragraph about each of your top values. Why are they important to you? Do you make an active effort to live them out in your everyday life? What things can you do to more actively incorporate your values into your life?

Think about it...

"It's not hard to make decisions once you know what your values are" ~Roy E. Disney

"Create the highest, grandest vision for your life, because you become what you believe" ~Oprah Winfrey

"With self-discipline, most anything is possible" ~Theodore Roosevelt

"Without self-discipline, success is impossible, period." ~Lou Holtz

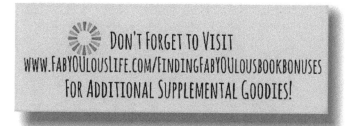

DON'T FORGET TO VISIT
WWW.FABYOULOUSLIFE.COM/FINDINGFABYOULOUSBOOKBONUSES
FOR ADDITIONAL SUPPLEMENTAL GOODIES!

Chapter 4

BUT WHY?

Okay, so now you have a grasp on who you were created to be and where you want your life to take you. That's great—but it isn't enough. There is one question that you need to answer in order to bridge the two. In order to move the person that you are today to the destination that you desire, you *must* answer the question *why?* It is your *why* that will serve as the catapult to get you to your Fab**YOU**lous life. It is your *why* that will serve as the fuel in your tank that keeps you chugging along through the long, dark night rather than leaving you stranded in the middle of a desolate desert waiting for the vultures to come pluck out your eyeballs. It is your *why* that will propel you forward even when everyone else tells you that you're crazy and that your dreams are nothing more than delusional fantasies that will never come to pass.

Why is your vision of your Fab**YOU**lous life so important to you? Why does it keep you awake at night as you ponder new ideas and possibilities? What is it about your vision that compels you to keep going—no matter what?

If your *why* is so that you can make a lot of money, buy a beach house and spend your days sipping umbrella drinks while ogling the pool boy, you might need to dig a little deeper. Not that any of those things are *bad* (not at all!) but our true and compelling *why* is something that resonates with us on a deeper, less superficial level. Why do you want to make a lot of money? Is it because you long to experience freedom and the ability to support causes that are important to you? Why do you want a beach house? Is it so that you'll have an inviting place for your friends and family to stay when they come to visit you? Why umbrella drinks? Do they represent fun and leisure to you at a time when you are feeling overworked and exhausted? Why ogle the pool boy? Does he get you excited about the prospect of finding a romantic partner with whom you can share your life, or does he make you feel youthful and energized instead of middle aged and tired? Whatever your *why* is, it is important that you identify the deeper and more meaningful reasons behind your desires.

When I think about my own *whys*, I come up with reasons that resonate deep within the core of my being. Reasons that when I truly spend time thinking about them bring me to tears. My experience of losing myself, battling an eating disorder, fighting my way out of a dangerous marriage (I *promise*, you really are going to read all of the gory details of my colossal collapse soon!) and rebuilding my life from a pile of broken bits and pieces so that I could take care of my precious sons and create a healthy and prosperous life for us, has instilled within me a driving desire to make sure that **no** woman ever has to feel lost within her own life the way that I did. I worked hard to turn my situation around but I know that I easily could have ended up with a very, very different story. It is the culmination of my experiences coupled with my unique passions and talents that stoke the fires of my why. I never want another woman to doubt her Fab**YOU**lousness. I want to help reconnect women with the incredible beings that they were uniquely created to be. This *why* is what gets me out of bed in the morning, energizes me to keep going when things are hard and drives me to continue stretching myself.

I have other *whys* too though. My big *why* is the one that I just laid out for you, but I have a few smaller *whys* as well. Sometimes, I struggle with the fact that one of my *whys* for developing my coaching/writing business is because I want to make money doing something that I love. I worry that the desire to make (a whole whole lotta) money somehow makes me a bad or greedy person. As I dig deeper however; I know that this simply isn't true. In fact, my personal belief about money is that money is simply a tool that makes you more of who/what you already are. Sure, if you're a bad or greedy jerk, money will just allow you to reach deeper levels of bad, greedy jerkiness. However; if you are a kind, generous and loving individual, having more money will simply allow you to be *even more* kind, generous and loving. I plan to make lots of money because I need that money to further the mission of Fab**YOU**lous Life Enterprises and to help lots of women to find their Fab**YOU**lous. I *also* want to make enough money to allow my sweet, supportive and oh-so-hardworking husband to retire. He has worked hard to create an incredibly successful painting business, but decades of climbing up and down ladders while hauling paint buckets has taken a toll on his poor, aching knees. I plan to make enough money to retire him so that he can sell his business (or pass it down to our boys) and enjoy the freedom to pursue his other passions. I also plan to help support my parents as they age so that they can enjoy their leisure years. It only seems fair after all that they've done for me. Additionally, I have charities and social causes that are important to me that I long to support in significant ways. Yes—I plan to make a lot of money, but I also plan to use that money for good; therefore, I don't feel one bit guilty about having "make (a whole whole lotta) money" as a part of my *why*.

Another *why* of mine is one that is a little more difficult to define. It has to do with my desire to create a meaningful legacy. I want to build a life that I can be proud of but also one that my husband, kids and parents can be proud of as well. I'll never forget the feeling that I got when I heard the pride in my dad's voice when (at a Christmas gathering for extended family) he told some other family members that one of his highlights of the year was attending a black-tie gala where I was honored as one of twelve *Colorado*

Women of Vision. I know for a fact that there have been *plenty* of times over the years when my folks had to have wondered if I'd *ever* get my act together, so it meant a lot to me to hear my dad brag on my accomplishment. I also was nearly moved to tears when I saw my youngest son's post about me on his Facebook account after I was featured in *Mind & Body Magazine* as one of forty Colorado "Superwomen" and I'll always treasure the big hug and kiss on the cheek that I received from my oldest son when I stepped off the stage after giving a speech at a large charity event. These moments, along with the floaty feeling that I get whenever I hear the pride in my hubby's voice as he introduces me to one of his friends or associates, is something that I can't even put into words. I try not to get too caught up in what other people think of me, but the opinions of *these* people *do* matter. I long to create a legacy that is worthy of their esteem. All of the awards, accolades or recognition in the world don't come close to providing the feeling that I get when I know that the people that I love are proud to have me in their lives. Every step that I take towards the FabYOUlous life that I have envisioned for myself is one in which I carry my love for these people with me and create a life that fully involves them to whatever extent they want to be involved.

So, now that you've read about a few of *my* whys, it is time for you to define your own, because the truth of the matter is—your FabYOUlous Life *will not* come to pass if you aren't clear on exactly *why* you want it to.

The process of pinpointing your why isn't complicated; it is simply a matter of drilling down your desires by asking the question *why* over and over again. If you're a mom, you've no doubt experienced this with your own children when they were young...

> Child: Mama, WHY can't I have a cookie?

> Mom: Because it is almost dinnertime and I don't want you to ruin your appetite.

Child: But WHY mama?

Mom: Because your dinner will make you big and strong but a cookie won't

Child: But WHY mama?

Mom: Because I love you honey and I want you to be healthy so you can become whatever you want to become when you grow up. Or…the more common reply used by moms throughout the ages: Because I said so. *THAT'S* why.

As exasperating as these constant *whys* can be when coming from an inquisitive four-year-old; the same technique can be very useful in helping us to drill down to our core motivations regarding our Fab**YOU**lous lives. I'll use an example from my own life as a guide for you to follow.

On my vision board, I have a photo of a big beautiful home on a crystal-clear lake. To find out *why* this is something that I passionately desire, I simply have to start by asking *why do I want a big home?* My answer to this question has several different parts to it. I want a big home because I want it to be able to hold my entire family and their families. I want my husband to be able to have an office and a gym because I know that both are important to him. I want there to be plenty of room for my sons and their future wives and children to come visit (okay—to be completely honest here, I'd love it if my sons would just move their future families in and live with me but that makes me sound like a crazy mom so I'll settle for visits—*lots* of visits*)*. I want my stepdaughter to feel like she can bring her partner anytime she wants to come spend time with her dad, and I want a place where my parents can live if necessary once they are ready to downsize. I want all of this and yet I don't want people having to crash on floors or wait 30 minutes for a bathroom, so therefore I need a *big* house.

Once I have these initial reasons identified, the next step is to ask *why* again...*why do I want my house to accommodate my family and future family?* This answer gets closer to the heart of the matter in that, I want this because my family is such an integral part of my happiness. Without close and loving ties to my husband, children and parents, it would be impossible for me to live my Fab**YOU**lous life. These people are my heart and I want to maintain close and loving relationships with them. I want a home that serves as a backdrop for creating memories and forging deep, committed relationships with one another. Now *that* is a *why* that will inspire me and give me a jump-start if my motivation ever starts to wane.

Don't stop there however. Continue to ask *why* until you feel like you have truly exhausted every motivation behind your desire. My next *why* could be *why else do you want a big home on a lake* to which I would answer that I want a big home because I plan to office from home and therefore need a designated work space (office) *and* I want the home to be on a lake because I plan to hold retreats and therefore need to be able to accommodate visitors and provide a beautiful place where they can enjoy activities such as paddle boarding, hiking etc. Additionally, there is just something in my psyche that comes alive when I am on or near water. When I combine all of these reasons, they make for a very compelling *why* behind my desire and provide more than enough fuel to keep me motivated to turn my vision into a reality.

To really add power to your Fab**YOU**lous life vision, go through every image on the vision board that you created in the last chapter (if you cheated and skipped that step, now would be a really good time to go back and get that vision board made—seriously, do it already!) and repeatedly ask yourself *why* about each image until you drill down to the most heart centered and meaningful desire behind each image. When you've done this and are crystal clear on exactly *why* your dreams and desires are so important to you, you will be exponentially more compelled to do whatever it takes to make them happen. You won't let any obstacle, difficulty or challenge stand in your way. You won't stop pushing until your Fab**YOU**lous life vision is no longer just a vision but is instead, a wonderful reality that you are living out on a daily basis. Knowing your *why* will keep you from settling for anything less than what you know that you desire *and* deserve.

FAB LAB

Observe it...

- Look at the images on your vision board. Are there any images there that don't *really* represent your Fab**YOU**lous life? It might sound crazy but I actually caught myself almost pasting a picture of a woman in a tailored business suit sitting at a big, mahogany desk in a very academic looking office (complete with a globe and shelves lined with big, leather bound encyclopedias) to my vision board. As I went to paste it down however; I felt a very definite catch in my spirit saying "what the heck are you doing? You don't want *that* life". Now, don't get me wrong—I absolutely intend to be a business powerhouse in my industry; however, my ideal office looks a lot more like a laptop on a table at a beachside café than a stuffy office with a big pretentious desk and *encyclopedias* (I mean seriously—do people even use those anymore?) and though I do don a business suit from time to time, my *ideal* business attire consists of light, flowy dresses in summery colors or cute capris, killer wedges and a trendy top (with an amazing statement necklace of course).

When I thought about what on earth nearly compelled me to paste that *other* image on my vision board, it dawned on me that there was something in me that associated success and prosperity with images of the offices that my college deans worked out of. Now, mind you—I have no desire to be a college dean or pursue *any* kind of career in academia for that matter. I do however, recall feeling particularly awestruck when I (as a recent college graduate) accepted a position with my university's admissions office and was then asked to attend a meeting in the university president's office. As I walked into his office that was lined with shelves filled with books and accepted a seat across from his ginormous mahogany desk, I thought to myself *"this* must be what success looks like". Well, that was true—for *him* and likely for anyone else who wanted to pursue a career in higher education. At that point in my life, I honestly had no idea what direction my professional career was going to take, but from that experience, I subconsciously imprinted in my brain, the notion that success meant business suits and mahogany desks. Obviously, (even though that image is almost a direct *opposite* of what I now want for my life) there was still a part of my psyche that felt like I *should* want that vision.

What about you? Are there any images on your vision board that are there not because you genuinely desire them but because you feel like you *should* desire them? Or...are there any images on your board that reflect what *other* people want for you rather than what you want for yourself? If, when you examine each image on your vision board, you cannot come up with a genuine, soul-centered *why* to justify the image, you need to remove the image and replace it with one that truly resonates with you.

Test it...

- Actually follow through and *do* the "Desire Drill-Down" activity that was outlined in this chapter. Really take the time to go through each and every image on your vision board and repeat the question *why?* until you have managed to dig past the superficial or material reasons for your desires and have instead arrived at the heart & soul, core reasoning behind your image. What do the umbrella drinks and pool boy *really* represent to you?

Record it...

- Now that you've taken the time to drill down deep to the core reasons behind your desires, it's time to do some journaling around them. Spend some time putting your *why's* down on paper. Write down exactly *why* each of your desires is important to you and the level of Fab**YOU**lousness that your life will reach once your desires are reality. Then, if ever you start to feel your motivation waning or you start to feel discouraged in the pursuit of your dreams, take out what you've written and read it out loud to yourself. Re-engaging with your *why* and reinforcing its significance can be a powerful way of increasing your willpower and providing you with the strength necessary to once again pick yourself up, brush yourself off and begin again in the direction of your Fab**YOU**lous life.

Think about it...

"There are two great days in a person's life—the day we are born, and the day we discover why" ~William Barclay

"He who has a why to live for can bear almost any how" ~Friedrich Nietzsche

"If your why is strong enough, you will figure out the how" ~Bill Walsh

"When you operate from your *what*, you try to convince people to act. When you start from your *why*, you *inspire* people to act"
~David Mead

"You lose your way when you lose your why"   ~Michael Hyatt

☀ DON'T FORGET TO VISIT
WWW.FABYOULOUSLIFE.COM/FINDINGFABYOULOUSBOOKBONUSES
FOR ADDITIONAL SUPPLEMENTAL GOODIES!

Chapter 5

WHAT THE...?

The next question that we want to explore on our finding Fab**YOU**lous treasure hunt is *what?* But, before you ask "what *what?*" I need to explain that our *what* has two different parts to it. First, we will answer the question *what needs to go?* and then we will tackle the second what—*what needs to GROW?*

I am a firm believer that nothing is ever truly neutral in our lives and that there is no such thing as "standing still". Sure, we may *feel* like we are stuck and going nowhere or we may *think* that nothing is going on with us, but that simply isn't the case. In truth, we are always either moving ahead or falling behind. Our universe is either expanding or it's contracting. Our thoughts, behaviors and attitudes are either moving us closer to our Fab**YOU**lous life or they are taking us further away from it. We are never truly at a stand-still because even if we feel like we are stuck—the rest of the world is moving on ahead and is therefore causing us to fall further behind. That is not to say that the quest to find your Fab**YOU**lous is a race—it certainly is not. It is however, vital that we understand that our thoughts and actions (or lack thereof) will either propel us closer to our Fab**YOU**lous life destination and expand our experience of Fab**YOU**lousness or, they will cause our experience to contract and shrink, moving us further away from our desired result. We *must* grasp the fact that our every choice, thought, word, behavior and action carries weight and has a direct impact upon the level of Fab**YOU**lousness that we experience in our lives at any given moment.

Often, our lives end up being less than Fab**YOU**lous because of clutter (internal and external) that is mucking up our ability to get clear and to focus on our true desired destination. This clutter might be in the form of negative self-images, defeating attitudes, disorganized living or work spaces, emotional chaos etc., and sometimes the quickest way to start moving forward again is to take stock and begin eliminating some of those things that seem to have mired us in their quicksand of stagnation. It is time to break free of some of these hindrances to Fab**YOU**lousness by taking a hard look at the things in our lives that need to GO.

Now, don't panic. This chapter isn't about beating ourselves up or making ourselves feel bad because we have negative things in our lives that we need to purge. The fact of the matter is that *no one* alive on planet earth is perfect—not the Dalai Lama, not the pope, not even your sister-in-law with the never messy house and perfectly behaved kids. We *all* have things that we need to eliminate from our lives and guess what...once we have those things eliminated, we will discover *other* things that need to be eliminated. That's just life. Thank goodness perfection isn't our goal here— that would be one giant, exhausting exercise in futility. Our goal instead is Fab**YOU**lousness and *that* goal is VERY attainable.

When we start to ponder the things in our lives that need to go, we need to do a bit of paradigm shifting before we start. We do not want to come at this exercise from the perspective of "I suck and these are the things in my life that make me suck". NO NO NO! That kind of thought process will do nothing but defeat us. Instead, we need to approach this exercise as a champion gardener would approach her beautiful, prize winning rose bush. The gardener would **never** come at her prized roses with a set of garden shears and just start whacking away willy nilly until her rose bush is nothing but a sorry looking stump sticking out of the ground. No...the gardener would instead, carefully approach her beloved roses with nothing but the best intentions for bringing out the most beauty and fragrance in her blooms. Yes—she will still use gardening shears, but those shears aren't wielded as if they are some kind of medieval torture device. Instead, the shears are intentionally and precisely used to remove only the parts of the rose bush that do not serve in its quest to yield the most fragrant and beautiful blooms.

This process of pruning is beneficial in our lives as well. We won't be using gardening shears (thank God!) but we *will* begin to examine our lives and lovingly begin the process of cutting away those thoughts, behaviors, possessions and attitudes that don't serve us in our quest for Fab**YOU**lousness. We will engage this process in the kindest, most loving way possible and recognize that this is not an exercise in beating ourselves up—it is simply an exercise that will begin to release us from any encumbrances that are preventing us from experiencing our full Fab**YOU**lousness.

This exercise of purposeful pruning was first introduced to me several years ago when I was the lowest point of my life and in desperate need of help. I was, at the time, trapped in an emotionally and sometimes physically abusive marriage, trying to be strong for my two precious little boys and yet wasting away from a dangerous and debilitating eating disorder. In short—life was AWFUL, and weighing in at 78 pounds (as a woman in her 30's), I was quite literally committing slow suicide in the form of Anorexia Nervosa.

For those of you who don't know—the eating disorder, Anorexia Nervosa has the highest mortality rate of *any* mental illness (yes, there it is—I was diagnosed with a mental illness. I was mentally ill with a condition that I was not managing. That's about as far away from Fab**YOU**lous as one can get), so once I was officially diagnosed with Anorexia, I was immediately assigned an entire team of professionals including a medical doctor, nutritionist and therapist. It was at one of my numerous therapy sessions that the notion of purposeful pruning first came up. My therapist encouraged me to stop viewing my life as a disaster (even though I was still pretty sure that it *was*) and to start viewing it instead as a work of art...a masterpiece even. He told me that my masterpiece *was* there but that it had been buried for too many years under too many layers of yuck.

This notion resonated somewhere inside of me because I remembered (from a college Philosophy course that I had taken years earlier) that at a healthier time in my life, I had been inspired by what the nineteenth century, German philosopher, Friedrich Nietzsche had to say about how to live. Nietzsche urged people to make their lives into original and magnificent works of art and to live as creatively as possible. I also remembered reading about the famous artist Michelangelo who, when asked how he created his incredible sculpture, David, implied that it was easy because he simply chipped away the stone that *wasn't* David. I absolutely loved the idea of living a life of my own creation and the notion that something beautiful could emerge from an ugly slab of rock simply by chipping away at the pieces that didn't belong.

Thus began my process of purposeful pruning. At first, I have to admit that I was overwhelmed because there were SO MANY things in my life that needed to go—awful attitudes, rotten relationships, bad behaviors and more horrible thoughts than any one person should have during an entire lifetime...or three. I was so overwhelmed that I was frozen. I didn't have a clue as to where to start with those pruning shears so instead of moving forward, I chose to remain stagnant and not do anything—well, anything *except* obsess over all of the things that I should've been changing, that is.

Lucky for me (though it didn't exactly *feel* lucky at the time); my therapist was like a bulldog and wouldn't let me just remain stuck in my self-made spiral of defeat. He used a clever analogy that I will never forget. He very bluntly told me that I needed to stop swimming in my own sh*t. He said that I was like a poor, sad, unhealthy little goldfish that was swimming around day after day in an unclean fishbowl. I was suffering the ill effects of spending weeks, months and even *years* swimming around in my own, self-created bowl of emotional, physical and spiritual sh*t. He pointed out to me that nothing in my life would become clear again until I started to take the necessary steps to clean my fishbowl. He then instructed me to pick one, tiny little sh*tty habit, thought or behavior that I could change quickly and easily. I wasn't supposed to think about any of my other, larger looming issues. I was simply supposed to pick one tiny aspect of my life that wasn't serving my best interest and focus on removing it from my fishbowl. So, I chose lip gloss. Yep—you read that correctly. One of the first concrete steps in my recovery from a debilitating mental illness that was hell bent on killing me, involved a simple tube of lip gloss.

You see, when I was at that rock-bottom point in my life, I had pretty much given up on myself and that included my outward appearance. I simply didn't care enough anymore to make even the smallest effort in the area of my looks. So, I decided that my ambivalence towards my appearance was the first thing that needed to go. Now, looking back, I realize that maybe I should have chosen something less superficial—something that dealt with my lousy attitude or deeper-seated feelings of anger, but at the time, I simply wasn't ready for all of that. Instead, I decided that I needed to get rid of my lack of concern regarding my physical appearance. That was when I decided to start wearing lip gloss again.

I don't remember the brand of the lip gloss, but I think the color was called "Sugared Bronze". It wasn't too pink and yet wasn't too dark either. Putting on that lip gloss was such an easy thing to do and yet it felt like such a big step in chiseling away at the lack of self-care in my life. Something else amazing happened too. When I put on that lip gloss and looked in the mirror, I didn't like the fact that my lips looked nice but were out of sync with my sad, sunken eyes and hollow cheeks. So, I grabbed my makeup bag and for the first time in ages, applied foundation, blush, eye liner and eye shadow. I wouldn't allow myself to apply mascara at that point because I was still spending way too much of my time in tears and streaks of black running down my cheeks wouldn't help my efforts any. Still, when I was finished with my makeup application, I looked in the mirror and was pleasantly surprised at the results. Taking the step to cut away at my ambivalence towards my appearance gave me a teeny, tiny little boost of confidence that I hadn't felt in a long, long time. It also gave me the springboard that I needed to start cutting other negative aspects out of my life.

What about you? What is one, tiny little spec of sh*t that you can take action to remove from your fishbowl TODAY? Don't overwhelm yourself by trying to cut out too much too quickly—it won't work (trust me on this one!) If, for example, you are feeling lazy and a bit overweight, don't try to cut out *all* unnecessary calories while also vowing to eliminate all TV watching and internet surfing. That radical of a change may work for a few days but it isn't something that will be sustainable over the long haul because it will end up feeling like punishment or worse—torture. It definitely won't feel Fab**YOU**lous. Instead, choose to eliminate 30 minutes of TV viewing every night and replace it with a walk around your neighborhood. Then, once that simple elimination starts to feel like the norm, you can look for the next tiny bad habit to prune from your life.

In my work with clients, as well as in my own life, I've seen this process of purposeful pruning lead to amazing and sustainable results. There is, however; one sneaky, camouflaged pitfall that I've seen many good people stumble over. This wolf in sheep's clothing is the failure to realize that not all things that need to be pruned from our lives are inherently *bad* things. For example, maybe you know that your Fab**YOU**lous life is one in which you are able to leave your stressful, full-time job in order to pursue a hobby that you would like to monetize and turn into a business. In this instance, it might be necessary for you to temporarily prune out some discretionary expenses so that you can start putting aside money to finance your dream. In general terms, lunches out with girlfriends, manicures or spa days are *not* bad or negative experiences; they may however, be things that you need to temporarily prune in order to move forward in your quest for Fab**YOU**lousness. Sometimes we must be willing to let go of the good in order to go for the Fab**YOU**lous.

As you start small (as I did with my lip gloss) you will begin to have small victories and those victories will help to propel you on to greater victories. Eliminating my ambivalence toward my physical appearance led to me slowly beginning to eliminate other harmful aspects of my situation. It certainly didn't happen overnight, but over time, this process of purposeful pruning helped me to eliminate feelings of anger and self-loathing, remove negative and harmful relationships from my life and do away with many self-destructive behaviors that had held me captive for far, far too long. By slowly and methodically pruning away these detrimental aspects of my life, I was cleaning out my fishbowl and making room for my Fab**YOU**lousness to grow and flourish. Those things that once served as a distraction were now gone, allowing me to focus my time, energy and attention on the aspects of my life that were positive and that I wanted to see bloom. Just as weeds can choke out a flower and prevent it from experiencing the warmth and radiance of the sun, so too can negative emotional and physical clutter prevent your Fab**YOU**lousness from experiencing the warmth and radiance of your loving attention. In order to see your Fab**YOU**lousness bloom, you *must* be willing to pick up those figurative garden shears and slowly go about the process of pruning in a loving and intentional way that will, over time, create magnificent and sustainable results.

As our fishbowls become clearer and clearer and our roses begin to bloom bigger and bigger, it is vital that we come to grips with the fact that we will *never* be able to eliminate *all* negative elements from our lives. It simply isn't possible. It *is* however, possible to take action TODAY on *something*. I have come a long way, make that a LOOOOOONG way from where I was when I first began my purposeful pruning process. I've done a good job of eliminating the biggest, scariest and most harmful attitudes and practices from my life, but that doesn't mean that my work is done. Currently, I am working on trying to eliminate my addiction to caffeine and my compulsion to check my email "one last time" before going to bed at night (which usually leads to me staying up an extra hour to respond to things that could easily wait until the next day, thus leading to my need for more caffeine in the morning—it's a vicious cycle!) Once I've eliminated these toxic elements from my life, I'm sure that I'll find *other* things to eliminate. That's how it works. I'm okay with this though because I know from past experience that with each of these eliminations, the masterpiece of my Fab**YOU**lous life is being revealed. The same will be true for you.

FAB LAB

Observe it...

- Take a look around your living environment. Are your surroundings neat and tidy or does it look like a cyclone has hit? How about your car? Your office? Your refrigerator? Your closet? Often, our outer world is a reflection of what is going on in our inner world. If we are experiencing inner turmoil, our surroundings will often suffer and conversely; if we are taking good care of our possessions and personal space, it is a good indication that we are taking good care of ourselves as well. Do your surroundings need a little purging? If so, take a good look at the mental and emotional clutter that you may also need to clear.

Test it...

- Set aside and hour to do some purging in your environment. Do you have piles of paper that need to be sorted? Are there condiments in your fridge that are four years past their "use by" date? Do you have clothes in your closet that no longer fit or are no longer in style? Taking time to purge your living/work areas can do so much to boost your spirits and clear out space for good energy to enter. Purge your physical environment and see if your emotional environment doesn't suddenly improve as well. Clean your fishbowl and stop swimming in sh*t.

Record it...

- Think about your life and your environment. In your journal, make a list of some of the hindrances in your lifestyle (debt, unhealthy habits, lack of sleep, people pleasing, etc.) that are moving you further away from living a FabYOUlous life. Make another list of some of the things in your physical environment (clutter, toxic people, unfinished projects, etc.) that are keeping you stuck in an un-FabYOUlous rut. Next—pick the smallest, most easily eliminated item from each list and choose ONE of those items to act on. Journal about your plan of attack and then take action. Give yourself plenty of time as you eliminate this first negative from your life, but once you feel that you've gotten it under control, move on to the next one.

Think about it...

"Elegance is elimination" ~Cristobal Balenciaga

"The wisdom of life consists in the elimination of nonessentials"
~Lin Yutang

"To become learned, each day add something. To become
enlightened each day, drop something" ~Lao Tzu

"You have to decide what your highest priorities are and have the
courage—pleasantly, smilingly, unapologetically—to say 'no' to
other things, and the way to do that is to have a bigger 'yes'
burning inside." ~Stephen Covey

"When we can become skilled at selectively knowing what to prune
out of our lives, what remains becomes stronger, brighter, clearer."
~Lisa Byrne

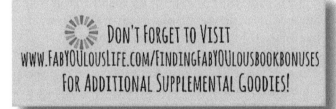

DON'T FORGET TO VISIT
WWW.FABYOULOUSLIFE.COM/FINDINGFABYOULOUSBOOKBONUSES
FOR ADDITIONAL SUPPLEMENTAL GOODIES!

Chapter 6

WHAT NEEDS TO GROW?

Yay you! If you made it through the last chapter and are still reading—congrats! You made it through the toughest chapter of the book and are well on your way to a Fab**YOU**lous life. In my work with clients, I have found that the pruning process is often one of the most difficult steps for women to take on their way to Fab**YOU**lousness. The tendency is either to take on too much too fast by trying to eliminate *all* negatives from life at once (and thus ending up burned out, frustrated and grouchy) or to become so overwhelmed that nothing is pruned and Fab**YOU**lousness becomes choked off by an overgrowth of unhealthy thoughts, habits and behaviors. That's why it is *so* important to start small and to gradually build upon success. Just as with those prized roses—pruning truly does lead to blooming.

Thankfully though, the often painful process of pruning isn't the *only* step that leads to Fab**YOU**lousness. Not only must we prune away the elements in our lives that need to go—we must also learn to fertilize and nurture the things in our lives that are positively serving our higher purpose of Fab**YOU**lousness. This process of *growing* is oftentimes a much more enjoyable experience than pruning, but don't think that just because it is fun, it can't be beneficial—nothing could be further from the truth.

So often in our society, we become focused (way TOO focused) on trying to get better at the things that we are bad at. This begins way back in elementary school. As a student, I always seemed to bring home great grades in subjects like reading, writing and speech. My grades in math however; were less than stellar (okay...WAY less than stellar...like, not even in the same universe as stellar). So, what happened? Yep—my teachers and parents forced me to spend SO much extra time trying to bring up those darn math grades. I missed recesses, after school play time, TV shows and phone chats with my best friend Mia, all because I was being forced to work on math problems. BLECH!!! I hated it and though I understand that their efforts were all well intentioned, guess what—I *still* suck at math. Being a mathematician was *never* a part of my entelechy. No matter how much I work at understanding math, it is never going to be one of my gifts. Now; that's not to say that the extra effort didn't help *somewhat*; I mean, I did make it through grade school, high school and college (all of which required math classes) but being *less bad* at math is definitely not the same thing as being *good* at math. I will *never* be good at math.

Fortunately, now that I am an adult and calling the shots in my life, no one can force me to spend hours agonizing over pages of math problems (just try it—I dare you). If I have complicated math issues, I call my accountant to take care of them or ask my hubby who is much more gifted with numbers than I am (always wise to marry someone who is strong in the areas where you are weak—it makes them feel needed!) Instead of constantly battling the areas in which I am weak, I have learned that I am much more successful and that my life moves forward much more quickly when I spend my time nurturing and developing the areas of my life in which I am already naturally strong. When I spend my time writing, speaking or teaching, I not only experience a great deal more success, I also have A LOT more fun and, it doesn't take a mathematician (thank goodness!) to understand the equation: success + fun = a Fab**YOU**lous life.

> ## *Success + Fun = a FabYOUlous Life*

So, how about it? What are you good at? Don't tell me nothing because if you believe that to be true, it means that you have been sold a big, rotten bill of goods and have bought into a lie that someone (who needs to be PRUNED from your life) has sold you. Believe me—there are PLENTY of things that you are good at. Are you good at being a mom and taking care of your kiddos? Awesome! Do you have a knack for picking out amazing looking outfits? Great! Do your gourmet cooking skills garner rave reviews from your friends? Perfect! Sometimes, if we are at a difficult point in our life, it can be a challenge to see all of the things that we are good at, but I promise you—those gifts *are* there and they are longing to be fertilized so that they can grow and flourish. Malcom Forbes aptly pointed out that "too many people over value what they are not and undervalue what they are". This is a habit that we must break if we are serious about finding our Fab**YOU**lousness— we must learn how to celebrate and make the most of our natural gifts and talents because those gifts and talents are key pieces in our Fab**YOU**lous life puzzle.

One easy way to discover our areas of giftedness is simply to think about the things that we enjoy doing. Usually, we get the most pleasure out of activities that we tend to be good at. For example; I *do not* enjoy math, but I could happily spend hours reading and writing. I *do not* get a rise out of domestic endeavors such as cooking, cleaning, organizing etc. I do however; enjoy hands-on creative activities such as knitting and sewing. I want to throw up at the thought of having to sing in front of a group of people; but I absolutely *love* speaking to large groups. In each of these instances, the things that I *enjoy* are things that I tend to be naturally good at. So—ask yourself what types of activities do you enjoy being engaged in? What do you do for fun? When you find yourself procrastinating on a job or project, what do you do instead? Perhaps, the thing that you're doing *while* you're procrastinating is the thing that you really *should* be doing in the first place.

Another way to uncover your gifts and talents is to think about the things that other people tend to compliment you on. Oftentimes, other people can be far better at seeing our Fab**YOU**lousness than we are. Are you constantly being told that you're a good friend? Maybe that means that you are gifted with empathy and compassion. Do people always ask for your recipes after you've prepared a meal? You're obviously gifted in the kitchen. Do you typically get what you want when dealing with salesmen or business colleagues? Negotiation skills might be high on your list of abilities. Maybe you always seem to make people smile and feel uplifted. Encouragement and cheer might be areas of giftedness for you. Don't discount any areas that seem to show up as strengths, talents or gifts in your life—even if you can't see how they might be impactful, they *are*, and with proper tending, *all* of your gifts can work together in harmony to create your Fab**YOU**lous life.

Finally, if you are looking for a way to really get a laser focus on the gifts that you possess; you might want to consider a strengths assessment. I would first recommend reading the book *Strengths Finder 2.0* by Tom Rath (*after* you finish reading this book of course!) Not only does the book provide hundreds of strategies to help you learn to apply your strengths in everyday situations, it also includes a special access code that will allow you to take an online strengths assessment. The online assessment is fun to take and it will provide you with detailed information regarding your top 5 strengths from an extensive list of thirty-four key strengths that are measured by the Clifton Strengths Finder tool. Once you've taken the test and received your results, you will have a great understanding as to the unique qualities and gifts that make you Fab**YOU**lous. The next step is to simply start rockin' what you've got and let those strengths, gifts and talents become the driving force in your life. There is a Japanese proverb that says, "raise the sail with your stronger hand". This means that in order to truly live a Fab**YOU**lous life, you must go after the opportunities that arise in your life that you are best equipped to excel at. Don't waste valuable time and energy mourning your areas of weakness—celebrate instead your areas of *strength*, for those are the areas that will lead to your Fab**YOU**lousness.

While discovering and building upon the positive aspects of your *personal* being is the first, most crucial activity in this chapter; it isn't the only one. You see, your personal attributes, skills and talents aren't the *only* things in your life that need to grow. You also have positive *outside* influences that can help to complement the Fab**YOU**lous things that are going on in your inner being. For example; when I went through my period of purposeful pruning, it became VERY evident to me and everyone who knew me, that I needed to prune my toxic relationship with my (now ex) husband. That unhealthy relationship was something in my life that definitely needed to GO. I am now however; happily married to a man who loves me and supports my dreams. He has brought love, laughter and security into my life and as a result, I am able to thrive in an environment where I am able to be the most Fab**YOU**lous version of myself and live a truly Fab**YOU**lous life. Obviously, despite the fact that my first marriage was a wreck, my *current* marriage is a blessing and is therefore something that I want to nurture and allow to GROW. I also have some very deep and supportive friendships that help me to be a better person and a thriving career that brings me great satisfaction and financial reward—these are two more aspects of my *outer* life that I most certainly want to see GROW.

Once you've identified the positive aspects of your *personal* being (gifts, talents, skills, passions etc.) take a good look at the outside forces that have made an impact on your life. If these forces make a positive difference and help propel you closer to your ideal Fab**YOU**lous life, they too are areas of your life that are worthy of fertilization so that they can GROW. If however, these forces do nothing but tear you down, weaken your resolve or lead you astray, they are aspects that need to be pruned. It's a delicate balance sometimes, but just like in that prize rose garden, fertilization *and* pruning are both required in order for you to truly bloom and reach your full potential.

As a final note on this subject. I feel that it is important to point out that not everything in your life that needs to grow is necessarily something that can be perceived as *positive*. Just as I mentioned in the last chapter that not everything that needs to be pruned from our life is inherently *bad*, so too is the fact that not everything that needs to be fertilized in our life necessarily *good*. For example—my experience of losing myself in an unhealthy marriage and struggling with an eating disorder that was slowly killing me was definitely NOT good. However; now that I am through that experience and am healthy; I can see that even that dark and difficult period in my life has served a higher and positive purpose. Telling my story and putting together programs based upon my experience of reconnecting with my Fab**YOU**lousness has helped countless other women in difficult circumstances. That scary and painful part of my past served as an impetus for change and a catalyst for creating a Fab**YOU**lous life, while also helping others to do the same. Though I clearly needed to prune the parts of my life that were contributing to my painful situation; learning to take that experience and GROW it into something that can help others, has become one of my greatest joys. As Jean Paul Sartre said, "freedom is what you do with what's been done to you". Having the ability to look at your difficulties with compassion and an intention to learn, may just lead you to your calling, like it did for me. I believe that it is *so* important for us to learn how to *use what has happened to us* rather than letting our past experiences *use us* if we truly want to experience the freedom of Fab**YOU**lousness.

You are unique (maybe I should say YOUnique!) and no one else on this planet has the same mix of gifts, talents, experiences and strengths that you have to offer. We are ALL Fab**YOU**lous, but Fab**YOU**lous in our own individual ways. We need to be able to

66

experience and express our own Fab**YOU**lousness while also enjoying and appreciating the Fab**YOU**lousness of others. Rock what you've got and admire the strengths of those around you. Appreciating our own gifts while admiring those of others, without being intimidated or feeling inferior, is a true mark of Fab**YOU**lousness.

FAB LAB

Observe it...

- Spend some time this week noticing people who are GREAT at what they do. Maybe it's an athlete on TV or a singer on the radio. Perhaps it's your child's math teacher who has a knack for making fractions fun, or your neighbor who makes the best zucchini bread that you've ever tasted. Whatever it is—make note of the individual's gift (and be sure to mention it to them—everyone loves a sincere compliment). Do you think that this level of greatness could have been achieved if the person didn't enjoy what they were doing? Is it possible that the activities that bring *you* the most joy might also be your greatest areas of giftedness?

Test it...

- Think about the things that you enjoy doing and compare them to the things that people most often compliment you on. Is there crossover between the two? If there is something that you enjoy doing, there is a good chance that you're good at it and if you're good at it, there is a good chance that other people admire you for it. If no one compliments you on the things that you enjoy doing, it is probably because you haven't put your talents out into the universe to be of service. Stop hiding your FabYOUlousness—the world needs your gifts! I firmly believe that the more you love doing something, the better you'll be at it and the further it will take you in life.

Record it...

- Instead of a "to-do" list, create for yourself a "TA-DA" list (or visit *FabYOUlousLife.com/FindingFabYOUlousbookbonuses* and download a free printable TA-DA list). This is a list of all of the things that you are good at, and things that you enjoy. This is NOT the time to be humble—this is a time to recognize your FabYOUlousness and to show gratitude for it! List all of the things that you know you're good at and all of the things that people *tell* you you're good at. Post this list somewhere where you'll see it every day so that it can serve as a tangible reminder of just how FabYOUlous you truly are.

- Make another list of things that you think sound fun but that you're not necessarily good at *yet*. These things will often turn into things that you'll *become* good at. If you are interested in something enough to try it—DO IT. You never know where it might lead. I tried golfing for the very first time ever last year and even though I wasn't *good* at it (it was my very first time after all) I was decent enough to know that I seemed to have a natural knack for it and that if I kept working at it, I could *become* good—and more importantly, I had a blast. Fun is a major key to FabYOUlousness and it is far better than knocking yourself out to get better at something that you hate. Once you have this list made, pick one thing on the list to *try*. This isn't about being an expert—it's about exploring your interests to see if they might lead to some untapped potential. If not, fine—move on to something else that sounds fun. You might just surprise yourself.

Think about it...

"Hide not your talents. They for use were made. What's a sundial in the shade?"   ~Benjamin Franklin

"Take your pleasure seriously"   ~Charles Eames

"The meaning of life is to find your gift. The purpose of life is to give it away"   ~William Shakespeare

"You have gifts to give the world. Find your voice and prosper" ~Beverly Mahone

"The Universe continually gives us gifts, but we have to open them"   ~Nancy Ashley

"Trusting your individual uniqueness challenges you to lay yourself open"   ~James Broughton

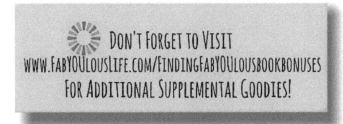

DON'T FORGET TO VISIT
WWW.FABYOULOUSLIFE.COM/FINDINGFABYOULOUSBOOKBONUSES
FOR ADDITIONAL SUPPLEMENTAL GOODIES!

Chapter 7

IF NOT NOW, WHEN ? IF NOT NOW, WHY?
DO YOU HAVE A WAIT PROBLEM?

I have to chuckle as I start writing this chapter because it strikes me a bit funny that I am writing about procrastination. It's not that I'm not qualified to write this chapter; believe me—I know A LOT about procrastination. In fact, for many years, I put the PRO in procrastinate. No, my reason for chuckling is because there was a time in my life when procrastination robbed me of so much Fab**YOU**lousness that I now have to laugh when I think about it because the only other option would be to break down and start sobbing over those lost days, week, months and yes—even *years*.

I'm sure that I'm not alone when I say that procrastination has been one of the biggest barriers between me and my Fab**YOU**lous life. It is pervasive in our culture. It is *so* easy to fritter away our time on things that will have no lasting positive impact on our lives. We have great intentions of doing all manner of Fab**YOU**lous things but then we get sucked into taking mindless Facebook quizzes (oh c'mon—I can't be the *only* one who has taken the quiz to find out which Grease character I am. I got Rizzo—not sure how I feel about that) or surfing the internet to see if our horoscope for tomorrow looks any more promising than today's. Believe me—I get it! It wasn't until my rock bottom moment when every area of my life (marriage, health, career, friendships, etc.) went plummeting head first off a cliff that I was forced to take a hard look at my situation and face the realization that my procrastination was causing me to miss out on far too many opportunities, connections and adventures. My unwillingness to confront my fears, act on ideas, follow up with contacts, pursue leads, etc. caused my life to come to a grinding halt and I became stuck in a rut that was so deep that it felt more like the Grand Canyon. It most definitely was *not* Fab**YOU**lous.

The thing is though, *everyone* is guilty of procrastination and there are as many reasons as to why we procrastinate (and *even more* excuses that we concoct to justify our procrastination) as there are procrastinators. It is an absolute epidemic and is likely one of the biggest hindrances keeping us from realizing our full Fab**YOU**lous potential. This procrastination habit is one that we MUST break if we truly want to find our Fab**YOU**lousness, but before we can kick the habit, we must first understand the reasons for its existence in the first place. When I was in treatment for Anorexia, one thing that was drilled into my head on a daily basis was the phrase "awareness allows change". This simple yet profound truth can also be applied to our battle with procrastination. Once we become aware of the reasons behind our self-sabotaging behaviors, we can take the necessary steps to overcome them and make the real and lasting positive changes that we need to make in order to truly live within the greatest expression of our Fab**YOU**lousness.

One of the most common reasons for procrastination is a condition that we all experience from time to time—overwhelm. How many times have we been faced with a project that seems so big and daunting that rather than jumping in and getting started, we check our email (for the sixteenth time in an hour) or surf the web for yet another entertaining cat video? In our mind, we know that LOLcats.com isn't getting us any closer to completion on our project and yet we just can't seem to tear ourselves away from those silly, box sitting cats. This condition is so common that I'd be willing to bet that nearly everyone has experienced it at least once, despite the fact that the antidote is so *simple*. Yes, you read that correctly—the solution is *simple* though not necessarily easy.

The solution when faced with this type of overwhelm induced procrastination is simply...get started.

I know, I know...I can feel your eyes rolling as you process what you just read. Believe me, my eyes have rolled plenty of times too. However; I've also experimented enough to know that getting started is often the most difficult part of a task and yet, once started, it becomes easier and easier to keep going. I guess Sir Isaac Newton knew a thing or two when he declared that a body at rest tends to stay at rest while a body in motion tends to stay in motion. I put this theory (Newton's first and second laws of motion, for those of you who want to look it up in order to procrastinate a bit longer) to the test almost every day as I work to train for a half marathon that I will be running soon. You see, I am not one of those people who just loves to spring out of bed in the morning, lace up her sneakers and head out for a pre-dawn five-mile run. NO. That does not sound enjoyable to me. In fact, it sounds downright awful. Truthfully, up until just recently, I have pretty much *hated* any kind of physical exertion and the thought of running one mile (much less 13.1 miles!) was enough to make me want to cry; and the notion of me completing a half marathon seemed completely ludicrous. Strangely though, I've discovered that the hardest part about my training regimen *isn't* the actual running of the miles—it's getting the shoes on my feet and my butt out the door. Once those two feats are accomplished, the rest comes much more easily. I am able to find my rhythm and log the miles. At first it was one mile (and I'd have to take walking breaks) but then, one mile turned into three and three turned into five etc. I have yet to accomplish my half marathon goal, but I am no longer overwhelmed at the mere thought of it. I now *know* that I will be able to do it—I simply have to continue lacing up my shoes, getting my butt out the door and *starting*. Having the discipline to do this has made my once overwhelming goal of running a half marathon now seem inevitable instead of impossible.

So, whether your overwhelming project is reaching a fitness milestone, writing a book, getting a graduate degree etc., you *must* get started. Once you do your part and get started, the universe will conspire on your behalf and bring about the necessary conditions and circumstances to aid you as you move your project toward completion. Scottish explorer W.H. Murray described this phenomenon best when he said, "The moment one definitely commits oneself, then Providence moves too...raising in one's favor all manner of unforeseen incidents and meetings and material assistance, which no man could have dreamt would have come his way". That might sound a little too "new agey" and woo-woo for some of you, but I have experienced it myself enough times to know that it is absolutely true. Take the small step to get started and I promise that you'll be amazed at where you end up.

While feelings of overwhelm can paralyze us and cause us to do nothing (or at least nothing *productive*...) there is another emotion that can stir up even more powerful feelings within us and therefore erect even more stubborn strongholds in our minds when it comes to procrastination. I'm sure you can guess the emotion that I'm talking about here is none other than the big F word...well okay—the *other* big F word. Yep—I'm talking about FEAR. The truth of the matter is, we are *all* afraid of something. I wish I could say that I've come so far in my quest of finding FabYOUlous that I am no longer afraid of anything; but that simply isn't true. You'd know that if you ever saw the way that I shriek like a little girl whenever I see a spider or the way I suffer a full-on anxiety attack at the thought of riding a Ferris Wheel (I'm totally fine with gnarly roller coasters, haunted houses etc. but I will lose my sh*t if you try to get me on a Ferris Wheel—seriously—don't try it. I'll hurt you and embarrass both of us).

Fortunately, spiders and Ferris Wheels probably aren't going to be big contributing factors as to whether or not I live a fully FabYOUlous life; but what about other fears like the fear of failure or even the fear of success? What about the fear of letting other people down or the fear of looking foolish? These kinds of fears are very real for many of us and can hold us hostage for far too long by preventing us from moving out of our comfort zones and into our Fab**YOU**lousness. You've heard the phrase "paralyzed by fear"—well, that's exactly what happens. We over think and over *feel* all of the negative things that we *might* experience if things go wrong. Or, on the flip side—we panic at the thought of the added responsibility or recognition that might come our way, were we to actually succeed. We place far too much value on the opinions of other people and then worry about not living up to *their* expectations for our lives, or we hold ourselves back from something that we'd like to experience for fear of falling on our face and looking like an idiot. In short, we fear changing anything that will take us out of our safe, *little* existence, despite the fact that we yearn for SO much more. It is a true Catch 22 that will ensnare us for years if we don't find a way to put an end to our procrastination and take concrete actions that will bring us out of fear and into Fab**YOU**lousness. We *must* figure out exactly what it is that we are afraid of, and find a way to deal with that fear so that we don't continue to use that emotion as an excuse to remain stagnant. If we are going to fear anything, we should be afraid of what our lives will look like in five years if we *don't* begin to take the steps to bring us more fully into our Fab**YOU**lousness. That, could indeed be a horror story of epic proportions.

As we think about our fears as purveyors of procrastination, I *do not* want to give the impression that I take this business of fear-busting lightly or that I think it is easy. On the contrary—I *know* that it is hard. I have struggled all my life with the fear of letting people down and with a huge—make that **HUGE**—fear of failure. These two fears combined are what kept me from stepping out of a situation that was slowly killing me, even though I knew in my heart, soul and mind that getting OUT was precisely what I needed to do. You see, I come from a long history of wonderfully loving marriages. My parents have been married for eons and both sets of grandparents before them were happily married until death they did part. Happy, loving marriages were a part of my "norm" growing up and when I married my first husband, I fully intended for it to be a lifelong commitment. To make matters even more challenging, I was, at the time, surrounded by holier than thou church members who constantly preached about the sanctity of marriage and a wife's role of loving submission within the marriage. These factors combined to make a deadly snare in my mind that had me convinced that I needed to put aside any thoughts of separation and instead wear a mask of contentment to hide the turmoil that was really going on in my life.

Unfortunately, my marriage wasn't quite what I had previously experienced marriages to be—not by a long shot. Instead of love, support and partnership, I found myself dealing with issues of manipulation, control and abuse. I knew in 2004 that I needed to escape the marriage but fear kept me from acting on it until 2007. I spent over *three years* trying to pretend that everything was okay (all the while dying on the inside) because I was scared of being "the one" to be a failure when it came to marriage. I didn't want my other family members and those church folks who kept preaching to me that "God hates divorce!" to look down on me—or worse yet, *pray* for me (please don't get me wrong here—I absolutely believe in the power of prayer/meditation/blessing and I think that it is the most beautiful gift that can be given when someone *sincerely* calls upon their faith in a genuine desire to bless and uplift another. Unfortunately, I've also seen prayer used as an innocent looking cover up for malicious gossip. Thank you but I don't need *that* type of prayer). In short, my fear of failure and fear of letting people down kept me from having the courage to advocate for myself and take the necessary steps to get my life back.

It now makes me sick to think that I let procrastination due to fear rob me of three full years of my life. I spent over 1,100 days feeling trapped, angry and hopeless all because I was afraid of looking like a failure and worried about what people would think of me. As it turned out, when my marriage finally did fail (and it failed gloriously—trust me, there is no better antidote to the fear of failure than to fail something SO magnificently that it will make every future failure seem small in comparison), the people who truly loved me, *still* truly loved me and the people who were *praying* (oh how I wish that there was a font for sarcasm!) for me disappeared.

There is no doubt that fear is scary, but we *must* learn to conquer it if we are ever going to experience our most Fab**YOU**lous life. Fortunately, I have learned (through much trial and error...*lots* of error) that there are ways in which I can reframe my fears and make them work *for* me as opposed to *against* me. It seems counter-intuitive but when I stop looking at my fears as hindrances to my progress and instead embrace the feedback that they provide to me as a tool that I can use as I strive for my goals; I find that I am able to *use* my fears in order to *lose* them. By putting my fears to work *for* me as opposed to *against* me, I am able to harness their power and let them serve as a catalyst of change in my life.

One powerful way to *use* your fear is to visualize it as a fierce competitor. I have big, Fab**YOU**lous dreams for my life; and, as I think about my dreams, I could easily get side-tracked and overwhelmed by all of the myriad things that could potentially go wrong in my quest to reach these dreams. *THAT* is exactly what fear wants to happen. Fear wants to keep me trapped in my hum-drum comfort zone and prevent me from taking any steps toward my Fab**YOU**lousness. To help counteract this, I picture myself as a fighter who is fighting *for* my dreams and fear as a competitor who is fighting to keep me *from* my dreams. Every time fear starts to rear its ugly head, I visualize myself punching it square in the face. Sometimes I'll even crank the song "You're Going Down" by Sick Puppies to get myself *really* fired up (laugh if you want but music can be a powerful motivator—especially hard, angry music). This strategy might sound a little extreme but it works for me because 1.) I am highly competitive by nature so picturing my fear as a *competitor* is incredibly motivating for me and 2.) as we pointed out earlier, visualization has been proven to be an effective technique for goal attainment, so we might as well put it to good use by visualizing ourselves kicking ass on our fears.

Another way to *use* your fear is to see it as a trainer. Just as a personal trainer can help us to develop our physical muscles by providing the resistance of weight training, fear also employs resistance that can help to us to develop. Every time we face down a fear and act *in spite* of it, we build a little more muscle in the areas of courage and confidence. The more "muscle" we build, the more resilient we become and the better prepared we are to face the next fear. The lesson that we learn from this is that fear IS NOT fatal and that it *can* be overcome. Every time we take a step forward in spite of the fear that is in our path, we gain confidence in our abilities. As we prove fear wrong, over and over again we begin to become successful in ways that seemed impossible before we began our resistance training. Feeling the resistance of fear and using it as a tool to develop our confidence is a powerful way to put our fear to good use.

Fear can also be the corrective lens that we need in order to help us better focus on what is truly important in life. When I was in my recovery from Anorexia and escaping from my toxic marriage, I was incredibly fearful about how I was going to provide a good life for my two little boys. I had no clue as to how I'd be able to cover the mortgage payment *and* keep food on the table (my boy's father was proving to be a dead-beat so I couldn't count on any help from him). I remember one night in particular when I tossed and turned all night long wrestling with the fear until I felt like I was drowning. Interestingly enough, I woke up the next morning (after sleeping for what felt like five minutes) with a crystal-clear idea as to how

I'd make it work. I absolutely refused to settle for anything less than a good life for my sons, so in order to help us get back on our feet financially, I decided to rent out the basement of our house. It had two bedrooms, a full bath and a living area—perfect for a single person who didn't need much space and couldn't afford traditional rent scenarios. This situation wasn't *ideal* (giving up the basement meant giving up my boy's main play area) but I knew that the situation was only temporary, and it was a solution that helped me to stay afloat until I was able to find a higher paying job. That time in my life now seems *so* long ago and my boys and I have come *so* far. Still, it was the fear of losing everything that caused me to become hyper-focused on the things that truly mattered the most to me—my sons and the ability to provide a comfortable upbringing for them. Fear caused me to ignore everything else at the time and focus like a laser beam on my immediate concerns. This focused attention is what allowed me to come up with a solution that worked—*and* gave me the courage to face down future obstacles. As an added benefit, it also provided me with a short-term solution that allowed me to keep my home, which I still have to this day. That home that I was once so scared of losing, is now a rental property that brings in monthly passive income while building equity and adding value to my financial portfolio.

Much research has been done on the subject of fears and the overwhelming conclusion is that when faced with these common, non-life-threatening (but no less scary) fears; the ability to face our fears is undeniably linked to enhanced levels of creativity and overall well-being. When we recognize that fear is a major contributor to our procrastination habit, we can take steps to mitigate it and thereby place ourselves back on a forward-moving trajectory in life. Refusing to do this, not only causes us to miss out on our FabYOUlousness, it can also diminish our health and overall well-being. In fact, studies have now shown that in just over the course of a single academic semester, procrastinating college students were much more prone to compromised immune systems, colds, gastrointestinal problems and the flu. Additionally, these students suffered more bouts of insomnia and tended to earn lower grades than other, non-procrastinating students. I don't know about you, but gastrointestinal issues, the flu and insomnia DO NOT sound Fab**YOU**lous to me. These students might have put off their bigger, more Fab**YOU**lous goal of a quality education in favor of more fleeting pleasurable pursuits (not that I know anything about the pleasurable pursuits of college students...wink) but much like the dreaded credit card bill, the time to pay up *always* arrives. Don't bankrupt your future dreams and Fab**YOU**lousness by frittering away the hours today.

Clearly, fear and overwhelm are two of the largest, looming reasons behind most people's procrastination habits but there are others as well—depression, unclear goals, burnout, laziness etc. It is important that we identify our own procrastination triggers so that we can put into place the appropriate measures to help us take action when that urge to visit LOLcats.com threatens to overtake us yet again.

While, I have found the aforementioned "Use it to Lose it" fear-busting technique to be the most effective way for me to deal with my own deeply rooted procrastination habit; there are other methods that also work well. Another strategy that I employ on an almost daily basis is one that I call "The 15 Minute Miracle". This method is especially effective when I'm faced with a task that I *really* don't want to do. I just convince myself that no matter how bad something is, I can probably survive doing it for 15 minutes. Then, I set a timer and get to work. It's amazing, but when I hunker down and commit to doing a task for a mere 15 minutes, I get an incredible amount of work accomplished and the 15 minutes seem to fly by. In fact, I often find myself getting into such a state of flow that I'll set my timer for *another* 15 minutes so that I can maintain my momentum. Sometimes I'll adapt this method and use another unit of measurement instead of time. For example, I would *never* get any writing done if I constantly thought about writing a book. Writing a book is way too big and overwhelming for me to fathom without taking myself to the brink of a nervous breakdown. Instead, I just tell myself that I will sit down and pound out a *page*. For me, the thought of writing an entire book is an anxiety attack waiting to happen, but a *page* is something that I can easily manage. A word becomes a sentence, sentences become a paragraph, paragraphs become pages, pages become chapters and voila— chapters become books. Chunking large tasks down into smaller, more manageable, bite sized pieces is the only way to get any big goal accomplished.

The bottom line is that if you truly want to find your Fab**YOU**lous, the time has come to put off the procrastination, set your timer and get the ball rolling. Don't be intimidated by the amount of time that it might take for you to reach your goal—that time is going to pass regardless of whether or not you make good use of it. Just think about how much more Fab**YOU**lous your life will be when you take the steps that you *know* you are being called to take. I think that Nike is onto something when they say, "Just Do It!" When it comes to finding our Fab**YOU**lousness, *doing it* is the only thing that will get us to where we want to be, and there is no better time to get started than NOW.

FAB LAB

Observe it...

- Check in with yourself on an emotional level. What Fab**YOU**lous things could you have accomplished in your life by now had you not procrastinated on them? How does this observation make you feel? It isn't a great feeling, is it? Why do you think that you have allowed procrastination to rob you of this Fab**YOU**lousness? What is it that has you feeling overwhelmed or fearful? Though it is natural to want to mourn the lost opportunities or wasted time that has passed through our fingers, it is much more beneficial to set our sights on a new Fab**YOU**lous endeavor or revive and recommit to an old one that still makes our heart sing and GET STARTED on it. It is not too late. You are not too old. You are not unworthy. You are Fab**YOU**lous and you deserve to experience the joy that comes from accomplishment rather than the defeat that comes from procrastination.

Test it...

- Pick a project that you'd like to complete but that feels overwhelming to you. Picture the angst, overwhelm, fear and frustration that you have associated with the project as a big, black cloud in front of you. Allow yourself a few minutes to really *feel* the emotions associated with the cloud. Now, imagine yourself on the other side of that cloud with your project completed. Imagine the elation, relief, satisfaction and pride that you'll feel once you've broken through the cloud and have your completed project in front of you. Next, set a timer for 15 minutes and take one step toward the completion of your project. It's only 15 minutes so it won't kill you, but it *will* help to give you some momentum toward your goal and a sense of accomplishment. Try setting a timer for 15 minutes every day until your Fab**YOU**lous project is Fab**YOU**lously finished. The bottom line is that the 15 minutes is going to pass no matter how you spend it and the Law of Diminishing Intent states that if you don't take action soon after the idea strikes you and the emotion is high, the urgency will quickly begin to diminish and the longer you wait, the less likely you will ever be to accomplish your goal. Think about how much more Fab**YOU**lous you'll feel if you spend that time consciously engaged in a project that is meaningful to you rather than scrolling through a website full of funny cats.

Record it...

- You procrastinate, I procrastinate, we *all* occasionally procrastinate. The challenge is to recognize when we are procrastinating and then figure out *why*. Start keeping tabs of the times when you are most prone to procrastination. What project/jobs are you avoiding? Why do you think that you are avoiding them? Spend time journaling about the Fab**YOU**lous things that you'd like to accomplish but haven't yet begun. These very things are likely to be an important part of your journey to Fab**YOU**lousness. It doesn't matter if the project will take an hour to accomplish or a year. If it is something that makes your spirit sing, and is something that you feel called to accomplish; you *must* get started. You *must* break through the resistance and begin to take concrete steps (even if they're just baby steps!) toward your Fab**YOU**lousness. You deserve nothing less. Journal briefly about the resistance that you are feeling because identifying the resistance will help you to put a finger on the reason for your procrastination. Most importantly though, journal extensively about the feelings of joy, empowerment, accomplishment and pride that you will feel once you've stopped procrastinating and have broken through the resistance. Journal about the ways in which your life will be different once you take control of your procrastination problem and fully act upon your Fab**YOU**lousness.

Think about it...

"Create a definite plan for carrying out your desire and begin at once, whether you're ready or not, to put this plan into action."
~Napoleon Hill

"Don't get stuck with the NOW you. Instead, use it as a springboard to the NEW you." ~Melissa Venable

"To change your life, start immediately, do it flamboyantly, no exceptions." ~William James

"Today is when everything that's going to happen from now on begins." ~Harvey Firestone Jr.

"This is your time, your world, your pleasure." ~William Stafford

"How we spend our days is, of course, how we spend our lives" ~Annie Dillard

"Procrastination is one of the most common and deadliest of diseases and its toll on success and happiness is heavy."
~Wayne Gretzky

"The best time to plant a tree is twenty years ago. The second-best time is NOW." ~Chinese Proverb

DON'T FORGET TO VISIT
WWW.FABYOULOUSLIFE.COM/FINDINGFABYOULOUSBOOKBONUSES
FOR ADDITIONAL SUPPLEMENTAL GOODIES!

Section 2

At first they'll ask you *why* you're doing it.

Later they'll ask you *HOW* you did it.

Eventually they'll ask you if you're hiring.

While the first part of *Finding FabYOUlous* was all about asking the questions that need to be answered in order to discover the FabYOUlousness that resides so gloriously within you, this second part of the book is all about practical application. This is where we dig into the nitty gritty of the "how".

You'll no longer be tasked with assignments from the Fab Lab because from here on out, every single chapter is an experiment in and of itself. You can follow through these chapters in the order in which they are presented or you can hop around to the ones that you feel most drawn to. To make things easier, this section is divided into four smaller sub-sections 1.) Your FabYOUlous Spirit 2.) Feeling Fab 3.) FabYOUlously Connected and 4.) Your FabYOUlous Purpose. These sub-sections represent the vital areas in life that together, create a solid foundation upon which to build your most FabYOUlous life. There are forty chapters divided among the four sub-sections. The important thing isn't whether or not you take the chapters in order—the important thing is that you remain open to the suggestions offered in each chapter and that you give each suggestion the opportunity to resonate with you. Some will, others won't, and that's okay. You don't necessarily have to incorporate every single suggestion from every single chapter into your life (though doing so would practically guarantee more FabYOUlousness than can be imagined) but it *is* important that you take the time to sit with each suggestion to see if it feels right with your spirit. If it does, great—add it as a regular practice in your life. If it doesn't, fine—go on to the next suggestion.

We've tackled the "who", "what", "when", "where" and "why" of FabYOUlousness—now let's get busy hammering out the "how".

"You are an infinite spiritual being having a temporary human experience"

Dr. Wayne W. Dyer

WHAT THE HECK IS SPIRITUALITY ANYHOW?

This is a question that I get asked a lot and admittedly, it's a difficult question to answer. I think that the difficulty lies in the fact that there are *so many* possible answers out there depending upon whom you ask. A Tibetan Monk is likely to provide a very different answer than a Catholic Priest would. A Wiccan Priestess will no doubt define spirituality much differently than would a Muslim Imam.

Does this mean that there is *no* correct way to answer the question *"what is spirituality?"* I don't believe so. Instead, I believe that this simply means that spirituality should only be defined by one's own *personal* experience of it. Connecting to our spirit is a highly individualized practice and yet it is one of the quickest ways that we can truly embrace, honor and radiate the Fab**YOU**lousness inside of us.

Research has long shown that spirituality (which can be either religious or non-religious) can provide us with a sense of connection to others as well as to something "bigger" that guides our lives. It can bring a sense of meaning to our lives and an inner peace that often contradicts the chaos surrounding us.

How then do we cultivate a spiritual practice that is right for us?

For some, spirituality might be synonymous with their religious faith. Others may consider themselves to be spiritual but not necessarily religious. Many experience spirituality while they are engaged in worship while others find spiritual connection while in nature or listening to music. There is no cookie-cutter "one size fits all" when it comes to spirituality—it is something that is deeply personal and highly individualized.

Though studies have shown that individuals with a regular spiritual practice receive numerous quantifiable benefits in the areas of physical and emotional well-being; not everyone knows where to begin when seeking to develop their spirituality. According to Ken Pargament, a leading expert in the field of the psychology of religion and spirituality, developing spiritually is a dynamic process involving three separate stages:

- **Discovery**—finding a form of spirituality to which we feel drawn
- **Active Practice**—can include attendance at religious services, meditation, chanting etc.
- **Struggle**—a time when life events cause us to question our beliefs

Often, the best way to discover the most personally meaningful way to connect with spirit is to begin with contemplation. Simply spending some quiet time alone to ponder the answers to the following questions can set you on the right path towards your own experience of spirituality. Find a quiet place and spend some time *feeling* out your answers to these questions*...

What role does spirituality currently play in your life?

What role would you like for it to play?

What or whom do you call on or turn to in times of difficulty?

What do you hold to be sacred in your life?

When do you feel the presence of the sacred most strongly in your life?

Are there spiritually significant items, symbols or practices that you feel naturally drawn to?

What or who has influenced your sense of spirituality?

Where are you when you experience the most inner peace? What are you doing?

Are there spiritual practices that you believe to be wrong for you?

How have you tried to develop your spirituality in the past? What roadblocks/struggles have you encountered?

How has your family and religious upbringing shaped your attitude towards spirituality?

How have key events from your life influenced your sense of the spiritual?

In what direction do you feel that your intuition or inner guide is leading you?

What do you feel that your purpose on earth is?

What kind of spiritual transformation/revival have you experienced in the past?

What judgments/negative perceptions towards spirituality do you harbor?

Why do you long to create and cultivate a personal, spiritual practice?

What are some do-able next steps that you can incorporate into your spiritual journey?

These questions aren't easy and you may not have immediate answers to many of them. That's okay. Revisit the questions often and spend time over a few days, weeks or months reflecting on your answers. Allow yourself to follow your spirit's lead as this is a process that needs to be *felt* as well as thought about. This process is also not a static, one-time deal. It is an ongoing, ever changing process that will likely lead you to different discoveries at different times in your life. This is all good and normal and if you allow it, this awakening of your true spiritual essence will guide you to a meaningful spiritual practice that will bring more peace, fulfillment, connection and Fab**YOU**lousness into your life.

*Based on questions by Ken Pargament

BECOME YOUR OWN B.F.F.
LEARN TO MASTURDATE

I don't remember where I first heard the term "masturdate" but I absolutely love it. I love it because 1.) it's a funny play on words that cracks me up and 2.) it is something that might seem a little strange and awkward at first, but eventually feels *sooo* good and may even be considered a religious experience.

Oh come on—this book is rated PG (or PG-13 at the very least)...get your mind out of the gutter (wink!)

Masturdating is essentially, the process of going out on dates with yourself so that you can learn to connect with your spirit and enjoy your own company. The important aspect of this is that when I say dates, I mean *dates*, not errands. Running to the bank, grocery store and dry cleaners by yourself is *not* a date—going out for a nice dinner (with wine) and then seeing a movie that you've been looking forward to *is*.

At first, many people have a hard time *dating* themselves. They feel strange sitting alone in a crowded restaurant or buying a single ticket to a concert because they don't want people feeling sorry for them and thinking that they can't get a *real* date. I only have one thing to say about this...GET OVER IT. Don't let the initial feelings of awkwardness or worry over what other people are thinking of you (because newsflash—most people *aren't* thinking of you) stop you from the joy and pleasure that is masturdating.

Just like in traditional dating scenarios when two people are learning about each other and trying to discover what makes the other person tick in the hopes of finding a love-match; masturdating does the same but on a solo level. Masturdating is all about spending time in your own company so that you can rediscover all of the things that you enjoy and love about yourself.

Not only is masturdating an eye-opening experience that helps us to reconnect with the activities that we enjoy, it also allows us the opportunity to experiment with new things without the worry of needing to please or impress another person. We are able to try new restaurants or experiences knowing full well that if we don't like them, we can get up and walk out without anyone judging us. On the flip side, if we discover a quaint little bookstore that we love, we can spend as much time as we want wandering the aisles without worrying about anyone getting impatient with us. By going on a date with ourselves, we are taking full responsibility for our own happiness and enjoyment, and in doing so, sending a powerful message to our psyches that we matter and that our pleasure is important.

In addition to the pleasure factor, masturdating has other benefits of a more spiritual kind. When we invest time and energy into our own enjoyment and lovingly treat ourselves with kindness and respect, we attract more of those enjoyable and loving feelings to us. When we put forth the effort to "woo" ourselves and shower ourselves with attention, we demonstrate to the universe that we are worthy of adoration—to which the universe responds by bringing us more opportunities to feel cherished and adored. It's a cycle that once you get on, you'll never want to get off.

Often when I talk about masturdating, people will assume that this is something that is only meant for singles—not for people who are happily coupled up. Nothing could be further from the truth. I am happily married to the world's greatest guy and still, I masturdate every chance I get. Sure—my honey and I go out on wonderful dates together and invest time in our relationship; but...going to yarn stores or quaint coffee shops just isn't his jam, so I spare him the agony of these activities and happily pursue them on my own. I firmly believe that having a solid, foundational relationship with oneself is the critical bedrock upon which all other relationships are built. Only by valuing and loving ourselves are we able to truly value and love others. Plus—when we develop a strong sense of respect for ourselves, we will learn not to tolerate anyone who gives us less than what we know that we deserve. Therefore, masturdating helps us to establish the boundaries and standards necessary for us to enjoy rewarding relationships with others.

Okay—now that I've convinced you of the value of masturdating, it's time to go to it. Here are a few suggestions to get you started...

- Go see that movie that you've been wanting to see but haven't been able to convince anyone else to go to. While you're there, be sure to buy yourself a large popcorn and a box of Junior Mints—this is a *date* after all.
- Pack a picnic basket (complete with a bottle of wine), grab a blanket and a good book and head to a park. Spend the afternoon nibbling, drinking, reading, resting and people watching. Give yourself bonus points if you leave your smartphone at home.
- Spend a day at the beach (or in the mountains, at a lake etc.) Get some sun and fresh air (and maybe a little exercise if you throw in a hike or swim)
- Take a class that interests you—pottery, website design, genealogy, photography, bonsai tree growing...whatever flips your switch.
- Enjoy breakfast *out of* bed. Grab the crossword puzzle from the newspaper and head out to breakfast by yourself. Enjoy some pancakes and OJ with a side order of peace & quiet.

The opportunities for masturdating are only limited by your imagination. Anything that you might *normally* do with another person is an opportunity to masturdate. Lose your inhibitions, do a little experimentation and allow yourself to experience all of the Fab**YOU**lous pleasure that comes from masturdation, you'll be *so* glad that you did.

FIND YOUR PLACE

Now that you've taken some time to "date" yourself and have (hopefully) learned to enjoy your own company, you need a special place where you can regularly go to feel supported, loved and inspired. We *all* need a place that we can call our own—a place where we can escape from the cares and stresses of the day and let our souls unwind and find delight. A sacred sanctuary of your own doesn't have to cost a lot of money nor does it require a multitude of material possessions; all it takes is a bit of creativity, imagination and inspiration to create a space that resonates with your deepest values, reminds you of your hopes and dreams and inspires you to reach for them. With a little intentionality, your chosen place truly can become, in the words of Joseph Campbell, "a sacred space where you can find yourself again and again".

Ideally, your entire *home* would be this place, but I'll confess, for me that just isn't the case. Don't get me wrong—I love the feeling of coming home at the end of a long work day or after a tiring business trip; and it thrills my heart to know that my home offers a place of refuge to my family and is filled with love and laughter on most days. However; my *personal*, sacred space isn't my home, it's the upstairs guest bedroom *in* my home. You see, as much I love my home, I share it with three other people...all of whom happen to be large males. My husband and college aged sons are the absolute loves of my life but they prefer Xboxes and weight sets to throw pillows and succulent centerpieces. In short, there is a serious overdose of testosterone at my house. We even have (I'm dead serious here) a Nerf basketball hoop duct taped to the wall in our family room.

So, because my home more closely resembles a frat house than a serene retreat; I have taken it upon myself to commandeer our upstairs guest bedroom and make it my own. Yes—there is still a bed for when we have overnight visitors, but there is also my computer desk, bookshelves, and storage containers for my knitting yarn. My bookshelves are filled with books that I love and that bless my spirit. My desk has on it, seashells from a family trip to Florida's Sanibel Island, a decoupage art piece made by my sweet-sister-in law and an empty Coke can that says "Superstar" on the side that my hubby gave to me after I was honored as one of twelve "Colorado Women of Vision" (the can wasn't empty when he gave it to me. I drank it. It was the most delicious Coke *ever*). The walls of the room are covered with framed photos from a family trip to Hawaii, my vision board and a cute (but cheesy) poster that my youngest son bought for me (at a thrift store). These things hold absolutely no intrinsic value for anyone else on the planet and yet to me, they are priceless.

In addition to the objects that mean so much to me, I also have an aromatherapy diffuser in my sanctuary room so that I can fill the air with uplifting scents and a little space heater so that I never have to feel chilly despite the fact that my men like to keep the thermostat in our house set ridiculously low. There is nothing particularly beautiful or *special* about my sanctuary room and yet whenever I set foot into it, I immediately feel more centered, grounded and alive. It is where I do most of my writing, blogging, reading and dreaming. It is where I am surrounded by reminders of good times with the people that I love most in this world and it is a place where I can just sink in, relax and refocus on everything that is truly important in my life.

I feel very fortunate to have an entire room that I can call my own (unless we have overnight guests, in which case the room reverts back to being the guest room) but I realize that not everyone has that luxury. Remember though—your space doesn't have to be large, it just has to be *yours*. A favorite chair in the corner of a quiet room can work just as well.

Since this is *your* personal space, you are the one who gets to decide where it is and what it contains. There is however; one suggestion that I think is very important, and that is to find a place where you are able to be *alone*. Even if you can't really find a place that is separate from your general living areas, try to find a quiet corner that won't constantly have people traipsing through your space while you are in it. Beyond this, there are no hard and fast rules as to what your space should look like—the important consideration is what the space *feels* like when you are in it.

Also, because this is *your* space; you get to decide how to make it special. Here are a few suggestions that you might want to incorporate in order to create a space that supports love, warmth, security, peace, joy and mindfulness...

- If your space is a part of a larger living area that is commonly used by others; you might want to invest in a pretty, decorative screen that you can put in place when you are in your sacred space. Explain to your family or roommates that you are not trying to keep them out, but that you are instead, trying to create a distraction-free zone where you can focus on your goals and emotional well-being and that in order to do this effectively, you need to be able to enjoy some solitude.
- Make sure that your space is well lit (preferably with natural light from a window) so that you won't have to squint while reading, journaling, knitting...whatever it is that you plan to do in your space. If possible, select a space that has natural sunlight from a window with a nice outdoor view.

- Only allow items into your space that hold a sacred value to you. Don't allow your space to become cluttered with too many knick-knacks. I love the sea shells on my desk because they remind me of good times spent with my family *and* of the future dreams that I have of owning a beautiful home on the beach. Maybe you love music and therefore want a guitar in your space or an artist's pad to encourage your creativity. Whatever has special meaning to *you*, make a place for it in your sanctuary.

- Create a sense of coziness and comfort. My personal space has a fluffy comforter that I can wrap up in if I'm cold (or if I'm just needing to feel cozy since I also have my space heater) and some soft, comfy pillows. I have a friend who keeps a pair of fluffy slippers under the chair in her space so that she can slip them on when she enters into her sanctuary. If you like candles, they can add a soothing ambience *and* comforting fragrance to your area as well (just be sure that you always extinguish them before leaving). Whatever makes you feel comfortable and supported should be included in your sacred space.

- Decide upon a soundtrack for your sanctuary. I love music but I have found that when I am in my sanctuary, some music is too distracting for me. Since I do a lot of writing, reading and meditating while I am in my sanctuary, I prefer to listen to soothing music that has no distracting lyrics so that I am not tempted to sing along. I have some wonderful Native American flute music as well as some hauntingly beautiful instrumental music that I play (via my iPhone) while I am in my space. I have other friends though who insist upon complete silence when they are in their sanctuaries and others still who have miniature water features in their spaces because they like the sound of gurgling water. Again, this is *your* space so only you can know for sure what kind of sound ambience you want to create.

- Consider adding a touch of nature to your space by bringing in a potted plant or two. Plants are great for helping to keep the air in your space clean because of their ability to remove toxins from the air. Additionally, plants help to create a sense of calm and a connection with nature. I am particularly enamored with tabletop succulent centerpieces but any kind of plant that appeals to you can be used. If you're not a fan of potted plants, you can receive many of the same benefits by bringing in a bouquet of beautiful, fresh cut flowers.

- The use of color can do a lot to enhance the vibe of your space. How do you plan to use your sanctuary? If you plan to use it as a place where you can partake in quiet, contemplative activities, you might do best by choosing a soft, calming neutral color palette for your space. On the other hand, if you want to use your space for more lively pursuits; an energizing mix of bright, playful colors might be what you want to opt for. Even if you can't paint the walls of your space, you can add pops of your desired colors by adding pillows, rugs, accent pieces etc. in your chosen color scheme.

- One of my greatest desires in life is to inspire women to live their most FabYOUlous lives. In order to do this, I, myself, need to remain inspired. One strategy that I employ to boost my own individual level of inspiration is to include items that I find to be personally inspiring in my sanctuary space. I've already mentioned the sea shells that remind me of my goal of one day owning a beach home, but I also have a small framed print of an inspirational quote that speaks to me and my vision board. Looking at these items never ceases to fill my tank and boost my levels of commitment and inspiration. Be sure to find items that do the same for you and include them in your sanctuary space.

- Often, when I am in my sanctuary space, I come up with fantastic, creative ideas. Unfortunately, I have also *lost* some great ideas because I wasn't prepared to record them when they came to me. This usually happens to me because I'm reading or meditating (or some other mentally engaging activity) and don't want to take the time to run grab a pen and notepad to record my thoughts. Don't let this happen to you! Because our sanctuary spaces are places where we are able to relax and let go of the stresses of the day, they are also places where creativity is uninhibited and therefore free to run wild. Make sure that you are prepared to capture the thoughts and ideas that come to you during your sanctuary time by having a small notebook and pen available, or, if you're more on the techie side, make sure that you have your smart phone handy so that you can record a voice reminder for yourself.

By creating *your* sanctuary, *your* way, you will design a space that calls to you and draws you in. Spend some time over the next week creating your sacred space and remember—it doesn't have to be *fancy* to be Fab**YOU**lous.

BECOME HEAVILY MEDITATED

"Sometimes I sits and thinks and sometimes I just sits"

~Satchel Paige~

How can something as simple as sitting still and quieting your mind be so stinkin' hard? Seriously? Everywhere you look there are articles citing the numerous benefits of having a meditation practice. These benefits are manifested in both, our physical *and* mental well-being and include (but are not limited to)...

Physical Health Benefits of Meditation

Enhances Immune System   Weight Management   Alkalizes the Body   Increases Blood Flow   Reduces Muscle Tension Improves Sleep   Increases Energy Levels   Lowers Cholesterol Increases Sex Drive   Reduces Headaches/Migraines   Lowers Blood Pressure   Fights Diabetes   Reduces Cortisol Levels Increases Oxytocin Levels

Mental Health Benefits of Meditation

Reduces Anxiety   Reduces Phobias/Fears   Alleviates Depression   Builds Confidence   Improves Focus   Stabilizes Emotions   Increases Intuition   Increases Creativity   Enhances Will Power   Reduces Anger/Rage   Improves Intelligence Promotes Inner Peace   Leads to Enlightenment   Cultivates Gratitude   Improves Memory   Enhances Relaxation   Assists in Discovering Life Purpose

Still, despite these myriad reasons to meditate, it is something that so many people (myself included) struggle with.

Why? What can possibly be so hard about this? How is it that I can put on my running shoes and go for a ten-mile run and yet for some insane reason, I have such a difficult time with sitting still and calming my mind for fifteen minutes?

This was a question that drove me crazy for a long time and I searched diligently for an answer. As it turns out, my hang-up with meditation stemmed from a big misunderstanding of what meditation actually was, and what components a sustainable meditation practice required. I was taking something simple and making it way, way too hard.

The truth of the matter is that there is really no *wrong* way to meditate. Even if you sit for ten minutes with your mind bouncing around from one meaningless thought to another the entire time—that's fine. The important thing is that you view meditation as a friend that you *want* to spend time with—not as an annoying boss that you feel *obligated* to spend time with. There is no set amount of time that you *must* meditate and no specific meditation technique that you *must* use in order to find nirvana. In fact, a meditation teacher once told me that there can be as many different ways to meditate as there are meditation practitioners. The key is to find something that works for you and stick with it.

As I conducted my own experimentation with meditation, I discovered that there were really only ten things that I needed in order to establish a sustainable meditation practice. These magical meditation components are...

1) **A goal.** What do you most hope to gain from your meditation practice? Relaxation? Increased ability to focus? Higher levels of concentration? Serenity? By picking out one particular benefit that you would like to manifest through meditation, you will have a

benchmark by which to evaluate your practice over time.

2) **A commitment to yourself.** Write it down if you must, but whatever you do, make sure that you make a commitment to yourself that you WILL allow yourself the time to begin and cultivate your new practice. Hold yourself accountable to your commitment.

3) **A set time of day.** As you begin your practice, it will be important to establish consistency. Having a specific time of day will help you to establish meditation as a habit. As you become more experienced with meditation, you will be able to add more flexibility to your routine, but when starting out, it is best to be consistent with the timing of your practice.

4) **A special place.** Again, having a certain place that you go to for your meditation will help to establish a routine. Pick a place in your home that is comfortable and private (hopefully you followed the advice in the previous chapter and have already established a location for your own personal sanctuary). You may even want to create a mini altar with candles and sentimental items. Even if you just pull a cushion off of your couch and sit on it in the corner of your living room—having a special place for your meditation practice will make it more meaningful and habitual.

5) **A *realistic* amount of time**. As a newbie to meditation, it would be foolish to try to commit to a four-hour long meditation practice. You *may* get to that level at some point, but for starters it will be difficult enough to maintain a practice that is only 20 minutes a day. In fact, it is suggested that true beginners start with a time of 5 to 15 minutes. Set a timer if you need to, but start out with a time limit that doesn't feel daunting. Five minutes is absolutely

acceptable. As you grow in your practice you will no doubt want to increase the amount of time that you spend in meditation, but starting out small will help to keep you from feeling overwhelmed and will help you to build upon the momentum of early success.

6) **Thirty days.** Commit to sticking with your new practice for thirty days. It takes time to find your rhythm and get in your groove so don't just give up after a week of floundering. Use the thirty days to figure out what time of day works best for you, what type of meditation you prefer and where you feel most comfortable practicing.

7) **A simple meditation technique.** One of the most common mistakes made by newbie meditators is attempting a meditation technique that is too complicated. According to former Zen Buddhist monk and author of *The Wooden Bowl: Simple Meditation for Everyday Life* (Hyperion, 1998), Clark Strand, a simple breath meditation is often the best starting point. To begin, says Strand, sit in a comfortable position (you may wish to use a cushion or folded blanket). Straighten your spine, relax your shoulders and take a few deep breaths. Gently close your eyes and allow your body to become still. Then, begin counting your breaths from one to four (count on the exhalation—the out breath). Try not to manipulate the breath in any way; simply observe and count. When your mind begins to wonder (which it will), don't admonish yourself—simply bring your mind gently back to your breath. Continue in this fashion for the allotted amount of time.

8) **Grace.** You won't start off as a perfect meditator. Heck, you probably won't even start off as a *good* meditator. That's okay. Meditation is about presence not perfection, so give yourself some grace as you

begin to build your meditation practice. If your mind wanders, don't get frustrated—many people have a difficult time staying focused during meditation and that's not such a terrible thing. In fact, scientists are now reporting in the journal, *Frontiers in Human Neuroscience* that wandering thoughts can actually be a *good* thing. In their study, MRI scans showed that people who allowed their thoughts to flow freely during a twenty-minute meditation session showed activity in more of the brain regions related to memory retrieval and emotional processing (both of which are key to managing stress) than those who remained focused. So…give yourself some grace and don't beat yourself up if you suffer from occasional bouts of "Monkey Mind" —it's normal.

9) **Evaluation.** After thirty days of meditation practice, give yourself a quick review. Go back and look at what your goal was when you first started. Are you feeling more relaxed? Has your concentration level improved? Are you more easily able to find and maintain focus during your meditation time? Be honest with yourself regarding the things that you'd like to improve upon or changes that you'd like to make to your practice, but also be proud of yourself for the positive strides that you are making.

10) **Thirty-six more days**. A 2009 study from the University College, London shows that it takes 66 days of consistent practice for anything to truly become a habit. By adding an additional thirty-six days to your initial meditation practice, you will be at the magical 66 day mark and your practice will feel like a normal and routine part of your day. This is a great time to celebrate your accomplishment by adding a bit more time to your practice or maybe trying a new form of meditation. The important thing is that by now, your

practice will be second nature to you and you will be reaping the numerous rewards.

It might sound cliché, but I truly do believe that if I can meditate, *anyone* can meditate. Still, on those days when it is particularly difficult for me to get centered, I will use a guided meditation to help ground me and get me into the right frame of mind. There are many guided meditation CD's on the market but I prefer to use the Simply Being Guided Meditation app on my iPhone. It is an inexpensive app that comes highly recommended by The New York Times, Self Magazine and Yoga Journal. I love that fact that this app allows you to determine how long you want to meditate (the shortest option is just five minutes) and that you can customize your meditation experience by determining if you want soft music or nature sounds playing during the meditation.

As you become more comfortable with your meditation practice, you may want to change things up a bit. You can try using mala beads to guide your meditation or begin using a mantra as your focus point. Some people are even able to combine meditation and fitness by participating in walking meditation or meditative yoga. I haven't quite mastered *that* yet, but I am happy to report that my meditation practice has become a natural part of my day that I genuinely look forward to. My monkey mind still runs rampant on occasion, but since incorporating meditation into my daily routine, I have found that my ability to focus has dramatically increased while my anxiety levels and penchant for impatience have dropped.

GO ON A SPIRITUAL DETOX

Do you find yourself in a perpetual bad mood these days? Are you experiencing a lack of energy that goes beyond just being tired and instead has you feeling genuinely *weary*? Are you bored with your life and frustrated with a lack of enthusiasm?

If you answered yes to any of these questions, there's a good chance that your life is in need of a good spiritual/mental detox.

Just as our physical bodies can begin to feel sluggish and unhealthy when they are subjected to too many environmental toxins or poor dietary choices; so too can our spiritual/mental state suffer when it is subjected to too much negativity, stress, or all-around ugliness. That's why it is crucial to our overall well-being that we take steps to detox our spirits on a regular basis.

While drinking healthy, **infused water** (water infused with lemon, cucumber and mint leaves is one of my favorite detoxification blends), eating healthy and organic foods and **dry brushing** your skin are Fab**YOU**lous practices for detoxing the *physical* body; what can be done to detox on a spiritual level? Here are a few suggestions to get you started…

10 FabYOUlous Ways to Detox Your Spiritual Life

1) **Tidy up your desk** or your car, or your closet…just tidy up *something*. It's so hard (if not downright impossible) to have a positive perspective on life when you are drowning in clutter. A messy, disorganized outer life is often an indication of a messy,

disorganized *inner* life. It's hard to find your FabYOUlousness when it is hidden under a pile of papers on your desk or shoved in a pile of old clothes at the back of your closet. Taking an hour to do some straightening up can work wonders for your mental state. Don't try to tackle your entire house (you'll just end up feeling overwhelmed and frustrated) but instead, pick one area where you spend a lot of time and tend to it. Once that area is cleaned up, you will notice a lightness in your spirit and will likely feel inspired to move on to another area. Don't try to do too much at once—just begin gradually to clean up your outer surroundings and notice how much cleaner your emotional state feels as well.

2) **Limit your exposure to bad news.** It has literally been *years* since I've watched a news program. I also don't read newspapers. Does this mean that I am completely out of touch with current events or uneducated on important social matters? Nope. It just means that my psyche isn't inundated with constant stories of murder and mayhem (or political mud-slinging since I'm typing this three days before an especially contentious presidential election). Whenever something truly important is going on in the world, I always manage to find out about it through social media, my friends or my own investigation. I learned a long time ago however; that exposing myself to too much "news", just caused me to be stressed out and cranky. I believe that we could all benefit from decreasing our intake of negative news (which makes up 99% of the news because let's face it—*good* news doesn't sell) and *increasing* our intake of positive, uplifting and inspiring content. Give your mental state a boost by feeding it with positivity—something that you're not likely to find much of in the nightly news.

110

3) **Get a little culture.** While you're cutting your intake of negative news, try upping your consumption of culture. Go to a museum, attend a poetry reading or enjoy a night at the symphony. While I'll confess that I'm a bit more of a baseball games and rock concerts kind of gal, I *do* enjoy attending performances by our local ballet company (I particularly look forward to their annual rendition of The Nutcracker) and taking in theatrical productions at our various stage venues. There is something so moving about live performances and they never cease to leave me with a sense of awe. The same can be said of great literature or art. Even my macho husband who watches WWE wrestling (I'm serious—he watches that stuff) enjoys attending these cultural gems with me. Give it a try yourself—I'm sure that your spirit will be filled.

4) **Surround yourself with the right kind of people.** We all know who the people in our lives are that we should limit our time with, but do we actually do it? Take a look at the people with whom you spend the most time. Are they positive and encouraging people who get you excited about your goals and eager to change your life for the better—or are they too busy gossiping about others and complaining about how much their life sucks? Life is too short and too precious to be wasted on people who drag you down and who don't bring out the best in you. If you're already feeling depleted and in a funk, the last thing you need is to hang around with people who suck the life out of you. Misery may love company, but misery only becomes *improved* in the company of positivity.

5) **Bond with an animal.** Yes—surrounding yourself with positive, uplifting people is one way to let go of negative B.S. (belief systems) but so is spending time with a special critter. There are many physical health

111

benefits of pet ownership, but the mental health benefits are just as impressive. Numerous studies have shown that bonding with a special animal is great for reducing stress and increasing happiness levels. Animals are social creatures just like we are and they love us without judgement or unrealistic expectations. If you are fortunate enough to have a pet of your own, you are blessed beyond measure, but even if you don't, you can still reap the benefits of an animal friendship by volunteering at your local animal shelter or pet sitting for your friends.

6) **Delegate.** I'll admit, this one tends to be a hard one for me, but I've discovered that few things make me feel more overwhelmed and in need of a spiritual detox than feeling like I have too many balls in the air. For this reason, I have had to force myself to get better at delegating certain aspects of my work and personal life. I will still handle critical tasks myself, but I have gained a great deal of freedom and peace of mind by delegating "busy work" to someone else. I've learned that I can send my sons (who both have their own vehicles) to run errands for me (if I bribe them with a little gas money) and have my local grocery store *deliver* my groceries straight to my front door. By delegating non-critical tasks such as these, I have gained time in my schedule and therefore, peace in my spirit.

7) **Recreate...for *real*.** Find something that you can do for fun, without concern about score, expense or how you look. Do you love to knit? Then knit. Do you love to sing? Then sing. Do you love to run? Then run. Do you love to read? Then read. Do you love to grow Daffodils? Then by all means, grow the prettiest Daffodils anyone has ever seen. We all need activities that help us to decompress and let go of the stresses

of the day. Obviously, our lives won't be very productive if we spend *all* of our time on recreational pursuits, but at the same time; our lives won't be very productive if we *never* spend time on recreational pursuits. Being able to truly cut loose and lose ourselves in the sheer enjoyment of an activity will help to recalibrate our levels of spiritual and emotional well-being and allow us to release toxic thoughts and behaviors that are holding us hostage.

8) **Laugh it up.** Few things feel as good as a genuine and hearty belly laugh. Laughter truly is the best medicine because it helps to provide a proper, balanced perspective on life, aids in relaxation and promotes healing. Unfortunately, when we are in desperate need of a spiritual/mental detox, it can be very difficult to find something to laugh at. This is why it is *critical* that we make the effort to bring laughter into our lives. Watch a funny movie, learn a few jokes, spend time with a funny friend—do whatever you need to do to ensure that you are getting enough Vitamin L in your life.

9) **Make inspiration a priority.** Keep your spiritual fuel tank from running on empty by surrounding yourself with inspiration. I do this by keeping my own personal vision-board front and center in my office (and on my computer's desktop background and iPhone wallpaper). I also keep inspirational books nearby and my iPhone loaded up with uplifting podcasts. I've created a life where I am able to plug into positivity at almost any time and from almost anywhere. This has been incredibly beneficial in my battle against toxic negativity and I am sure that the same can be true for you.

10) **Get out into nature.** It is hard to clear your mind and detox your spirit when you are cooped up in a cubicle

all day long. For this reason, it is *imperative* that you learn to escape into nature on a regular basis. Go for a hike or splash in a lake. If you live in a city, you can still visit a park and enjoy a picnic under a tree. Let yourself breathe the fresh air and feel the sun on your face. If you're able, slip off your shoes and walk barefoot across the grass. Nature has a unique way of grounding us *and* providing a sense of connection to all things.

By being intentional in our efforts to detox our spiritual/mental lives, we open ourselves up to a world of positivity and possibility. Take the steps necessary to ensure that you regularly cleanse your spirit of negative B.S. (belief systems) so that you are unencumbered and able to more fully experience your most FabYOUlous life.

BASK IN THE BEAUTY

"Beauty behind me, beauty before me, beauty beyond me, beauty beneath me"

~Navajo Prayer~

There's no denying it—the world can be an ugly place sometimes. We turn on the television to see news of riots, bombings and all manner of atrocities. We hear vile language and messages of anger and violence coming from the music on our teenager's iPod and we see our oceans and natural areas littered with garbage and toxic waste. So. Much. Ugliness. How then do we, in the midst of all of this ugliness, find and celebrate beauty? How do we create a world in which beauty surrounds us and resides *within* us?

Well, the first step to finding and cultivating beauty is to understand that it *is* there. We may have to squint, clean our glasses, and squint some more, but if we look closely enough and are intentional in our seeking, we can always, *always* find something beautiful to celebrate. This is so, so important because beauty elevates us beyond the mundane and exists as an expression of the divine. Beauty (whether in nature or of human creation) lifts our spirits, stirs our hearts and engages our intellect. The more we seek it out and let it permeate our souls, the more profound and essential beauty will become to us. Also—the more beauty we draw into our lives—the more beauty *we'll have* to draw into our lives. We find what we look for. If we look for beauty, the Universe will supply more and more beauty for us to discover.

If you are in a place (physically or spiritually) where you find it difficult to find and recognize beauty; try a few of these suggestions for inviting more beauty into your life.

- Keep a book of beautiful photographs or poetry on your desk or nightstand. Look at it regularly.
- For God's sake—turn off the TV. Seriously, when is there ever anything *beautiful* on TV? Like, never. Instead, turn up the volume on some beautiful music. I just discovered a kind of music called Wholetones. It is music that is recorded at specific frequencies so as to promote healing, consciousness, relaxation, mindfulness and more. I honestly don't know if any of those claims are true or not but I *do* know that the music is gorgeous, rich and mesmerizing. A quick Google search for "wholetones" will help you to find it if you are interested in learning more.
- When you wake up in the morning, open your window *before* you open your smartphone browser. Throw open the shades and let some sunshine in. Close your eyes and let the sun drench you for a few sacred seconds. Or—if you have to wake at some ungodly hour *before* the sun rises, look at the stars or moon with a sense of awe. Starting your day in this manner (instead of with an onslaught of emails or cranky Facebook political rants) can help to set the tone for the day and open you up to more beauty as the day moves forward.
- Bring a flower, seashell, rock or water feature into your work area. Whenever you start to feel your spirits lag, take a few moments to really look at the object and contemplate its beauty. Let it serve as a small reminder of the beauty of nature that surrounds us.
- If you live in a city where it is difficult to enjoy nature, take a look instead at the skyline at night. Notice the lights against the night sky. I've seen many beautiful sights in my

lifetime but few can rival the nighttime view of New York City from atop the Empire State Building.

- Watch a sunrise or sunset. Okay—I'll confess that I'm rarely up early enough to take in a sunrise, but I absolutely love going for an evening walk around the lake near my home and watching the sun set behind the crystal water and purple mountains. I've done this many, many times and yet I am completely awed and overwhelmed by the beauty—every. single. time.

- Remove dirty, broken, cluttered or ugly things from your living areas and work spaces.

- Invest in some beautiful stationary/note cards and use them to correspond with friends and family members instead of always sending boring old emails.

- Sign up for an art class or learn to play an instrument. Learn to create your own beauty.

- Plan a vacation to a place that is well known for its beauty. Mountains, beaches, deserts, prairies—they all have an abundance of beauty to offer. As you plan your trip, search the web for images of your destination and keep these images on your desktop for moments when you need a beauty boost.

As we look for beauty in objects, our surroundings and nature, let's not forget to also look for it in our fellow human beings. I'm not talking about physical beauty here (because honestly—what *is* that even?). Instead, I'm referring to the kind of beauty that radiates from one's spirit and heart. Even those with broken hearts and shattered spirits, still have beauty to offer this world. Even those with whom we vehemently disagree on important issues, still have beauty to offer this world. In order to live our most Fab**YOU**lous lives, we must be willing to squint past the ugly and focus our attention instead upon the beautiful. It's there—I *promise;* just look.

DITCH THE DRAMA
TO FIND YOUR DHARMA

Drama, drama, drama. It's EVERYWHERE. It's on our televisions, in our schools and FILLS our Facebook feed.

I'll confess that I enjoy losing myself in a good drama occasionally. Tuning in to watch Keifer Sutherland play President Kirkman on the TV show *Designated Survivor* is something that I look forward to every week—it makes my life seem so much more sane compared to espionage, terror attacks and finding out that your teenage son may (or may not) have been fathered by another man. A little bit of drama as a means of finding entertainment can certainly have its place in our life. It's an entirely different story however, when the drama isn't just on the TV or movie screen and is, instead, a prevalent component of our everyday existence.

Drama manifests itself in our life as a reactive response to what's going on around us. While our emotions are neither good nor bad—they're just feelings that emerge within our bodies in response to circumstances—*drama* is what occurs when we allow our emotions to overwhelm us, causing us to blame and oppress others *or* to victimize ourselves. Sometimes we perpetuate drama by lashing out at someone on Facebook who voices an opinion that we don't agree with or by stirring up trouble amongst a group of friends when we feel as though we've been slighted. Other times, the drama is more subtle and passive-aggressive in nature. Regardless of its expression; drama is nearly always damaging to our sense of well-being and prevents us from living in the fullness of our personal power and Fab**YOU**lousness.

How then do we break our addiction to the chaos and stress brought about by drama? How do we detach from the insanity and rise above the mud-slinging? It's not always easy, but the more we make a concentrated effort to do so, the happier we will be. We need to learn to move the needle from the low energy, low vibe, drama side of the scale to the joyful, centered and purpose filled *dharma* side.

This then begs the question, what exactly *is* dharma? Well, on the insanity spectrum, dharma is about as far away from drama as one can get. It is an ancient Sanskrit word that (despite not having an *exact* English translation) means "the path" and can be understood as one's personal life path or calling. Most traditional spiritual teachers agree that dharma is connected to the underlying order of the universe, so one clue to discovering whether or not you're following your dharma might be to ask yourself if you feel that the universe is supporting you in what you do. To follow your dharma means to align yourself with the most evolved level of your own consciousness in a way that is supported by and connected to Universal truth.

In simpler terms—living your dharma means consciously living the life that you were created to live in a way that nourishes your spirit, expresses your gifts, supports others and connects to the Universe.

Making the transition from living a life of drama to a life of dharma isn't easy but it can be done, and it is a shift that will bring more mindfulness, connection, expansion and meaning to your life than you ever thought possible. Thankfully, there are some steps that us mere mortals can take in order to help ease the transition from drama to dharma…

Simple Steps to Ditch the Drama and Find Your Dharma

1) **Bring attention to your awareness.** Often, when we are experiencing drama in our lives, the drama is really serving as a wall behind which feelings of pain and

rejection are hiding. Dharma is experienced when we are able to stand outside and witness our emotions with less attachment. This doesn't mean that we don't still feel the feelings—it just means that we don't become overwhelmed by them, thereby perpetuating negative reactions. Instead, living in dharma means understanding that we have the power to *choose* how we want to feel in any given moment, thus, we have the power to *choose* our behavior in response to our feelings.

2) **Get out of your head and into your body.** Drama requires a lot of over-thinking, mind twisting, second guessing and manipulation—all things that happen in our *head*. When you are ready to move from drama to dharma, try pressing the mute button on your thoughts for a while and instead, try shifting your focus to the sensations happening within your body. Take a deep breath and *feel* the air enter your lungs. Stretch and *feel* the tension in your muscles release. Despite whatever is going on around you, you have the ability to control what is going on *inside of* you.

3) **Ask for divine guidance.** Often, we get so caught up in trying to figure out how to make our lives work that we end up forcing solutions that aren't really solutions or trying to manipulate outcomes that end up taking us further off course. Rather than always thinking that we know what's best (which inevitably leads to more self-inflicted drama), it's time that we learn to humble ourselves and ask for divine guidance from that which is greater than us. Whether you prefer the term God, Spirit, Universe, Angels or some other identifier doesn't matter. What *does* matter is the recognition that there is a power greater than us and that that power is available for any of us to tap into at any time for guidance, connection and serenity.

121

4) **Meditate.** We've already committed an entire chapter to meditation but it gets mentioned again here because it is so, so vital when it comes to living a life of dharma. Stillness is a gift and silence allows us to tune into the frequency of divine guidance. When we are still, we are better able to sense the Universe's guidance and thereby live in a state of dharma rather than drama.

5) **Pursue passion and purpose.** When children are bored or stuck doing something that they don't want to do, they cause drama (picture a three year old who does NOT want to be drug through one more store and the fit that inevitably ensues when she is forced to comply). As adults, we like to think that we are more mature than that, but sadly, that often isn't the case. We may not throw ourselves onto the floor in a wailing, red faced fit (though some of us might!) but still, we have a tendency to create drama and chaos in our lives when we are not able to express our true desires and follow our passions. This is why, it is so crucial that we take the steps necessary to find our FabYOUlousness and to release it into the world to do its work. When we are living in the fullest expression of our FabYOUlousness, we are living our dharma.

6) **Make a commitment to yourself—and _keep_ it.** Once we commit wholeheartedly to finding our FabYOUlousness and letting it be the guiding force in our life, we open ourselves up to all of the power and abundance of the universe. As we honor the commitment that we make to living a life of dharma, we will naturally rise above all of the drama around us because we will be able to see it for what it is—a distraction from our higher purpose. Honoring our commitment to ourselves allows us to recognize and

avoid the quicksand pit of drama that threatens to pull us down and suffocate us.

7) **Walk it out.** Living a life of dharma means understanding that we are all physical bodies inhabited by a divine essence. Whether or not we allow that essence to be the guiding force in our life is up to us. Once we say that we want to ditch the drama and live out our Fab**YOU**lous dharma, we must take the appropriate actions to do so. This may mean distancing ourselves from toxic "friends" or replacing unhealthy habits with new, life-affirming behaviors. While some of these shifts might seem difficult at first, the more we start to move closer to our life of dharma, the more we will find ourselves *wanting* to make these positive changes. The ability to harness our self-discipline and "walk our talk" when it comes to moving from a life of drama to one of dharma is what will set us apart and help us to rise above the drama of the masses, and in so doing, experience our most Fab**YOU**lous life.

When it comes right down to it, living your dharma simply means knowing the inner truth of your Fab**YOU**lousness and fully living into that truth. The more we make this our aim in life, the less inclined we will be to put up with or engage in any drama that threatens to overtake us.

SELF CARE SO YOU DON'T LOSE YOUR SH!T

It happened. I'm not proud to admit it; but all the denying, justifying and excuse making in the world won't change that fact that it happened. I (a forty-something year old wife, mother and successful career woman) had a meltdown. Not just any meltdown mind you; I had a full blown, two-year-old-throwing-a-temper-tantrum kind of meltdown, complete with tears, slamming doors and a few words that aren't fit for print.

To be completely honest, I don't even remember what exactly triggered my meltdown. Someone must've said or done something terrible...right? I mean...grown women don't just fall apart like that for no reason, do they? Surely someone had to have committed some grievous crime against humanity in order to spark such an epic fit on my part...right?

Unfortunately...no. The reason that I can't remember the event that precipitated my meltdown is because the event wasn't a big deal. I'm sure that it was something that on any other normal day, would have flitted right past me without notice. This however, was not a normal day. On this particular day, I was exhausted, overwhelmed, stressed out, burned out and at my wit's end with everyone and everything. What's worse is...I had no one but myself to blame for my situation. I am the one who had stopped taking care of myself. I am the one who was burning the candle at both ends (and in the middle) and I am the one who allowed my own emotional and physical needs to be put on the back burner so that I could focus on other "more important" things.

I've learned the hard way that neglecting my own needs for too long will—sooner or later—lead to disaster. Neglecting my own well-being is one of the quickest routes to chaos and the only way to remedy the situation is to make my own self-care a priority again. How about you? Where does caring for your own emotional and physical health fall on your to-do list? As mothers, wives, career women, daughters, etc., we make every effort to care for the people, things and projects that are important to us—isn't it about time that we add ourselves to that list? Self-care is not *selfish*—it is vital to our well-being and allows us to better care for those who are depending upon us. Ask yourself the following 25 questions to determine if you are in need of some personal pampering...

Self-Care Test

1) Do you get enough rest?
2) Do you eat foods that taste good and nurture your body?
3) Do you go to the doctor for your annual physical?
4) Do you get regular exercise?
5) Do you connect with friends on a regular basis?
6) Do you have good posture?
7) Do you drink at least 6 glasses of water a day?
8) Do you enjoy regular quiet time?
9) Do you take vitamins?
10) Do your clothes reflect your personality and style?
11) Do you regularly unwind in a nice bubble bath?
12) Do you take time to learn about new things that interest you?
13) Do you take time to read for pleasure?
14) Do you associate with positive, upbeat people?
15) Do you have a cute hairstyle that you feel good about?
16) Do you make time for spiritual growth?
17) Do you make time for hobbies?
18) Do you allow yourself to cry when it is warranted?

19) Do you set goals and review them regularly?
20) Do you regularly treat yourself to facials, manicures, pedicures etc.?
21) Do you keep your closet organized?
22) Do you splurge on yourself occasionally?
23) Do you plan your day the night before?
24) Do you keep an inspiring "dream file" or vision board?
25) Do you celebrate your successes—big and small?

If your test results indicate a deficit in the self-care department, try a few of these quick and simple ideas to put yourself back at the top of your priority list. Not only will you feel better and get more enjoyment out of life, you'll also be better equipped to handle crisis situations when they arise and to care for the people who are depending upon you.

Self-Care Suggestions

- **Eat a banana.** Not only are bananas a great pick-me-up food (they are loaded with quick-fuel carbohydrates), research shows that eating a banana can also elevate your mood.

- **Call your mom**—unless your mom is an overly critical nag, in which case, call your sister, best friend, sweet aunt etc. Fill her in on all of the amazing things that are happening in your life and then listen enthusiastically as she fills you in on hers. It is always good to have someone that you can count on to be your cheerleader and a supportive shoulder to lean on.

- **Belt out a tune.** Whether you are alone in your car or taking a shower, singing has been proven to relieve stress, boost the immune system and release the same feel-good chemicals that sex and chocolate do. To compound the benefits of singing out loud, try following it up with some sex and chocolate!

- **Make time for yourself.** Turn off your phone (the world won't end—we promise), brew some tea, find a good book and allow yourself to just chill for a while. Even 30 minutes of uninterrupted "me time" can make a huge difference in one's outlook and attitude.
- **Visit a makeup counter and get a free makeover.** Maybe you'll discover a new lipstick color that you love (and we all know what a good lipstick can do for our psyche!)
- **Get outside.** If you can't get outside for some reason, open a window and take a deep breath. The combination of fresh air and sunlight will do wonders for your spirit and help to clear your mind.
- **Lift your spirits with aromatherapy.** Try taking a whiff of lemon, wild orange or peppermint essential oils for an instant, mood lifting burst of energy.
- **Organize your desk or closet.** Donate the items that you no longer need or that no longer suit you. Not only will your donation benefit someone else, it'll help you to make room for items that you truly love.
- **Take a luxurious bath infused with lavender essential oil and soothing bath salts.** To make this a truly decadent experience, light some candles and play some soft, relaxing music.
- **Ask for help when you need it.** No one should have to shoulder all of life's burdens alone. When things are hard—ask for help. Chances are good that you'll find others who care about you and who are more than willing to pitch in and lend a hand.

Being good to ourselves truly is the best thing that we can do to be good to others. When we are feeling rested, supported, healthy and balanced, we will be better able to help ensure that those we love are feeling the same way. Don't put off caring for yourself—make your own self-care a priority in your life TODAY.

THE UP-SIDE TO FEELING DOWN

No one doubts or questions the value of feeling good. It's a state that we all strive for and go to great lengths to maintain. Research has shown that feeling good has physical benefits ranging from reduced instances of cardiovascular disease to lower blood pressure, *and*, Law of Attraction enthusiasts (of which I am one!) tout the benefits that feeling good has on raising one's vibrational frequency, and therefore, one's ability to manifest joy and abundance.

This is all well and good, but here's the deal—no one feels *good* 100% of the time. Like it or not, we are *all* going to be faced with days that just plain suck. Sometimes there are legit reasons for the suckiness (sore throat, blown alternator on your car, root canal, job stress etc.) but sometimes, something is just *off* within our spirit which results in us feeling down.

It today's society, negative emotions are viewed as "unhealthy" and are often shunned, suppressed or medicated. *However;* the word "negative" is a misnomer as it refers to emotions because, as we have pointed out in previous chapters, emotions are neither positive nor negative—they simply *are.* They are tools in our psyche that help to direct our behavior and guide us as we identify opportunities or potential pitfalls along the path to our FabYOUlous goals. Emotions—both those deemed *positive* and *negative*—are crucial instruments of survival and, in fact, the human species would have disappeared long ago without them. By understanding better how and when to effectively deploy *all* of our emotions, we can learn to better navigate our relationships with ourselves and with others. On the flip-side, keeping our emotions bottled up without having an effective outlet can lead to eroded relationships *and* physical health. How then do we successfully cope with so-called "negative" feelings of anger, shame, envy, regret, fear, sadness or boredom in a way that honors the valuable feedback that they present to us, without allowing ourselves to become overtaken with negativity? One way to navigate this conundrum is to start reframing our experience of these emotions so that we are able to see the *up-side* of feeling *down* and capitalize on the positive aspects of these seemingly negative feelings.

Capitalizing on the Positive Aspects of Negative Emotions

Anger: Hoo boy! This one is a biggie. The word *anger* is only one letter short of *danger* and the *emotion* of anger is just one small action, word or thought away from a potentially dangerous situation. *However;* despite the potential volatility of this emotion; much *good* can come from anger. In fact, I personally credit *anger* as the catalyst that led me to take the necessary actions to remove myself (and my sons) from a very toxic situation and turn our lives around.

Anger is probably the most misunderstood of all of the emotions. It most often occurs when we feel undervalued, and it prompts us to reassert our value by lashing out, threatening harm or withholding benefits. According to psychologist Aaron Sell, "the primary benefit of anger for an individual, is preventing oneself from being exploited". If we know that we deserve better than what we're getting, anger can provide the motivation to take necessary action. Yes—unchecked and unmanaged anger can lead to irreparable destruction, but an *appropriate* level of anger expressed in an appropriate way at an appropriate time, very often leads to us getting that which we desire and deserve.

Unlike many so-called negative emotions that encourage us to *avoid* situations (think fear, depression etc.), anger typically is a motivator *of* action. It can boost confidence, risk taking and self-assertion. It will cause people (individuals and groups) to rise to the occasion when threatened with the possibility of losing something valuable. In my own experience, it was the threat of losing my (figurative) voice, sense of personal identity and control over my own life choices that made me *angry* enough to take a stand and remove myself and my sons from an unhealthy marriage and toxic situation. It also had the side benefit of earning me a reputation as one who will not be pushed around or manipulated and therefore garnered me a level of respect that I had not previously experienced.

Yes—anger is a tricky, two-edged sword but it most definitely has a place within our repertoire of emotions. Left unchecked, it can wreak havoc on individuals and relationships, but with proper management and expression, it can be a powerful catalyst for positive change. The up-side of anger comes when we are able to channel our anger and use it bring about a breakthrough as opposed to a break*down*.

Regret: Who among us doesn't have things in our life that we regret? No one—that's who. It's popular to say, "no regrets" but in truth, we *all* have things that we wish we wouldn't have said or done (or regrets over things that we wish we *would have* said or done). In fact, research shows that regret is likely the most common "negative" emotion that human beings tend to experience.

Regret emerges when we think about how different things could be *if only* we had made other choices or behaved differently. We ponder what *might have been* if only we had handled things another way.

Regret can be an especially difficult emotion to cope with, but that doesn't mean that it doesn't have positive aspects from which we can benefit. In fact, many of our greatest life lessons can come to us as a by-product of regret.

As human beings, one of the most effective learning tools that we have at our disposal is our immense propensity for screwing up. Mistakes make excellent teachers and because of this, our emotions highlight our blunders by adding regret to the mix in order to *make sure* that we really learn our lessons. Research shows that when our mistakes are made more painful by being tinged with regret, they are more memorable and therefore more effective in inducing us to make necessary behavioral changes.

Regret (and its trusty sidekick, *anticipated* regret) shapes our behavior by either motivating us to fix whatever mess we've caused, or go to great lengths to *avoid* future messes (thus the reason we watch what we eat, stop smoking or use birth control). Regret also requires us to take personal responsibility for our behavior since feelings of regret arise when outcomes of a situation are made worse *because of* our own actions (or inaction, depending upon the situation).

Though regret can be an incredibly painful emotion to process, its up-side is the fact that its powerful emotional pull makes it an excellent molder of future behavior. Some of our most poignant life lessons come to us through our regrets; therefore, regret is one of our most effective tools for shaping a meaningful life.

Fear: Few emotions render us more incapacitated than fear. We fear failure, embarrassment, pain, loss and heartache. Oh, and spiders...we definitely fear spiders. Research has shown however, that there is a direct correlation between a person's level of creativity and their ability to face and overcome fears. For this reason, it is crucial that we all learn to get a handle on our fears so that we can live our most Fab**YOU**lous lives.

Despite its bad rap, fear does have its up-side. In fact, if it weren't for fear, most of us would be dead. Fear is a defender that shields us from danger by heightening our awareness and preparing us to escape treacherous situations if need be. It's what keeps us from walking too close to the edge of a massive cliff or from leaning too far over a balcony railing on the 37th floor. Fear is what prevents us from taking unnecessary risks and therefore, fear promotes self-preservation. Even in less life-threatening situations, fear has its benefits because it causes us to think through all possible scenarios and weigh the various outcomes of our actions, thus allowing us the opportunity to extend the appropriate amount of risk.

Remember, without fear, we'd all be dead; but with *too much* fear, we might as well be.

Shame: This is a difficult emotion for people to process because feeling shame implies that one did something shameful...and that's hard for a lot of people to own up to. Still, whether we want to admit it or not, shame is something that we've *all* felt at one time or another.

Social cohesion is imperative in order for a society to survive; therefore, members of a society must learn to adhere to accepted cultural and moral norms. When we veer too far away from socially acceptable behavior, shame is what brings us back into line. The emotional discomfort of shame causes us to look inward and examine the motivations behind our actions. This introspection is what helps us to modify our behavior and act in a more acceptable way the next time we are faced with a potentially shame inducing situation.

As might be expected, there is a great deal of shame about feeling shame, and yet its up-side is that it is an emotion that enables us to live peacefully within our society. Without shame, we would never be able to trust others—or ourselves.

Sadness: Too many people will do whatever it takes to avoid feelings of sadness and yet, sadness often brings with it the opportunity for healing and growth.

Feelings of sadness come as a response to loss and are an indication that restoration is needed. Sometimes when the loss is great (such as the death of a loved one) sadness can guide us to seek help and to reach out to others in an effort to ease our suffering.

Despite what one might think, research shows that accepting and acknowledging feelings of sadness can actually reduce levels of depression, and that sadness is, in fact, a very healthy response to difficult situations. Additionally, according to science, sadness has an up-side in that it makes us more rational in our thinking and reduces forgetfulness and gullibility. While none of us would willingly seek out reasons to be sad, the experience of sadness is one that deepens our human experience and teaches us to be compassionate and generous with others.

Envy: It has been said that comparison is the thief of joy, and while that may be true, feelings of envy *can* bring about certain benefits if we allow them to.

Whether we like it or not, much of our success is dependent upon our relative status within a group. This is how it has always been and this is how it will likely always be. Our levels of happiness and self-satisfaction are greatly influenced by our comparisons of ourselves to others. The discomfort that we experience when we feel like we don't stack up to those around us can leave us feeling a mix of resentment, shame and frustration—a potent mixture that when combined together creates envy. None of us is immune—I personally experience this when I am participating in a race and see all of the "real" runners dash on ahead of me or when I look at bestselling authors and wonder if my writing will ever be recognized at that level.

While envy can certainly be a destructive force if taken too far, it also has real, tangible benefits. Though I certainly don't *enjoy* feeling envious; I know from my own personal experience, that envy is a very powerful motivator for me and one of the most effective ways of getting me to step up my game; and I am not alone in this. Niels Van De Ven, research psychologist at Tilburg University, found that inducing feelings of envy enhanced a subject's persistence and performance on a creative task *even more* than admiration did. Obviously, admiration feels better in the moment but the sting of envy was more effective at lighting the fire of ambition.

Taken to extremes, envy can have dire personal and relational consequences, its up-side however, is that when kept in perspective, it can be a powerful motivator for self-improvement.

Boredom: I feel very fortunate because boredom is something that I rarely experience. This is because I absolutely *hate* being bored so I've learned how to prepare myself for potentially boring situations (I even took my knitting with me to the DMV once—I completed an entire slipper while I was waiting).

Boredom is a feeling that is so aversive that people will actually administer electric shocks to themselves in order to avoid spending fifteen minutes alone with their own thoughts (hence the reason solitary confinement is such a horrific punishment in prisons). As bad as this may be—boredom does have an up-side in that it is a very clear indicator that something in our life needs to change. If we find ourselves bored in a relationship or on the job, it is time to start looking for ways to either infuse some excitement into the situation *or* change the situation altogether.

Boredom also has value in that it can lead us to our passions and purposes by clearly highlighting those things/jobs/relationships/ situations/etc. that we are *not* passionate about. By using boredom as an indicator of where your passions *do not* exist, you can gain clarity on where they *do*.

Despite their sometimes negative associations, *all* emotions have both positive and negative aspects—it is up to us to make the conscious decision to capitalize upon the positive rather than dwell upon the negative. There are, however; times when finding positivity is nearly impossible and feelings of negativity become more than just passing annoyances. If you find yourself in a dark, negative frame of mind and feel unable to reverse the trend or reframe the emotions, *please* take steps to get help. Talking to a trusted counselor, spiritual advisor, coach or friend can be the first step to help put you back on a path to positivity and Fab**YOU**lousness.

☀LOVE YOUR SPIRIT WITH YOUR BODY☀

As we wrap up this *Fab Spirit* section and move into the *Feeling Fab* section of the book, it seems like a chapter melding together our nebulous, floaty spiritual side with our down-to-earth, flesh & bone bodies would make a good segue from one realm into the other. Fortunately, this link isn't difficult to make because, despite being very different aspects of our being, our spirits and our physical bodies are perpetually working together to create our Fab**YOU**lous human experience.

Subconsciously, we know that when our spirits are high and life is good, we *feel* good within our bodies. Conversely, we've likely also experienced times when our wounded psyches have manifested into illness or discomfort within our bodies. The reverse of these is also true—when we are feeling physically strong and well, it is easier to find spiritual ease, but frustration with or pain in our physical bodies can wreak spiritual havoc in our lives. This constant dance between our spiritual and physical aspects can either be an angry mosh-pit of violence or a beautiful and flowing ballet. The good news is that we can learn to direct the dance by popping out of autopilot mode, tapping into our bodies, becoming aware of the physical sensations that our body is experiencing and looking for clues within those sensations.

Here are ten great ways to do this very thing—learn to free your spirit by loving and listening to your body.

1) **Know thyself.** It is hard to know what is happening within your body if you aren't familiar enough with

your body to know what is *normal* for you. Is that kink in your neck *always* there? Does your asthma *always* act up after a run? In order to understand the clues that our body is sending us, we must first be able to determine the difference between our *normal* state and abnormal physical occurrences.

A simple body scan done on a regular basis can be a powerful tool to tap into the power of your physical being. No, we're not talking high-tech MRI scans here (thank goodness—getting sucked into that god-forsaken tube is enough to trigger a full-on panic attack for me). Instead, we're just talking about a simple check-in with your body. This can be done simply by laying down, closing your eyes and exploring any sensations that you are experiencing. Start by focusing your attention on your toes and then work your way up your body. Do this enough times to allow yourself to become intimately familiar with the way your body is *feeling* so that you'll instantly know when something feels *off*.

2) **Get centered.** The abdomen is often referred to as the "core" of the body and we use it for both, strength and grounding. The next time you feel yourself getting stressed or anxious about something, take your hands and place them over your belly. Then, take a few deep breaths and allow the tension to leave your body as you feel yourself become more grounded.

3) **Check in.** Another effective way to beat stress is to perform an hourly check-in with yourself. Take a deep breath, noticing where tension is being held in your body—this could be the shoulders, jaw, brow, neck or abdomen. As you notice areas of tenseness, allow them to soften as you breathe in deep slow

breaths. After releasing this tension, do a few easy stretches and correct your posture as you go back to your task. Set a timer on your smartphone to remind yourself to do this quick check-in every hour—or even more often if you are going through a particularly stressful period.

4) **Make daily tasks sacred.** We all go through so much of our day on auto-pilot. Our brains are wired to make our daily tasks into routine actions so that we can focus our attention instead on new and creative endeavors. However; when we pause and bring our awareness to these seemingly mundane tasks; we create mindfulness and allow our routine tasks to take on a special kind of sacredness. For example, the next time you wash the dishes, instead of hurrying through the task, take time instead to feel the warmth of the water and the squish of the soap suds in your washrag. Smell the fragrance of the dish soap and notice how the light bounces off the bubbles of the suds. Bringing your full attention to even the most routine of tasks will engage your spirit and bring a sense of mindfulness to your day.

5) **Raise your E.Q.** We are all familiar with the initials I.Q. for Intelligence Quotient and may have even taken tests to see just where we fall on the I.Q. scale. How familiar are we with our *emotional* intelligence though? How would we rate on the E.Q. scale? One way to elevate our spirit is to elevate our emotional intelligence—which is our ability to understand and manage our emotions. This can be done simply by learning to listen to the moment to moment clues that our body sends us regarding how we are feeling. By understanding that emotions are neither good nor bad, we can learn to detach from them a bit and formulate better responses to them. By becoming

141

more in tune with the feelings that our emotions cause within our physical bodies, we can better learn to control emotions that might otherwise have been disruptive to our psyche. This ability to feel, detach and observe our emotions will serve us well as we cultivate appropriate responses to those emotions— especially the difficult ones.

6) **Strike a super pose.** Research conducted by Amy Cuddy, social psychologist, has shown that there are certain poses that we can hold in order to reduce stress and increase confidence (a clear indication of the correlation between our physical selves and our spiritual selves). One such "power pose" has been dubbed the "Superman Pose". To experiment with this pose, try standing like Superman, with your back straight, chest forward, heart open and hands on your hips. Hold this pose for two minutes before heading into a potentially anxiety inducing situation (like a job interview or sales negotiation). The power from your pose will spill over into your confidence level and be evident in your words and actions.

7) **Get plenty of Vitamin L.** We all know that laughter *feels* good but now research proves that the benefits of laughter go beyond just the psychological boost that we get from a good chuckle. A study out of Loma Linda University found that laughing for short periods of time can help to reduce stress levels and increase short-term memory. The University of Maryland published *another* study showing that laughter can protect against heart disease. With so many great benefits, it is vital that we make laughter a regular part of our life. Spend more time with people who make you laugh and do more things that induce laughter (watch funny movies, go to comedy clubs etc.). We all know that laughter is highly

contagious so sharing a laugh with others isn't only good for you—it's good for everyone.

8) **Move it, move it.** As it turns out, King Julian of the movie *Madagascar* was on to something when he sang "I like to move it move it" (if you haven't seen that movie, PLEASE go rent it! You'll experience plenty of laughter which—as you now know from reading the previous entry—is so good for you!) Sadly, most of us spend way too much time during the day sitting on our duffs. This lack of movement causes us to experience tension, stress and stiffness. Don't become a slave to your chair! Your body and your spirit will thank you if you make it a point to get up and move your body. Change your posture, stand up and walk around, open up your chest, do some simple stretching—anything to get the blood and good energy flowing again. Not only will you feel better physically; movement will give a boost to your spirits as well.

9) **Savor life.** When our emotions feel difficult or stressful to us, it is so easy to get sucked into a spiral of negativity. How often though, do we allow positive and happy feelings to elevate us to new heights? Typically, we are much more prone to wallowing in misery than in savoring joy. This needs to change! The next time you feel good, notice how the positive emotions are manifested in your physical body. Do you feel relaxed? Is there a warm feeling in your chest? Do you catch yourself grinning? When we become aware of the effect that positive feelings have on us, it will allow us to broaden our perspective and induce these positive feelings more often. This process has been coined the "Broaden and Build Theory" by researcher, Barbara Frederickson and is what causes us to want

to stop and savor a sunset or relish the aroma and taste of our morning coffee. Learning to truly savor the good that we have in our life is a key indicator of our likelihood of living a truly FabYOUlous life.

10) **Have a heart.** One of the most essential components of physical and spiritual well-being is the ability to nurture a loving heart. This can be done with a simple practice of placing your hands on your heart, thinking of someone whom you wish to bless, and in your mind, sending loving, peaceful and healing thoughts their way. Not only does this practice put good energy out into the universe, it also has a calming, soothing effect on you.

Clearly, the spirit and the body are permanently intertwined and able to affect change upon each other. By implementing a few of these practices, you can better meld the two to work together in harmony—one with the other.

Feeling Fab

"Most people have no idea how good their body is designed to feel"

Kevin Trudeau

DECRAPIFY THE TEMPLE

I'm sure that you've heard the whole "your body is a temple" metaphor before but, how much do you really *believe* it? Do you treat your body like the temple that it is or do you treat it more like a landfill?

Here's a newsflash—*every single thing* that we do in our lifetime requires the involvement of our body. No matter how badly we may sometimes want to—we can't escape our physical body. It makes sense then, that in order to live our most Fab**YOU**lous lives, we *must* take care of our temple.

If you are health conscious at all, you no doubt spend at least *some* time thinking about the things that go *into* your body. We all know that good nutrition is a vital component of Fab**YOU**lousness. How much time however, do you spend thinking about the stuff that comes *out* of your body? Chances are that (unless you are an eleven year old *boy*) you don't give much thought to that crap (haha! Pardon the pun!). This is a shame though because in order for our bodies to function at their highest level, nutrition *and* detoxification need to be working together in harmony. We take in what we need (air, food, water), use it to fuel our bodies, and then expel the excess.

Activities as simple as breathing and sweating (and yes—peeing and pooping for those of you who are on the same maturity level as that eleven year old boy—I myself often fall into this category) are automatic processes that our bodies use to get rid of waste and toxins. However; in a modern society that is filled with pesticides, chemicals, processed "foods" and pollution; the toxic load on our systems is higher than it has ever been. This is why it makes sense for us to work to keep as many toxins *out* of our bodies as possible. In the last section, we devoted an entire chapter to detoxifying your spirit, but now it is time to try the following suggestions for simple ways of detoxing your *body*...

- **Just add water.** This is one of the absolute easiest ways to help your body get rid of toxins. Keep your body hydrated throughout the day by chugging good ol' H2O. To maximize the health benefits, swap the ice water for room temperature water *or* hot water with lemon. If you're like me and need a little variety, herbal teas, fresh veggie juices and kombucha all count toward our daily water intake. According to the Institute of Medicine, the average woman needs nine cups of water per day while the average man needs thirteen cups.

- **Fill up on fiber.** Your colon will thank you if you do your part to help keep it "clean" by eating high fiber foods such as apples, pears, sweet potatoes, blackberries, peas, dried beans, brown rice, figs, prunes, ground flaxseed, whole rye and almonds. These and other high-fiber foods will help to keep your system "regular" by acting as "intestinal brooms" that help to "sweep" out waste. Beware though—if you're not used to eating fiber-rich foods, you might want to add them to your diet gradually so that your system will have time to adapt to the change.

- **Purify the air you breathe.** Start switching your household cleaning products to those made with natural ingredients and look for paints that are low on volatile organic compounds (like the Sherwin Williams Harmony line). Also try to rid your home of plastic and vinyl products that can emit potentially carcinogenic gases. If you enjoy burning candles, choose those that are made of beeswax, soy or palm oil with cotton wicks. You can also clean your air by introducing plants into your living space. The plants that are best for purifying the air include bamboo, English Ivy, Gerbera Daisies, Chinese Evergreen, Mother-in-Law's Tongue and Peace Lily.

- **Breathe Deep.** Now that you've taken some steps to purify your air, it's time to start breathing it in. Just a few deep, slow breaths can increase your oxygen intake and aid in detoxification. Even though breathing is a natural response that happens automatically, *deep* breathing is something that requires a bit more intentionality. Here is a brief "how to" for yoga's three-part breath technique: 1.) inhale through your nose and expand your abdomen 2.) expand your diaphragm next and then 3.) exhale and continue with the next round. As you start to get a feel for this technique, try to make your exhale a bit longer than your inhale. Imagine yourself pushing all of the stale air out of your lungs as you prepare to take in more, fresh, invigorating, energizing oxygen.

- **Stick out your tongue—and *scrape* it.** Okay—I know that this sounds weird, but trust me—you should be doing it. Ever notice how gross your mouth feels in the morning when you first wake up and how terrible that morning breath can be? Well, there's a reason for that. The reason is that overnight, metabolic debris (that is meant to leave your body) builds up on your tongue. In Ayurvedic medicine (Ayurveda is a Sanskrit word that means "the science of life" and Ayurvedic medicine is an ancient, holistic healing system that originated in India and is based upon the belief that health and wellness depend upon

149

a delicate balance between the mind, body and spirit), this "tongue fuzz" is known as ama and removing it is a simple yet incredibly effective way to rid your body of toxins. All you need is a simple tongue scraper that can be purchased in the dental health area of most drugstores for less than five dollars (though honestly, using a spoon works too). Then, just use the device to scrape your tongue first thing in the morning before you eat or drink anything. Adding this simple step to your daily hygiene routine will prevent this toxic "tongue fuzz" from being reabsorbed back into your system.

- **Reduce your alcohol & caffeine intake.** I have several friends who happen to be physicians and guess what—they all drink an occasional glass of wine and start their days off with a cup (or two) of coffee. I found this interesting since I've heard that both alcohol and caffeine can be detrimental to our bodies. So—not wanting to unnecessarily miss out on alcohol and caffeine myself, I asked these friends what gives? As it turns out-they all subscribe to the "everything in moderation" philosophy. The thing is—we often misinterpret what exactly "moderation" means. According to my physician friends (*and* information that I found online), *moderate* alcohol consumption means one glass of wine *or* one beer *or* one shot of whiskey (NOT one glass of wine *and* one beer *and* one shot of whiskey!) for women daily and roughly twice that amount for men. In Ayurvedic teachings, however; alcohol is considered as *tamasic* (meaning a food that is thought to promote pessimism, laziness, doubt and criminal tendencies) and leads to heaviness and lethargy. For this reason, it is beneficial to reduce our intake if we are looking to detoxify our body.

As far as caffeine is concerned, it is best to keep consumption to a minimum because caffeine has been linked to stress, anxiety, heart disease, fibromyalgia, insomnia and a variety of other non-Fab**YOU**lous problems. Unfortunately, if caffeine is a regular staple in your life, cutting back can lead to some ugly withdrawal headaches. To help mitigate this problem, try stepping down your consumption gradually by switching from coffee to green tea to non-caffeinated herbal teas over a period of weeks. It is also best if you can forego the artificial sweeteners. Personally, I like adding honey to my tea but Agave nectar is another option as it is a light, liquid sweetener that comes from a cactus plant and is low on the glycemic index.

- **Indulge in a massage.** We all know how wonderful a good massage can feel, but the benefits go far beyond just the relaxation aspects. Massage is a valuable tool for boosting immunity *and* it improves our internal detoxification process by stimulating blood circulation and the flow of lymphatic fluid in the body. If regular massages seem like an expensive indulgence, look for massage therapy schools in your area—they often provide professional level massage services at a fraction of the cost.

- **Sweat it out.** When we sweat (perspire, glow…whatever you want to call it) we are expelling toxins from our bodies. In fact, whenever my husband feels a cold coming on, he intentionally spends more time in his gym's sauna in an effort to "sweat it out" (and incidentally—he rarely ends up getting a full-blown cold). Another way to increase our sweat output obviously involves vigorous exercise (which also benefits our cardiovascular system as well as our muscle health) but if you already spend a fair amount of time exercising, you can add the hydrotherapeutic technique to help boost your perspiration output. To do this, simply alternate five minutes in a steamy shower with thirty seconds of cold water and repeat this cycle three times; then, get under your warm bed covers for thirty minutes.

- **Eat organically as often as possible.** It's no secret that a majority of our food has been injected, sprayed or filled with pesticides, hormones, fillers and all manner of toxic ick. To lighten the toxic load on your body, try to be conscientious as you select the food that goes into your system. If you eat animal products, look for those that are organic because pesticide residues concentrate and magnify in animal tissue. As for your fruits and vegetables, it is especially important to choose organic when shopping for those produce items that tend to be the most heavily sprayed: peaches, celery, broccoli, leafy greens, apples, grapes, peanuts, berries and cucumbers. Unfortunately, organic food items often tend to cost more than inorganic, but frequenting farmer's markets, joining food co-ops or growing your own produce are ways to help keep those costs down.

- **Try a fast.** This suggestion certainly isn't for everyone and you should definitely consult with your doctor before exploring this option. If your doctor gives the okay however; juice fasting is a time-honored detoxification therapy that allows the body to use the energy that it normally devotes to digestion and use it on detoxification instead. A juice fast consists of consuming three to five glasses of freshly extracted vegetable and fruit juice daily and drinking water and caffeine-free herbal teas at will. Some juice combinations that are popular among fasters include apple/celery, tomato/arugula/lemon, apple/kale/ginger and carrot/spinach. If, however; you choose to fast on fruit juice alone, dilute it with pure water to reduce the sugar content. If you choose to explore the fasting option (again, with your doctor's blessing) be sure to get plenty of rest during your fast because your body will likely not have as much energy as normal.

GIVE TOXINS THE BRUSH OFF

I know that we just dedicated the entire previous chapter to various detoxification strategies, but there is one technique that I left out because I love it so much that I wanted it to have its own separate chapter. This technique with which I am so enamored is dry brushing.

Dry Brushing is an Ayurvedic cleansing technique that has been used for centuries and has proven benefits not only for one's skin, but for one's insides as well. It is a very simple practice that only takes five minutes a day and costs nothing once a brush has been purchased.

The benefits of Dry Brushing are numerous and include...

- Helps to release fatty deposits (also known as CELLULITE) under the skin's surface. Can I get an AMEN here ladies?
- Helps to slough off dead skin cells and other impurities from the skin's surface. It also aids in the renewal of new skin cells which results in brighter, smoother skin.
- Stimulates blood circulation.
- Rejuvenates the nervous system by stimulating nerve endings in the skin. Not only is this good for you, it also feels Fab**YOU**lous.
- Assists in lymphatic drainage which is one way that your body releases toxins and metabolic waste.
- Helps to strengthen your immune system.

- Increases muscle tone.

There are several other benefits to Dry Brushing, but these seven should be enough to convince you to begin your own Dry Brushing practice. Just like anything though, Dry Brushing is only effective if/when it is done correctly. If you're ready to give Dry Brushing a try (and seriously…there is no reason not to) here are the steps you need to get started…

Dry Brushing for Health

Choose a natural bristle brush (synthetic bristles may be too hard/sharp and may damage the skin). A brush with a long handle will make it easier to reach your back, ankles etc.

Start on dry skin before bathing.

Start with the soles of your feet using swift, upward strokes. Brush from your feet up your legs and towards your heart. Dry Brushing movements should always be directed towards your heart except for when done on the back where you should start at the top of your back/shoulders and brush down to your lower back. Brush strokes should be directed towards the heart because that is the natural direction in which lymphatic fluid flows through the body.

Start with light pressure until you adjust to the sensation and then begin to apply firmer pressure as you brush.

Start with gentle, circular motions and then use longer strokes.

After you've brushed your legs, move on to the thighs, stomach, back and arms. Use a gentler stroke on the tender skin of the breast/chest.

Do not brush over inflamed skin, open wounds, sunburns or skin cancer.

Brush for 5-7 minutes or until your skin is rosy and tingles.

When you are done brushing, it is time to rinse off in the shower to wash away any dead skin cells and impurities.

Keep a separate Dry Brush for everyone in the family and be sure to wash it periodically.

Dry brushing is just one simple way to help you feel more fit and FabYOUlous and because of its simplicity, there is no reason not to give it a try—TODAY.

DRINK TO YOUR HEALTH

Water. The average adult body is nearly 65% water. The earth's surface is nearly 71% water. We drink it, we bathe in it and we swim in it. Still, many of us are not getting enough water on a daily basis to sustain optimal physical health.

The critical importance of water to the human body was recently made very clear to me when my oldest son had to receive IV fluids due to a severe case of dehydration brought on by a bad case of the stomach flu. It was incredible (and terrifying) to me to see just how quickly the body of a healthy and strong twenty year old began to shut down as a result of not having enough water in his system. Fortunately, quick action on the part of medical professionals kept my son from needing to be hospitalized, but the experience was enough to get me to take a closer look at the crucial role that water plays in our overall health.

Just as plants wilt without adequate water—so do humans. As the principal chemical component of our bodies, water flushes toxins out of our vital organs and carries nutrients to our cells. Adequate water intake also cuts our risk of heart disease by nearly 50% and helps to prevent dangerous blood clots and painful kidney stones.

As if these important health benefits weren't enough reason to increase your water intake, there are numerous other important benefits to be gained by drinking more water...

1)   **It boosts your mood:** The next time you feel your mood taking a nosedive for no good reason, drink a glass of water—even if you don't feel thirsty.

According to the *Journal of Nutrition*, mild dehydration (so mild that you don't even notice it) can usher in fatigue, mental fogginess and a blue mood. Consider these symptoms your body's way of alerting you that it is getting low on fluids. If you prefer something with a little more flavor, you can try downing some Gatorade. Drinks (like Gatorade) that have a little bit of sodium can make you feel better more quickly. The sodium will trigger pleasurable sensations in a slightly dehydrated brain.

2)   **It boosts your energy:** Not only does staying well hydrated boost your mood, it will boost your energy level as well. In fact, fatigue is often the first tell-tale sign of dehydration. Not to worry though: drinking an ice-cold glass of water should do the trick to re-hydrate you. A study published in the *Journal of Physiology* points out that the cold temperature makes liquid pass through the stomach to the intestines faster for speedier absorption.

3)   **It prevents wrinkles:** Ladies—did you catch that? Something as simple as drinking more water can help to prevent wrinkles. Skin contains hyaluronic acid which stores water and gives skin a healthy, plump appearance. Even one day of dehydration can sap that plumpness and make it easy for skin to crease and wrinkle while we sleep.

4)   **It can help to whittle your middle:** A three month study on this subject found that study participants who drank two 8 oz. glasses of water before meals consumed fewer calories than those who did not drink prior to eating. In fact, those who drank the

extra water lost nearly five pounds more than those who didn't pre-drink. According to Registered Dietitian, Amy Jamieson-Petonic, "having water before a meal reduces unintentional overeating because your body can easily mistake thirst for hunger".

5) **It improves brain function:** A recent British study confirmed that sipping water before a challenging task (giving a speech, taking a quiz, etc.) helped to improve performance. Additionally, Army research has shown that well-hydrated women are better able to concentrate during boring tasks. Scientists say that even mild dehydration can cause your brain to operate less efficiently.

With so many tangible benefits like these, it is easy to see that adequate water intake is a vital part of maintaining optimal physical health. The question still remains though, how much water is really *enough*? According to the *Institute of Medicine*, adequate water intake for men is roughly thirteen cups a day while women need approximately nine cups. There are, however; other variables that may skew those totals a bit. Follow these guidelines from the Mayo Clinic to ensure that you are getting enough water on a daily basis...

Mayo Clinic Guidelines for Water Consumption

- If you exercise or engage in activities that make you sweat, add an extra cup and a half to two cups of water to your fluid intake.
- Women who are pregnant or breastfeeding need additional fluids. The Institute of Medicine recommends ten cups a day during pregnancy and thirteen cups a day while breastfeeding.
- Hot, dry or humid weather can cause perspiration which will require additional fluid intake.

- Vomiting and diarrhea cause the body to quickly lose additional fluids (as was the case with my son) so it is especially important to stay well hydrated during illnesses such as the flu.

While chugging some crystal-clear water is the easiest, most effective way to naturally re-hydrate your system, it's not the only way. **Some other ways to up your fluid intake include...**

Turning up the heat with spicy food. Eating hot, spicy food will have you reaching for your water glass more often, thus increasing your water consumption.

Swap out your soda for fruity, sparkling water. Yes, believe it or not, soda *does* contribute to your overall fluid intake but not nearly as much as water—plus, soda has a plethora of extra calories and negative effects on health. By swapping out your sugar laden soda for some fruity, sparkling water, you will still get a shot of fizz and flavor without all of the bad-for-you elements of soda.

Savoring another cup of coffee or tea. Contrary to popular belief and according to British Sports Medicine researchers, these drinks *are* hydrating and can offer a bit of flavorful variety when it comes to proper fluid intake.

When an action as simple as drinking more water can have such a positive impact on one's overall physical health, there is no reason not to incorporate it into your daily routine and make it a habit. Start off with adding one more glass of water to your day and build from there. It's a simple habit but it can make a Fab**YOU**lous difference.

INFUSE YOUR WATER
INFUSE YOUR HEALTH

Okay—I know that in the previous chapter I just gave a boatload of reasons as to why we should all be drinking a lot more water. Here's the real, honest-to-god truth though…I personally am not a huge fan of plain ol' water. Sure, I crave it after I've gone for a run or when it is especially hot outside, but in normal, everyday conditions, I find water to be a bit too *blah*.

Thankfully, while scrolling through Pinterest one day, I found several posts on the benefits of drinking *infused* water. Infused water is just plain ol' water that has been infused with natural flavors. These flavor infusions not only add a little pizazz to the water's flavor, they also provide additional health benefits (on top of those already provided by the water itself). Upon discovering the range of benefits from consuming infused water, I immediately went out and purchased a special flavor-infusion water bottle (yes—they're a thing) and began experimenting with different fruit combinations. While I love the simplicity of my infusion water bottle, these fruity concoctions can also be made in any glass jar or pitcher (don't use plastic because the high acidity levels of many citrus fruits can cause plastic to break down over time). For the best fruity flavor, I like to make my water before going to bed and then refrigerate it overnight so that it is ready to grab as I head out the door for work the next morning. Don't let your water sit for more than 48 hours though because the fruit will begin to break down and the water might start to taste funky (I notice this the most when using strawberries).

As I type this chapter, I am currently sipping strawberry/pineapple water and it is *delicious* but here are some other wonderful water infusion recipes that are grouped according to their most significant health benefits...

Immunity Boosting

Blueberry + Lemon   Pear + Raspberry + Rosemary Sprig Raspberry + Lemon   Lime + Orange + Lemon   Strawberry + Kiwi   Blueberry + Lemon + Cucumber   Honeydew Melon + Cantaloupe

Regulation of Blood Sugar Levels

Grapefruit + Lemon   Peach + Cinnamon Stick   Peach + Blueberry   Apple + Cinnamon Stick   Grapefruit + Raspberry Orange + Cinnamon Stick   Raspberry + Mint Leaves + Lime

Fat Burning/Digestion Aid

Green Tea + Mint Leaves + Lime   Watermelon + Peach Grapefruit + Orange   Watermelon + Mint Leaves + Lime

Detoxifying

Lemon + Cucumber + Mint Leaves   Cucumber + Lemon + Lime   Strawberry + Orange + Blueberry   Pineapple + Apple + Cantaloupe   Grapefruit + Cucumber + Lime

Stress Reducing

Lemon + Cucumber + Mint Leaves   Blueberry + Coconut Water Lemon + Ginger   Strawberry + Mint Leaves + Cucumber + Lime   Mint Leaves + Lavender + Lime

By infusing my water, I'm enjoying added health benefits but best of all—the flavors are so delicious that I now find myself drinking far more water than before. I'm sure that you'll find the same to be true for you as well.

☼ SLEEP YOUR WAY TO THE TOP ☼

No, this is not a chapter about using sex as a way of currying favor with your boss—*ick*! Seriously—DO NOT do that. Instead, this is a chapter about all of the magnificent benefits of sleep and how to ensure that you are getting enough zzz's to maximize your health and stay on top of your game.

Admittedly, this chapter is a bit of a challenge for me to write because sleep has been a struggle for me for most of my adult life. It's not that I *don't* sleep—it's just that I don't prioritize it the way that I should. My night owl tendencies often get the best of me and I'll find myself wide awake at 2:00 A.M. despite knowing that I have to wake up at 6:00 A.M. Still, despite being bad at sleep, I know just how amazing I feel and how much better life seems to cruise along when I am well rested; so, for this reason, I have become much more deliberate about making sure that I get an adequate amount of sleep...*usually*.

While I especially love the emotional health benefits associated with being well rested (less crabbiness, better relationships as a result of being less crabby, reduced anxiety levels and heightened levels of optimism—just to name a few); the "behind the scenes" physical health benefits of sleep are quite impressive too. Adding an extra hour of sleep to your routine can reduce blood pressure by as much as 8 to 14 points in just six weeks (according to Harvard Medical School researchers) *and,* that extra hour of shut-eye can cut your odds of dangerous plaque buildup in your arteries by 33%, making you less likely to suffer a heart attack (based on reports in

165

the *Journal of the American Medical Association*). Additionally, getting enough sleep (7-8 hours a night) on a regular basis will (according to a University of California, Berkeley study in the journal, *Nature Neuroscience*) reduce your risk of dementia and Alzheimer's disease, *and* make you 83% *less* likely to catch a cold.

These are all incredibly compelling reasons to make sleep a priority, and yet, despite these proven benefits, it is estimated that more than 60% of us get fewer than seven hours of solid sleep per night. What gives? Why is good sleep so elusive for so many of us and what can we do to reverse this trend? Here are five common causes of sleep deprivation and strategies on how to overcome each one...

- **Night time is YOUR time.** Yep—I'll confess, this is my biggest reason for not getting enough sleep. I tend to view the night time as the time when I finally get to do all of the things that I want to do but didn't have time to do during the day. I'll read, knit, play around on my laptop, etc. I *love* my "me time" but it definitely cuts into my sleep time. The thing is though; "me time" is beneficial in its own right and something that we all desperately need in order to live FabYOUlous lives. In order to not deprive myself of my "me time" but still get the sleep that I need, I now try to grab small, scheduled bites of "me time" throughout my day. I'll take 15 minutes at lunch to do some knitting or listen to a recorded book during my drive to work in the morning. These small bits of personal time accumulate and pay off in much the same way that short intervals of exercise can (over time) add up to big fitness benefits.

  Another way to get your "me time" in is to set the alarm on your phone for a predetermined amount of time (20-30 minutes usually works well) and use this time to do the chores that tend to eat up your evenings, *but* don't do the chores all by yourself. Instead, make it a ritual that during this time, *everyone* in the household pitches in and helps out. Children can help unload the dishwasher while your hubby makes the school lunches for the next day and you fold the laundry. Once the timer goes off, everyone wraps up the chore that they were working on and uses the rest of the evening to relax. This gives everyone a sense of contribution to the management of the household *and* gives you back precious minutes of "me time" that you now don't have to use at midnight.

- **Your "monkey mind" won't stop chattering.** Why is it that when the lights turn *off*, our brains turn *on?* This "monkey mind" phenomenon strikes most of us from time to time and boy can it be a challenge to deal with. It seems that as soon as our head hits the pillow, we start to obsess about every item on our to-do list or we replay the mental tape of every regret that we've ever experienced. Then, to make matters worse—we look at the clock and start to stress out about how many hours of sleep we're *not* getting. It's a vicious cycle—the more anxiety we feel, the less we sleep and the less we sleep, the more anxious we feel.

The next time you get a case of "monkey mind madness" take solace in knowing that you're not alone and that most everyone experiences this phenomenon on occasion. Then, in an effort to relax your mind and quiet the chatter, try listening to some soft, soothing music. You can plan ahead by downloading a relaxing playlist to your smartphone or MP3 player so that you will have it handy when you need it. Then, listen to the music in the dark and allow the soft melodies to ease your mind. Personally, I have to use music that is strictly instrumental because I find vocals to be too distracting when I'm trying to sleep. If your music library is more death metal than meditative, just do a quick google search for meditation music and you'll find an abundance of options that can be easily downloaded to your device.

Another way to get yourself off of the hamster wheel of worry is to shift your wakeful beta brainwaves to the slower, more restful waves that come on as you begin to get drowsy. According to Bruce O'Hara, Ph.D. professor of biology at the University of Kentucky, any kind of meditation that focuses on breathing can help to facilitate this shift. O'Hara speculates that even just five minutes of meditation can help move the brain into a more relaxed state that is more conducive to sleep.

- **You're *allergic* to sleep.** Okay—you're not *really* allergic to sleep but that doesn't mean that your allergies aren't keeping you awake at night. Lying down can wreak havoc for allergy sufferers—mucus drainage collects in your throat which triggers a cough and your nasal passages become congested making it difficult to breathe. You toss and turn (and snore) all night long so it's no wonder you wake up feeling exhausted rather than refreshed.

While a *real* solution to this problem may require the intervention of an allergist, there are a few steps that you can take in order to find some relief. First, if you are allergic to pollen, keep your bedroom window closed until your particular allergen is no longer in season. If however, your allergies are brought on by indoor allergens, be sure to vacuum your bedroom regularly with a vacuum that has a special HEPA filter and don't forget to wipe down surfaces to keep dust at bay. Additional help might be found by using a saline nasal spray during the day but if not, a prescription nasal spray (possibly in conjunction with an antihistamine) might help you to breathe more freely and therefore sleep more soundly.

- **You're addicted to electronics.** Hey—I get it. I love my iPhone and laptop too. However; as convenient as these devices may be during the day, they are incredibly detrimental when it comes to sleep. First off, whether you are working on a report for work, updating your Facebook status or playing Candy Crush, you are being stimulated by whatever is going on, on your device and (obviously) stimulation is *not* conducive to sleep. Secondly, the short wavelength (blue) light that is emitted by most devices suppresses melatonin (your body's sleep-inducing hormone) production. A study at Brigham and Women's Hospital in Boston recently found that compared to those who read printed books, users of electronic devices at bed time felt less drowsy in the evening, took longer to fall asleep and were sleepier and less alert the next morning—even after getting a full eight hours of sleep.

To eliminate the sleep disrupting effect of blue light, be sure to power down all electronic devices at least an hour before hitting the sack. If this seems too impossible for you (again, I get it!), consider purchasing a pair of glasses with amber lenses and wearing them at night when you use your device. Amber lenses have been shown to block short wavelength light, thus resulting in better sleep for those who wear them while using electronic devices before bedtime.

- **Your best friend is keeping you up.** Oh how we love our pets. I have three cats (yes, I'm *that* lady) and I adore them. I do not however let them sleep in my room anymore. I used to, but I got tired of them walking on my face at two in the morning or meowing to be let outside at ridiculous hours. Now they have to find somewhere else to sleep at night and as a result, *my* sleep is much better. A University of Kansas Medical Center survey found that 63% of pet owners who slept with their pets more than four nights a week had significantly lower sleep satisfaction than those who kept the critters out of the bedroom. At first, my kitties didn't like being banned from my room (they would put their paws under my closed door and rattle the door in an attempt to get my attention—this stopped after I threw a shoe at the door and scared the bejeesus out of them) but it didn't take long for them to adjust. Dogs are likely easier to train than cats but regardless of whether your furry friend is a dog, cat, ferret or Guinea pig (people don't really *sleep* with ferrets or Guinea pigs, do they??) making a special bed for your best friend that is outside of *your* bedroom will increase your sleep quality, thereby making you a less cranky pet owner. It's a win-win situation for everyone.

While these suggestions address some of the most common barriers to sound sleep, here are a few more suggestions that will help you to get some good, quality shut-eye and therefore, feel far more Fab**YOU**lous during your waking hours...

- **Wiggle your toes.** When stress makes it difficult for you to drift off, try wiggling all ten of your toes for sixty seconds. Reflexology experts say that this move helps to unblock energy channels in the feet and spark a relaxation response that spreads throughout your entire body, helping you to quickly fall into a deep, restful sleep.

- **Speaking of toes**—to drift off more quickly, try covering your toes with a warm pair of socks. Studies show that wearing socks to bed improves your circulation which helps to usher in sleep.

- **Be grateful.** A recent study found that heart patients who wrote down three things that they were thankful for before hitting the sack showed reduced levels of inflammation, improved their overall mood *and* got better sleep.

- **Turn down the heat.** Research shows that the ideal room temperature for sleeping is around 65 degrees. Set your thermostat to this temperature before turning in at night for an optimal sleep experience. Or—invest in a programmable thermostat that will automatically adjust the temperature for you.

- **Take a bath.** You can speed up the drowsy factor at night by taking a warm bath. The rapid cool down that your body experiences after getting out of a warm tub promotes relaxation and results in feelings of drowsiness.

- **Dim the lights.** Exposure to bright lighting can fool your body into staying awake. As you begin your nighttime routine (washing your face, brushing your teeth etc.) keep the lights low. If it seems *too* dark, try using indirect light from the hallway.

- **Stretch.** Showing your muscles a little love can help you to unwind and release the tension from the day. Combine stretching with deep breathing for an even greater relaxation effect.

- **Rub your ears??** It may sound crazy but practitioners of Traditional Chinese Medicine say that firmly rubbing your earlobes with your thumbs and index fingers for thirty seconds will stimulate acupressure points in the earlobe that relieve stress and return the body to a calm, peaceful state. This relaxation will then help you to drift off to sleep more quickly.

- **Inhale some lavender essential oil.** Long used for its sleep-inducing qualities, lavender essential oil can be inhaled or spritzed onto your pillow to help usher in sound sleep.

- **Eat a sleep-inducing snack.** The key to this suggestion lies in the timing of the snack (eat at least 30 minutes before you plan to turn in for the night) and the type of snack. Light snacks like mozzarella cheese or plain yogurt contain Tryptophan which is an amino acid that helps the body to produce serotonin, a brain chemical that is responsible for healthy sleep.

- **See the light, but then black it out.** Research shows that spending time outside during daylight hours helps to boost your body's production of melatonin which is responsible for keeping your body on a regular schedule. At night however, experts agree that the darker your bedroom, the better it is for your sleep. Keep your room dark by using black out curtains and by covering any bright electrical displays.

- **Bond with your friends** (outside of bed!) According to experts at the University of Chicago, close friendships contribute to better rest because feeling connected to others helps to reduce the stress and sadness that often inhibits sleep.

- **Create a bedtime routine.** If you do the same things every night before going to bed (take a bath, brush your teeth, read a book, etc.) your brain will begin to

172

associate those things with sleep and will therefore start winding down as you start your routine each night.

- **Use a flame meditation for relaxation.** A survey from the National Sleep Foundation reveals that sixty-three percent of us are so stressed that we toss and turn all night long. A simple remedy for this is to incorporate meditation into your bedtime routine. A very effective, sleep inducing meditation technique is called the dancing flame. To do this meditation, simply snuggle into a comfy chair and soften your gaze as you look at a lit candle for five minutes. Focusing on the gently flickering flame stimulates the brain to release alpha waves which create a relaxed, meditative state that can cut the risk of restless sleep in half. Just be sure to extinguish the candle before you nod off.

- **Make sure that you have the right kind of pillow.** If you suffer from a sore neck during the night, snore or are prone to bouts of sleep apnea, the wrong pillow might be the problem. Your predominant sleep position should determine the type of pillow that you use at night. If you tend to sleep on your side, opt for a pillow that is fluffy and that will keep your neck parallel to your mattress. Back sleepers on the other hand don't need as much support and should therefore select a flatter pillow because too much plushness can pitch the chin forward toward the chest and inhibit breathing. Stomach sleepers should opt for the thinnest pillow (or no pillow at all) to keep their necks from overarching.

Sleep is a vital ingredient in the recipe for a Fab**YOU**lous life. Make sure that you prioritize it appropriately so that you can reap the benefits of a well-rested mind and body.

WALK YOUR WAY TO FABYOULOUS HEALTH

As a runner, I personally have overlooked the benefits of walking because I figured that *surely* running had to be better for me (how did I become such a running snob??) I am now however, starting to learn that that is not necessarily the case. Sure—running has some added cardio benefits and might help you reach your fitness goals a bit more quickly; however, running can also be extremely hard on the body and lead to joint problems and other injuries. This information about the benefits of walking appeals to me because though I don't intend to give up on running (participating in a half marathon is still on my bucket list), I am excited to hear that walking is a viable option for me on those days when my body just isn't up for a run.

Walking is one of the easiest and most enjoyable forms of exercise, but don't let its simplicity fool you into thinking that it lacks the punch of other, more high-intensity workouts. In fact; walking is one of the most effective exercises to help keep age related health problems at bay, and walking just twenty minutes a day can do wonders for your overall well-being.

One benefit of walking is the fact that it doesn't require a bunch of fancy fitness equipment. A good, comfortable pair of **shoes** is really **all you** need to get started, though adding a **pedometer** can help to track how much you are moving and help you to set and reach your fitness goals. If a pedometer or tracking device (my favorite device is my **Garmin Forerunner**) isn't in your price range, you can also

175

download a free pedometer app (like *Runtastic*) for your smartphone. Having your smartphone with you as you walk is also a good idea because it gives you the ability to call someone if you run into problems like rain or you get lost (don't laugh—it has happened to me!) I also love the fact that having my iPhone with me allows me to listen to podcasts or music as I walk, and studies have shown that adult walkers who listen to music as they walk, tend to exercise 21% longer than those who walk in silence. Additionally, listening to your favorite tunes as you walk has been shown to improve thinking skills. A recent Ohio State University study has shown that the mix of exercise and music is a potent combination because exercise makes you feel better emotionally and physically while music stimulates your creativity. Combining the two heightens the benefits of both.

In order to rock your walk and truly maximize its physical fitness benefits, try a few of these simple tips...

Pick up the pace. You don't need to run, but walking as quickly as you can without losing the ability to carry on a conversation or sing along to your favorite song, will increase the fitness benefit of your walk.

Nibble on some dark chocolate beforehand. The antioxidants in dark chocolate are especially beneficial to walkers because they help to ease discomfort— even in folks with chronic leg pain.

Move in short bursts. You don't need to walk for an hour at a time. If you have five or ten minutes during your lunch hour, take a walk. Then, in the evening after supper take another short walk. Those minutes will add up quickly over time.

Don't forget your water. Take along a bottle of water to avoid dehydration. This is especially important during warm weather. Water is better than sports drinks if you are going on a short walk because the calories in a sports drink can negate the weight loss benefits of the walk. Sports drinks are more appropriate if you are going on a particularly long or strenuous walk because of the extra energy that they can provide.

Switch it up. Avoid boredom by varying your walking routes, but make sure that you stay safe by walking in well-lit and populated areas. For a fun change of scenery, find a trail with hilly terrain. Not only will it offer a bit of variety but the more challenging terrain will also increase your heart rate and help to strengthen your joints.

Add some weight. Those without neck, shoulder, back, knee or ankle injuries can try adding hand or ankle weights as they walk. The added resistance will build muscle more quickly and increase the number of calories burned.

Chin up. Keeping your head up and focusing on a far-off object such as a house or tree in the distance (and keeping your gaze fixed on that object) will trick your brain and body into thinking that you're walking a shorter distance than you really are.

Some people really enjoy walking with friends while others prefer to use their walk time as "me-time". Personally, I fall somewhere in the middle. On normal walks, I prefer to go it alone so that I can catch up on my favorite podcasts. However; I live in the gorgeous state of Colorado where we have an abundance of beautiful hiking trails to explore. If I am planning to take on an unfamiliar trail or a more challenging hike, I always go with a buddy.

There's nothing complicated about adding walking to your fitness routine and it is something that you can start small with and increase your distance over time. Despite its simplicity, the benefits of walking are numerous and immediate. Here are just a few of the good things that you'll begin experiencing if you add walking to your fitness regimen...

- **Weight loss.** Probably the most popular reason for anyone to begin *any* new fitness program is so that they can lose some weight. Well, walking just happens to be great for weight loss. Not only will burning the extra calories help you to lose weight, but walking also thwarts disease triggering inflammation caused by extra fat—especially belly fat. Research shows that overweight adults in their 40's and 50's who walk briskly most days are just as healthy as their thinner peers who don't.

- **Spark brighter ideas.** If you are feeling uninspired or are in a creative funk, head outside for a quick walk. When researchers at Santa Clara University in California asked volunteers working on a creativity test to either take a short stroll or stay seated at their desk, they found that the individuals who went for a stroll came up with twice as many innovative solutions and subjectively better ideas than those who remained seated. This seems to indicate that walking helps the mind shift from intense focus to stream-of-consciousness mode, allowing fresh associations to come to the surface.

- **Boost confidence.** A recent Gallup poll has determined that people who were regularly active (even with low stress workouts such as walking) had more positive self-images regardless of their weight or appearance. This is because physical activity triggers your body to release endorphins which are brain chemicals that boost feelings of confidence and contentment.

- **Train your brain.** Not only does regular aerobic exercise (which includes brisk walking) make you healthier; according to researchers from New Zealand's University of Otago, it can also make you *smarter*. This happens because aerobic exercise promotes the growth of new brain cells and improves connections between neurons so that they work more effectively.

- **Strengthen bones.** Women can lose up to 20% of their bone mass during and after menopause. Walking puts pressure on your bones (especially in fracture-prone areas like the legs and hips) which in turn helps to strengthen them and stimulate new bone growth.

- **Ease achy joints.** A new *Arthritis Care and Research* study reveals that you can reduce your knee-related pain and physical limitation by 18% for every 1000 steps (roughly half a mile) you take. As the researchers explain, walking strengthens joint-protective muscles and encourages the release of pain thwarting chemicals, keeping your knees healthy and osteoarthritis free.

- **Rev your memory.** Walking increases blood flow to your brain and decreases the inflammation that is linked to memory-impairing brain plaques. This results in a 27% drop in the likelihood of developing dementia.

- **Add years to your life.** Studies show that adults who stay active by walking, live as long as hard-core fitness buffs. Every minute of walking (even at a leisurely pace) extends your life by SEVEN minutes. This is because walking strengthens your heart and improves oxygen flow throughout your body.

When you combine the ease of walking with the numerous and significant benefits that it provides, there is no denying that it should be a key component to any fitness program. Start small—just stroll down to the end of your block and back, but start TODAY. A year from now—you'll be so glad that you did!

TAKE A STAND FOR GOOD HEALTH

There's bad news on the health front for all of us who spend our days at a desk, sitting for hours on end while we work on a computer or shuffle papers. Though we might feel as though we are out of harm's way as we work at our nice, safe office in our cushy swivel chair—we are WRONG and the culprit that is putting us at risk is the very chair that our butts are glued to day in and day out.

Actually—it's not so much the *chair* that's to blame as it is the *amount of time* that we spend sitting in it. According to a study from the University of Queensland, inactivity is the biggest risk factor for heart disease in women ages 30 and up—even more so than high BMI (Body Mass Index) and high blood pressure levels. Additionally, James Levine, M.D., Ph.D., and author of *Get Up! Why Your Chair is Killing You and What You Can Do About It* (Palgrave Macmillan, 2014) says that prolonged sitting can be more harmful to our health than smoking because although smoking is unquestionably harmful, only a fifth of the people in the U.S. smoke while the vast majority of adults and children are seated for much of the day. Therefore, the total health impact of sitting is *greater* than that of smoking because far more people are affected.

Studies have shown that sitters are more prone to thirty-four chronic diseases and conditions including obesity, type 2 diabetes and cardiovascular disease than those who are more active. Even those who engage in the recommended thirty minutes of moderate to vigorous activity a day, but are otherwise sedentary, have a higher risk of chronic disease than someone like a UPS driver who is up and down all day long, but who gets *no* additional exercise.

So...what do we do about this? I mean, we can't all become UPS drivers, right? Fortunately, a career change is not necessary—all we need to do is take a STAND against sitting. A study published in *Medicine & Science in Sports & Exercise*, stated that blood flow in leg arteries impaired by sitting can be reversed simply by taking a five-minute walking break every hour. Just get up and walk around your office, deliver a message to a coworker in person rather than by email, or take a phone call while standing instead of sitting. These small but consistent changes can make a significant difference over time. In fact, standing up at least once every two hours (though every hour is preferable) is linked to a 10% drop in the risk of endometrial cancer, an 8% drop for colon cancer and a 6% drop for lung cancer. This is because movement reduces the levels of cancer-linked inflammatory chemicals throughout the body. Our brains also benefit from these walking breaks because physical activity helps to move oxygen through the bloodstream which nourishes brain tissue at a cellular level.

So, incorporating more standing and movement into our routine is clearly the best way to fend off the negative health consequences brought on by sitting for too long—but what about those times when we just can't leave our chairs? Even if we must remain seated for a longer stretch of time, there are still a few things that we can do to make our sitting less detrimental. The first thing that we can do to improve our health while sitting is to use our muscles. Frequently sucking in our stomach or squeezing our thighs together for five seconds will help to increase circulation as will doing a few simple, seated stretches. If we have a bit more freedom to move about in our chairs, it is beneficial to also try some twisting and turning because according to Susan B. Lord M.D., a physician who is also a yoga instructor, "twisting and turning the body increases blood flow and lymphatic drainage which enhances detoxification of the body". Lord suggests the following simple twist to try at work: Sit facing forward, turn to the right and grab the top of your chair with your right hand, turning your body as far as you can in that direction. Then switch sides. Bending over to touch your toes also has cleansing benefits because letting your head fall below your heart encourages circulation which is also a critical element of detoxification.

Additionally, it is important to note the role of posture while we are sitting. Obviously, good posture prevents back pain and helps us to look slimmer; however, the perks of good posture don't stop there. According to a new study in the journal, *Health Psychology*, people who were asked to sit up straight while doing stressful tasks, reported feeling more enthusiastic, excited and strong; whereas slouchers felt sluggish, stressed and unmotivated. Straightening our spines makes our minds think that we are focused and ready to go. This little mental cue leads to an overall improved mood.

While sitting is simply a fact of life for most of us in our modern culture—it doesn't have to be a drag on our overall health. Simply taking a few steps (literally) can drastically improve your well-being without jeopardizing your productivity at work. Give it a try—take a STAND for your health...you'll feel Fab**YOU**lous.

There's an App for That

If you need a little extra help remembering to add more movement into your day, never fear—there are some great apps and programs that are designed to do just that.

- **Stand App:** This Mac app is geared specifically toward people who sit too much. It is a free app that reminds you to take a break *and* provides thirty quick exercises to follow to get your blood flowing and posture perfected. Find it at www.getstandapp.com.

- **Time to Move:** This app cleverly suggests random breaks with suggested exercises you can do *at your desk*. Exercise time is tracked, and you get a daily total at day's end to see how much exercise you racked up. Find it on iTunes or on Google Play for Android.

- **Coffee Break:** This is a cool little Mac app that tells you when you've been sitting in front of the screen too long. You'll get a reminder message and your screen will dim when it's break time. It lights back up once you've walked the dog or refilled your coffee mug. Find it on iTunes or apple.com.

- **Big Stretch Reminder:** This is a highly customizable program for Windows and Linux platforms. It lets you choose types of breaks and the lengths. It also lets you set reminders for the purpose of the break. Additionally, you can choose levels of alert intrusiveness and it will (if you choose) display a countdown indicator. Find it at monkeymatt.com/bigstretch

SIT & PLANK--EASY RIGHT?

Oh my gosh...SOOOOO wrong! Ugh! I am a forty-something year old woman who considers herself to be in decent shape. I run regularly (and even WON my age group in a recent 5K!) and I'm not overweight. Though I feel pretty good about my cardio fitness due to the running, I've always felt like I should be doing more in the way of strength training. Problem is...I hate strength training. Seriously...*HATE* it. So, rather than trying to become a gym rat like my husband and sons; I decided to come up with my own little strength training routine that I could do at night before taking my bath. I decided to start out with something *easy* like a minute-long plank followed by a three-minute wall sit and then ten push-ups. Sounds simple enough doesn't it? Well guess what...it's NOT easy!

When I first began this program, my one minute plank was the worst. I thought that planking would be a good way to strengthen my core but instead, it caused a lot of pain in my lower back. As it turns out, I was doing my plank incorrectly and was therefore doing more harm than good to my body. I didn't want to give up though because I knew that planking was better for my abs than doing crunches and that a good plank would help to tone and tighten my tush while also strengthening my upper arms (no bat wings for me!) So, I talked to a friend of mine who is a personal trainer and got the skinny on how to plank properly so as to gain the most benefit while reducing the pain and risk of injury. Little did I know that the secret to the perfect plank lies not so much in the amount of time spent holding the plank, but in the *form* of the plank. Though I started out with the intentions of *only* holding my plank for a minute, I quickly learned that a minute (sixty measly seconds) was actually too long for me. I would make it about half way through my minute and then I would either start to let my lower back sag or I would lift my pelvis...both in an attempt to fight the fatigue that was setting in. So, the first step that I had to take towards improving my plank was reducing my time to 30 seconds. I have to confess that this was a little humbling for me because I felt like a wimp for not being to hold my plank correctly for one lousy minute...but whatever.

My next step was to make sure that my form was correct...every. single. time. This is definitely easier said than done, but SO important.

To do a basic plank you first want to get into to push-up position but with your *forearms* on the ground instead of your hands. Your elbows should line up directly underneath your shoulders. Make sure that you keep a neutral neck and spine with no sagging or raising of the pelvis (both are natural tendencies once fatigue sets in). Create a strong, straight line from head to toe and tighten your abdominals and glutes. Look down at the ground at a spot right in front of your hands (this will help you maintain a neutral neck position.) Hold this position, but once your form begins to suffer it is time to stop. There is no benefit (and as I discovered, can be possible harm) in doing an incorrect plank.

Rather than trying to hold the plank for too long and doing it incorrectly, my trainer suggested a routine of holding the plank for ten seconds, resting for ten seconds and repeating this five times. As you do this routine, your core will begin to strengthen and you'll be able to hold the plank for longer intervals or will be able to move on to more advanced versions of the plank (many of which can be found online). The great thing about planking however, is that even if you never progress on to other planking variations; this basic plank will be sufficient for the development of solid core stability.

My next challenge was the wall sit. This one was easier for me than the plank and yet I still couldn't believe how hard it was to hold my sit for a full three minutes. I mentioned this to my trainer and she laughed and told me that the wall sit (also known as the Roman Chair) is actually used as a disciplinary action in the military due to its level of difficulty; therefore, I shouldn't feel *too* bad for finding it to be a challenge. That made me feel a little better. Still, I knew that the wall sit was great for strengthening the quad muscles so I wanted to keep it as a part of my routine.

To correctly do a wall sit, you basically want to form two 90 degree angles with your body. One at the hips and one with your knees. Find a wall and lean against it with your feet shoulder width apart and approximately 2 ft. from the wall. Ease your body down the wall until your knees are bent at a 90-degree angle (don't go beyond 90 degrees otherwise you risk injuring your knees). Hold this position for the allotted amount of time.

By the time I finished with my plank and my wall sit, I was SHOT so I decided that I would do my push-ups at another time. Now I do my push-ups in the morning and my plank/sit routine in the evening. In the short time that I've been doing this, I have noticed an improvement in my core strength as well as in my leg strength. I feel like this has been a good addition to the cardio that I get through my running and I love that it doesn't take a lot of time.

Try adding these simple moves to your fitness routine—they'll leave you feeling fit and FAB.

CUTE, CUDDLY & GOOD FOR YOUR HEALTH

Whether they say "meow", "woof" or "Polly want a cracker", our pets play such a significant role in our lives. They selflessly provide us with unconditional love, faithful companionship and endless entertainment. One of the biggest benefits of pet ownership however, might be the incredible health benefits that we as pet owners experience.

It doesn't take a super genius to understand that taking your pup on a daily walk is not only good for him, but good for you as well. A study from the University of California, Berkeley found that pet owners are far less likely to be overweight simply because they move a lot more than those without pets. In fact, it has been shown that dog owners walk nearly *twice as much* as non-dog owners. All of this walking and moving helps to whittle your middle and is therefore good for your pooch and your *pooch*.

In addition to the benefits to your mid-section that you gain when you take Fido for a daily stroll, you're also helping out your brain. There is mounting evidence showing that exercising (yes, walking your dog at a brisk pace counts) for 30 minutes a day, five days a week can lower your risk of developing Alzheimer's disease—even if you have an increased genetic risk. Exercise slows age-related changes in the brain and helps to ensure that you have plenty of healthy neurons and very little of the "sticky" protein that forms troublesome plaque in the brain's memory center. So, the next time your pup wants to go out for a walk, take him, and be grateful for the memories that you're making *and* keeping.

We love our animal friends with all of our heart, which is a good thing considering just how healthy they are *for* our hearts. According to the American Heart Association, sharing your home with a pet (or pets) drops your risk of heart disease by as much as 30%. This significant decrease in risk is due in large part to the relaxing effects that our pets have on us. I am the owner of three ornery cats and even though their absurd shenanigans keep me laughing on a regular basis, it is their cuddles and purrs that *really* get to me. This calming effect that our pets have on us is a wonderful safeguard against stress and (according to research from the State University of New York at Buffalo) helps to reduce dangerous blood pressure spikes by nearly 23%. No wonder cuddling with my Daisy girl always feels so good after a long day at work.

Speaking of feeling good...pets have been shown to have therapeutic effects on physical aches and pains too. In fact, surgery patients who cuddle with a pet during recovery, require 50% less pain medication than those without an animal's companionship. Cardiologist Stephen Sinatra, M.D. points out that "when you interact with an animal you love, your body receives a rush of pain-relieving endorphins". Additionally, a Miami University study shows that "pets reduce cortisol, a stress hormone, while boosting oxytocin (a pain-easing, mood lifting chemical)" which according to psychologist Denee Jordan, helps to strengthen your immunity and resistance to germs.

While the physical health benefits of pet ownership are significant, the *emotional* health benefits are no less valuable. As already mentioned, pets are great for reducing stress and increasing joy but did you know that they might even make your marriage stronger? It's true! Recent research out of Canada shows that couples who have a dog tend to feel closer to each other than couples without a canine companion. Additionally, couples who share a pet tend to resolve arguments more easily and report higher levels of marital satisfaction. According to sociologist, Terri Orbuck, Ph.D., "the unconditional love that you get from a dog rubs off on your relationship" resulting in more loving feelings between spouses. Dog owners also tend to be closer to neighbors and have stronger social connections, which can alleviate feelings of depression and isolation.

All of this is great news *if* you own a pet; but what if you *don't* have an animal to call your own? You can still enjoy the benefits of critter companionship by offering to pet-sit for a friend or by volunteering at your local animal shelter where there are plenty of animals in need of your love and affection. Or, if you *are* ready to take the plunge into pet ownership, you can check out the cool site *PawsLikeMe.com* to take a quiz and find a compatible dog at nearby shelter based upon your responses to questions about your personality, daily life and habits.

Yes—pets can add so much joy, love and *health* to our lives without asking for much in return. Make your pet a treasured member of your family by making sure that he/she is spayed/neutered and receives regular vet checkups. Then; how about picking up a new squeak toy or bag of treats on the way home from work tonight? Your pet will love you all the more.

HUG & KISS YOUR WAY TO FABYOULOUS HEALTH

Okay—it doesn't take a rocket scientist to know that hugging and kissing *feel* good. There are few things in this world that I crave more than physical affection. Whether it is a hot & steamy make out session with my hubby or big bear hug from one of my sons, I thrive on the exchange of love and affection between two people. It wasn't until recently however, that I discovered research that shows that not only do these physical exchanges feel good; they actually *are* good. I was excited to read that there are numerous documented physical and emotional health benefits to good ol' hugging and kissing—something that I intuitively suspected but now have scientific data to support.

Obviously, we don't need an excuse for showing affection, but if your sweetie wonders why you're extra lovey-dovey all of a sudden; just tell him that you're doing it for the sake of his health and then rattle off a few of these FabYOUlous health benefits...

- **Hugging is a great immunity booster.** Friendly hugging lowers the levels of cortisol in the body. This is good news because cortisol is a stress hormone that attacks the cells that ward off diseases like cancer. Also; the gentle pressure on the sternum and the emotional charge from hugging activates the Solar Plexus Chakra. This stimulates the thymus gland which regulates the body's production of white blood cells, which keep you healthy and disease free.
- **Hugging and kissing eases tension in the body.** It does this by promoting blood flow in the body's soft tissue, thereby aiding in the relaxation of tensed muscles.

This helps to combat pain and improves your blood circulation.

- **Hugging protects your heart.** According to researchers at the University of North Carolina at Chapel Hill, hugging helps to lower blood pressure and slow your heart rate. This helps to protect your heart since elevated heart rates have been linked to cardiovascular disease.

- **Hugging and kissing burn calories.** Okay, so maybe hugging isn't a *huge* calorie burner, but hugging your loved ones *does* burn approximately 12 calories (which is about 1/4 of an Oreo cookie). This means that every time you hug and kiss someone, you are helping to manage your weight...as long as you don't keep offsetting the hugs with Oreo Cookies, that is.

- **Hugging balances out the nervous system.** A study of the electrical properties of the skin of someone giving and receiving a hug shows a change in the skin conductance. Hugging seems to have an effect on the moisture and electricity in the skin and thereby suggests a more balanced state in the nervous (parasympathetic) system.

- **Hugging and kissing help boost the memory.** Hugging releases oxytocin (a hormone that produces feelings of relaxation, trust and psychological stability) into the bloodstream. This has been shown to improve memory function while also reducing tension.

- **Hugging eases the aging process.** According to researchers at Ohio State University, hugging and physical touch become increasingly important as we age. "The older you are, the more fragile you are physically, so contact becomes increasingly important for good health", University Psychologist, Janice Kiecolt-Glaser told USA Today. Studies have shown that loneliness, particularly with age, can increase stress levels and have negative health consequences. By hugging someone, we instantly feel closer to that individual and decrease those detrimental feelings of loneliness.

- **Hug and kiss yourself happy.** Holding a hug for an extended time stimulates serotonin levels within the body. This results in heightened pleasure and mood levels.

In addition to these eight health benefits, hugging and kissing have definite relationship benefits as well. In fact, recent studies show that a warm embrace might just be the key to a monogamous relationship. According to the research, men in relationships who were given a dose of the bonding hormone oxytocin, were more likely to *avoid* standing close to a beautiful woman that they had just met compared with men who *weren't* given oxytocin. Clearly, there is no *guarantee* of fidelity, but this research shows that a good cuddle might just keep your guy from having eyes for anyone but you.

Hugging is great but let's not forget about kissing. Locking lips with your sweetie can also help to kick your romantic relationship up a notch. A recent Oxford University study found that kissing is more effective than sex at keeping long-term passion alive within a monogamous relationship. "Kissing is more intimate and more indicative of relationship quality than sex" says Oxford researcher, Rafael Wlodarski. Kissing has been shown to release dopamine, oxytocin and serotonin in the body and these powerful hormones and neurotransmitters are key ingredients when it comes to helping people to feel aroused, connected and content in a relationship. Sheril Kirshenbaum, research scientist and author of the book *The Science of Kissing* (Grand Central Publishing, 2011) warns that couples in long-term relationships should work hard to make sure that kissing doesn't fall by the wayside over time because of the strengthening of emotional bonds that it induces. Kirshenbaum says that you should "kiss your partner every day. Even if it's not passionate, the feel-good chemicals will still be there".

So...as you do your push-ups and take your vitamins every day, you might also want to think about adding a little more love and

195

affection into your fitness routine. Not only will it make you (and the object of your affection) happier—it just might make you a little healthier too...and that is Fab**YOU**lous news.

"I define connection as the energy that exists between people when they feel seen, heard and valued; when they can give and receive without judgement; and when they derive sustenance and strength from the relationship"

Brene Brown

10 SWEET SOMETHINGS TO WHISPER IN YOUR PARTNER'S EAR

We ended the previous section talking about the health benefits of hugging and kissing, so let's continue on in that vein by exploring the ways in which loving *words* can help to deepen your connection to your partner.

Sure...roses, diamond rings and sappy love songs all convey unmistakable messages of undying love; but who has the time and energy to go to those lengths on a daily basis? Not me—that's for sure. Fortunately, there are far easier (and yet still very effective) ways to keep the love and romance alive in our relationships—all we need to do is use our voice and utter a few simple phrases that will communicate just how much we care. Try out a few of these loving phrases the next time you want to make sure that your honey is feeling the love.

You're so gorgeous/hot/sexy

We all want to feel desired. Make sure that your sweetie knows that he/she still has what it takes to get your motor revving.

I miss you

Even if you just saw him/her this morning and will see him/her again when you get home from work, a few simple texts or voicemails during the day to let your love know that he's/she's on your mind will never go unappreciated. Mix it up by sending photos or jokes that will make him/her smile. Here's one to start you off...

"What's the difference between snowmen and snow women?"

"Snowballs".

HAHAHA! It's a little PG-13 but it never fails to crack me up.

Please/Thank you

No one likes to be taken for granted and yet sometimes we use more common courtesy with strangers than we do with our loved ones. Make sure that your sweetie always knows that he's/she's appreciated.

Do you remember that time we...?

You and your honey have logged lots of wonderful memories from your time together. Show him/her that those moments still hold a special place in your heart by bringing them up. Take this a step further by dragging out the photo album or old ticket stubs for a jog down memory lane.

How was your day?

This might not sound all that romantic, but when asked with genuine interest, it will show your partner that you are sincerely interested in what he/she has going on in his/her life. Of course, this one only works if you follow it up by truly listening and responding to what he/she tells you.

I'm sorry/You're right

Okay, I'll admit...this one can be TOUGH. Sometimes we just don't want to admit that we are wrong (even when we are absolutely, dead dog wrong). Still...being willing to admit our faults (we all have them) and apologize when we've screwed up (we all do) shows our sweetie that we care enough about him/her and the relationship to eat crow and make amends when necessary.

What do you think?

Our partners have thoughts and opinions just like we do. Asking them to share those thoughts and opinions with us shows that we value what they have to say.

Let's Meet in the Middle

No matter how much we love our honeys, there are going to be times that we just do not agree with them. Rather than stonewalling or bullying your way to a resolution, show your partner that you care more about the relationship than the issue at hand by being the first to offer up a workable compromise. This will show your partner that you are willing to take the high road to work things out because you love and cherish their happiness as much as your own.

How can I help you?

Sometimes we all just need a helping hand. Whether your man is overextended at work and just needs someone else to mow the effin' yard or your girl is working through emotional issues with her extended family and needs a sounding board to bounce thoughts off of—your genuine willingness to help bear some of his/her burden will speak volumes as to your love and level of commitment. You might not be able to fix every issue or right every wrong, but you *can* show your love that you are on his/her side by being willing to do whatever you (reasonably) can to lend support.

I love you

Sometimes nothing says it better than those three little words. Make sure they are the last words your sweetie hears before he/she drifts off to sleep at night or before he/she leaves the house in the morning. Make the words stick by whispering them in the *left* ear because the left ear is controlled by the right side of the brain—the

201

side responsible for processing emotions. Add even more punch to your words by topping them off with a kiss.

CHECKLIST FOR A FABYOULOUS PARTNER

Did the last chapter leave you thinking "this is great Melissa and I'd *love* to say all of these wonderful things IF ONLY I had someone special to say them to"? Okay. I get it. I get it because I've been there.

I'll confess—I haven't always been great at picking winners when it comes to love. I've fallen for great looks/no brains, charming personality/no job, great job/self-absorbed...you get the picture. It wasn't until my first marriage fell apart that I finally took the time to get intentional about the qualities that truly mattered to me in a partner.

In order to establish what qualities were absolute non-negotiables for me, I first had to get crystal clear on the qualities that *I myself* wanted to possess and *then* I had to think in terms of qualities that a partner could have to complement those qualities of my own. I had to promise myself not to settle for something less than what I knew that I wanted and deserved...even if it meant being alone for a while (which it did). I had to visualize my perfect partner in my mind before I even knew if he existed. I had to think about the kind of partnership that I wanted to be involved in and what *my* contribution to that partnership would be. All of this forethought wasn't necessarily easy—but in retrospect, I can see that maintaining my standards and waiting for the right man to come along was DEFINITELY worth it.

One thing that really helped me in this partner picking process was having a clear and defined list of qualities that were vitally important to me. These qualities were so important to me that I had decided that if any guy lacked *even one* of the qualities—he wasn't the guy for me. It might sound cut-throat or rigid, but I had already spent far too many miserable years with the *wrong* man, so I was no longer willing to compromise on things that were important to me. Besides, I had finally gotten to the point in my life where I truly felt okay on my own. If I was going to share my life with someone, it was going to be with someone who added value to my life and made me want to be a better person. My list didn't include specifics on outer traits like looks, income level etc. but it *did* cover crucial *character* traits that were deal makers/breakers for me. As it turned out—the list worked. I found a partner who is by no means perfect, but who is absolutely perfect for me.

If you are currently single but longing to find your Fab**YOU**lous partner; consider making a list of your own and then set your intention on finding a partner who meets your criteria. Here are the twelve non-negotiable qualities that were on *my* list...use them if they apply, but feel free to add qualities that are important to *you*. Most importantly—DO NOT SETTLE. You are far too Fab**YOU**lous to be with anyone less than what you want & deserve.

My Perfect Partner Must...

- **Accept the fact that my sons and I are a package deal.** My boys are my number one priority and I will only be with a man who can accept that fact. I expect my perfect partner to support my role as a mother and to be willing to nurture a loving relationship with my sons.
- **Have chemistry with me and be nice.** I want to feel sparks when we kiss and chemistry when we are together. I want to feel a thrill when my man walks into the room. I also expect common courtesy and genuine kindness. Courtesy & kindness will go a long way in keeping the passion alive in our relationship.

- **Be compatible with me.** I know that the saying "opposites attract" may be true—but I'm looking for more than just attraction. I want to be with someone with whom I share common interests. I want a partner who will share my love of sports, travel, music and cultural activities. I don't expect my partner to take up knitting or running (two things that I enjoy) but I *do* expect to be able to enjoy activities like baseball games and concerts together.

- **Allow me to be my own person.** I am DONE trying to be someone that I'm not just to appease someone else. My perfect partner must accept me for who I am and allow me to have my own thoughts, values and opinions—even if/when they differ from his.

- **Have a great sense of humor.** A relationship without laughter is NOT FabYOUlous. My perfect partner must have a fun sense of humor that isn't mean or condescending. I love a good joke and someone who can laugh easily. I *especially* love someone who can laugh at himself.

- **Have similar morals and values.** Yes—we are individuals and have our own individualized belief systems but I want to be with a man whose values align closely with mine. We don't necessarily need to support the same political party or read the same kind of books, but I *do* want to be with someone who has similar values when it comes to things like family, faith and finances.

- **Be humble enough to apologize when he's wrong and gracious enough to accept an apology when *I'm* wrong.** There is nothing that is more emotionally exhausting than being with someone who must ALWAYS be right...even when they are 100% dead wrong. We are human. We make mistakes. I will do my best to own up and take responsibility for my mistakes but I expect my partner to be willing to do the same.

- **Be absolutely faithful to me.** I will not tolerate a cheater. Ever. Period.
- **Understand that I have lofty goals and aspirations and be willing to support me as I strive to turn my dreams into reality.** I need a partner who is not intimidated or threatened by a strong, ambitious woman. There are things that I want to accomplish in this lifetime and I fully intend to make them happen. I want to be with a man who is capable of encouraging my dreams while also pursuing dreams of his own. I don't want to feel like my man is in constant competition with me—instead, I want the two of us to be each other's biggest cheerleaders as together, we turn our dreams into reality.
- **Share the load.** A partnership is just that—a partnership. No one person should be expected to shoulder the burdens of a relationship alone. I expect my partner to contribute financially, emotionally and physically to our relationship. Whether it is dealing with the family budget or divvying up household chores, I expect my man to do his part. I spent WAY too many years trying to keep things afloat while being drug under by someone who wasn't willing to do his part to make the relationship successful. That is NO way to live and I am not interested in that type of parasitic relationship again. I expect my man to help me carry the load so that we can also share equally together in the *rewards* of our union.
- **Be willing to seek help if/when it is needed.** Relationships can be tough and sometimes even the most loving couples need a little help. I want to be with a man who loves me and values our relationship enough to be willing to seek the outside guidance of a counselor if it becomes necessary.
- ***Grow* with the flow.** Life is unpredictable and sometimes sh*t just happens. I want a partner who is flexible enough

to bend without breaking and adaptable enough to adjust the sails when things get off course. We are a team and together we can create a Fab**YOU**lous life if we understand that relationships are a balance of give & take and that the synergy created through our relationship allows us to be stronger together than we would be as separate individuals.

If you think this check list sounds rigid—you're right; it is. However; I believe with all of my heart that more women would be involved in far more Fab**YOU**lous relationships if they would decide ahead of time on the non-negotiable standards that they expect a partner to meet and stick to their guns rather than sacrificing their standards in order to avoid being alone. Being single is **NOT** bad—being in an unhealthy relationship with the wrong person *is* (trust me—I'm an *expert* on this one). Yes, my list might be rigid and my standards high but, I am okay with that because I know that I deserve a man who meets these criteria—and guess what...I found him. It took some time, but I found him. I also know that there is nothing on this list that I myself, am not also willing to contribute to the relationship.

So...if you are still hoping to find the perfect partner to spend your life with; get out a pen and some paper and start listing the attributes that are important to you. Once your list is complete, start picturing your partner in your mind and imagining your life together. Your perfect partner might not arrive immediately, but I do believe that he/she will arrive when the time is right. Give it a shot—you've got nothing to lose and a Fab**YOU**lous relationship to gain!

FINDING LOVE...AGAIN

In the first two chapters of this section we've covered cultivating your relationship by using edifying words, and creating standards when it comes to looking for love. What if you *had* love though? What if you had it and somehow lost it? Hey—it happens. We've *all* had our hearts shattered at some point; most of us more than once. I remember one particularly difficult heart break from my early years. It was Valentine's Day during my senior year of college and my long-time boyfriend and I had broken up the week before. At the time, I lived in a sorority house and all of my sorority sisters were receiving beautiful bouquets and stuffed animals while all I got was...well, let's be honest here, all I got was *drunk*.

Since that day all those years ago, I've experienced some pretty decent Valentine's Days but I've *also* experienced the post-divorce loneliness of wondering if I would ever enjoy a happy Valentine's Day again.

Thankfully, I no longer have to worry about that. My first marriage may have been a disaster but I didn't let the trauma from that experience prevent me from finding love again. It might not be *easy,* but becoming romantically fulfilled again after a devastating loss (be it divorce, break-up or even death) *is* absolutely possible.

If you think that you are ready to test the waters and explore the possibility of discovering love again, here are a few tips that can help you in your pursuit.

Seven FabYOUlous Tips for Finding Love...Again

1) **Stabilize your life.** Loss is hard. Even if the loss was necessary (as in my case—I *needed* to divorce my first husband in order to preserve my sanity) it can still leave you reeling. Experiencing the *death* of your loved one is particularly devastating. Don't even *think* of entering into another romantic relationship until you've had the time and taken the steps to heal yourself both emotionally and physically. Let yourself grieve, seek the help of a therapist—do whatever you need to do to get yourself back on stable ground. It is impossible to make appropriate judgements and decisions while in an unhealthy state. Save yourself and your potential partner a lot of heartache by making sure that you are emotionally and physically healthy enough to enter back into a romantic partnership.

2) **Enjoy what you've got.** There are a lot worse things in life than being single...trust me—A LOT worse. In fact, being single can be pretty darn awesome. Rather than focusing on what you perceive to be lacking in your life, shift your attention to all of the amazing things that are currently *present* in your life. Do you have amazing kids? If so, love them! Do you enjoy good health? If so, be grateful! Do you have friends and family members who love and support you? If so, you are more fortunate than you realize. By showing gratitude for the incredible blessings in our lives, we not only feel better about ourselves and our circumstances; we also open ourselves up to receive even more blessings.

3) **Understand that rebounding is great in basketball—but not so much in love.** Heading from one romantic relationship straight into another can be

210

a recipe for disaster and disillusionment. Too often, a failed relationship leaves us feeling emotionally beat up and our self-esteem takes a hit. Jumping headfirst into *another* relationship might provide a temporary boost to our self-confidence, but rarely will it result in long-term love and commitment. Rather than trying to get over one relationship by hurrying into another, try instead to allow yourself enough time to recuperate from your loss. This will make it possible for you to move into another relationship from a place of strength and wholeness rather than out of desperation.

4) **Be willing to be vulnerable.** This one is particularly difficult for me. I tend to be one of those people who likes to keep my heart closed off rather than allowing someone else the opportunity to break it. This might *sound* like a good defense mechanism, but in reality, it makes it difficult for me to truly connect with others on a deep, emotional level. In order to *really* find true love again, it is vital that you get to a place where you can feel good about opening yourself up and giving love away without the expectation of receiving it in return. This isn't easy because it requires a tremendous amount of self-confidence in one's ability to handle possible rejection. However; the ability to be vulnerable with another person is a key component to any lasting relationship, so it is something that must be mastered if you want to find real and lasting love.

5) **Apply the "Butterfly Effect" to your love life.** The Butterfly Effect simply states that if you find yourself in a meadow filled with butterflies flitting all around you, you will have much greater success at attracting the butterflies to you if you sit still and allow them to land on you than you will if you go running through the meadow with a net trying to snare them. When applied to your love life, this principle simply means

211

that having patience and allowing relationships to happen and develop naturally will lead to greater success than chasing after them with frantic and hurried desperation. Be patient and be still—eventually the right butterfly *will* land on you.

6) **Look for love in the right way *and* the right places.** Your next *true* love most likely will be someone who shares your interests (it's hard to cultivate a lasting relationship with someone with whom you have nothing in common) so it only makes sense that your best way of finding that person is to develop your own interests. Whether you enjoy camping, kayaking, break dancing (do people still do that?) or poetry slams—your best bet for finding love is to keep doing those things that you love to do. While you are participating in these activities, be open to meeting others who are also enjoying them. You'll exude happiness because you are doing something that you enjoy, and that happiness might just attract another fellow poetry slamming, break dancer who turns out to be the love of your life.

7) **Remember that actions always trump words.** People can *say* anything but behavior is what reveals true character. People are who they are. Thinking that you can change someone into something other than what they are, will only lead to frustration and heartache. When looking for love, remember that *behavior* is the true litmus test of whether or not a relationship has potential. Pervasive characteristics (those recurring patterns of thought and behavior that guide actions) matter. Don't believe someone who tells you that they are a great catch until their actions *show* you that they are a great catch.

The bottom line is, don't despair if you haven't found "the one". Instead, head out for drinks with some of your single friends, join a softball league or schedule a day of pampering for yourself at a local spa. When you are truly ready for love, it *will* find you. Just keep these seven tips in mind as you open yourself up to the Fab**YOU**lous possibilities, but most importantly—LOVE YOURSELF FIRST. Until you are able to truly love yourself, no one else will be able to love you in return.

IT'S LOVE IN ANY LANGUAGE

"I love you." Everyone loves to hear those three little words, but they can sound even sexier if whispered in another language. The next time you feel like turning up the heat with your honey, try adding a little international flavor to your sweet nothings with these eight different translations.

French: Je t'aime (zhuh tem)

Spanish: Te amo (teh ah-moh)

Japanese: Watashi wa anata o aishite-imasu (wa ta shee wa a na ta o a ee shee tee ee ma su)

Italian: Ti amo (tee ah-moh)

Esperanto: Mi amas vin (mee ah-mahs veen)

Hawaiian: Aloha au ia 'oe (ah low ha wow ee ah oh ay)

Russian: Ya lyublyu tebya (yah lyoo blyoo tee byah)

Swahili: Nakupenda (nah koo pen da)

As you practice your newly acquired multi-lingual skills, be sure to whisper your sweet nothings in your sweetie's left ear. Studies show that we process terms of endearment better in our left ear because it's controlled by the "emotional" right brain.

FAMILY MATTERS

When it comes to our personal relationships, our connection to our family ranks right up there with our relationship with our romantic partner. As a child, I was blessed to have grown up in a very close-knit family. My mom and dad loved my brother and I, *and* they loved each other. Additionally, I grew up with the tremendous blessing of having all four of my grandparents nearby and very involved in my upbringing. Despite some craziness during my teenage years (for which I will now and forever blame *Buddy Kittle—I'm pretty sure he won't ever read this, so it's safe to blame him—ha!) I grew up blissfully unaware of the difficult challenges that many families faced. Oh sure, I'm sure that mom and dad had their moments of wanting to strangle each other (as all married couples experience from time to time) and lord knows that they had *plenty* of moments of wanting to strangle *me*—but overall, we were a happy and for the most part, functional family.

As a child and teenager, I took my nice, stable, loving family life for granted. As an adult, however; I now have a much greater appreciation for the sacrifices and efforts that my parents made on a daily basis to ensure that my brother and I grew up in a secure and loving environment. A supportive family unit is *so* crucial to the emotional well-being of every member of the family. If there is strife between members, every individual in that family suffers as a result.

If you are feeling as though your family isn't as close as you'd like, or maybe you're just a little out of sync these days, keep the following points in mind to help strengthen that all important familial bond...

- **Labels hurt.** Most of us can look at our own families and immediately identify that one family member who is always getting into trouble. For me, that family member is my brother. HA HA! Okay—I'm lying. I'll confess that *I* was the family member who was more prone to pushing the limits, breaking the rules and getting into trouble (thanks a lot *Buddy Kittle!) While I like to think that I was just a bit more spirited and headstrong, I'm sure that the word "troublemaker" was on the tips of everyone's tongues during my teenage years.

  How about you? What labels have stuck with you? Are you "the quiet one" or maybe "the showoff"? Perhaps you were "the smart one" who then felt pressured to maintain a ridiculous GPA or "the pretty one" who fell into a depression whenever a rogue pimple appeared. Yes—over time, even seemingly positive labels can have a negative effect on our self-esteem if the pressure to live up to the label becomes too burdensome.

  Labeling our family members is dangerous because it prevents us from seeing and appreciating their full range of Fab**YOU**lousness and instead confines them to predetermined boxes with a set list of expectations. It simply isn't fair to ascribe a single faceted label to a brilliant, multi-faceted human being.

- **Time is a treasure.** I know, I know...we all *know* that we need to turn off the television and spend more quality time with our family members, but how many of us actually *do* it? How many of us miss our son's football games because we are too wrapped up in a project at work (I'm guilty of this one myself) or how many of us hear about our child's first steps or first words from the nanny rather than experiencing them firsthand?

As a mom with a full-time job, *I get it*. The pressure to be a good parent *and* successful professional is immense and exhausting. Still...making our family a priority and then working our schedules to reflect our priorities is a juggling skill that we *must* try to master. Maybe we can't make it to *every* football game, but do we at least make the effort to personally connect with our child to hear firsthand how the game went and how he felt about his individual performance? Maybe we missed our little one's first steps but do we make every effort to ensure that we make a big deal out of her second and third steps?

The time that we spend together as a family doesn't have to be extravagant or expensive. A simple game of Uno or Jenga (or better yet—*Jenga with a Twist*; visit the *www.FabYOUlousLife.com/FindingFabYOUlousBookBonuses* website to download your own free printable download of this fun, family friendly game. Just be sure that you don't accidently download the *Drunken Jenga* printable unless your family members are all of legal drinking age) around the kitchen table can forge bonds that will last forever. It is important that we savor every moment that we can with our families because years have a way of slipping away in the blink of an eye. Before you know it, your sweet little four year old will be cruising Main Street on the back of *Buddy Kittle's motorcycle while wearing a toga. Don't let those years pass without forging plenty of happy memories and supportive bonds.

- **Knowledge is power.** How well do you *really* know your family members? Can you name your teenage son's favorite band or the position he plays in football? Do you know if the fella your daughter is dating is any relation to

*Buddy Kittle? Do you know what book your spouse is currently reading? We live with our family members and think about them numerous times throughout the day but how well do we really *know* them? Make the effort now to really start listening to your family members and paying attention to their interests, hopes, fears and aspirations. I cannot imagine anything sadder than having a family full of strangers; so whether you eat dinner together three times a week or spend a lot of time driving your kids around to activities, use that time together as a chance to learn more about the things that are important in their worlds—you might be surprised at some of the interesting things you learn.

- **Have FUN.** When was the last time you and your family had a genuinely good time doing something fun together? If you have to stop and think about the answer to this question, it has been TOO LONG. Grab a Frisbee, head to a water park, work on a jigsaw puzzle...just do *something* together with your family that is FUN. It is so easy to slip into a soul sucking routine of waking up, dashing off to work/school, coming home, eating take-out, doing homework, vegging in front of the TV, going to bed and waking up to do it all over again...day after day after day. Is it any wonder that our family life is suffering from a lack of connection and enthusiasm? Try breaking out of this dull, hamster-wheel of an existence by infusing your family time with a little fun. It doesn't have to be extravagant or expensive (though I am a big proponent of family vacations), just something to get everyone laughing and relaxing together. These simple moments of shared enjoyment will be moments that form your family's most cherished memories.

With a little concentrated effort and a dash of creativity, your family life *can* go from drab to FAB and every member will benefit tremendously from the added attention and affection.

*Disclaimer—just in case Buddy Kittle *does* ever read this, I feel like I should point out that even though I got into more trouble as a result of Buddy's high school hijinks, I also had more FUN with him than any person should be allowed to have. I guess it's all just a matter of perspective. Thanks Buddy!

THE CASE FOR HAPPY FAMILIES

While a close connection to family is certainly good for our spirit, there are numerous studies that show how beneficial a happy family life is to one's overall health as well. In fact, it has been shown that a fun and supportive family dynamic can even add years to one's life expectancy. So, that being the case; it's a no-brainer that we should do all that we can to ensure that our family is a place of safety, acceptance and fun. To crank up the FAB in your fam, remember the points from the previous chapter and then add these five crucial keys to the mix.

1) **Spontaneity:** A 30-year study of over 16,000 strong families found that the happiest families made it a point to surprise each other with fun activities. These activities weren't necessarily elaborate; instead, it was the element of surprise that made them special. To incorporate more spontaneity into *your* family life, take the family on a spur of the moment ice cream run (a favorite in our family—even big, young adult sons will gladly join in if it means free ice cream) or warm up the oven and bake a batch of unplanned cookies together. Enjoyable, unexpected moments like these can create a fun sense of unity without requiring a lot of effort.

2) **Affection:** Hugs or high-fives, it doesn't matter how your family chooses to show affection for each other but the happiest families *are* affectionate. According to Richard Eyre, co-author of *Teaching Your Children*

Values; physical affection is a hallmark of happy families. Happy families seem to instinctively know when to offer a supportive pat on the back, comforting hug, playful butterfly kisses or a celebratory high-five.

3) **Traditions:** They can be silly or more meaningful, but special traditions are an important component for family bonding and give family members a sense of intimacy, security and belonging. So, whether it's bedtime stories every night or root beer floats after the first day of school, establishing traditions that are unique to your family will bring everyone closer and increase feelings of connection and well-being.

4) **Cheerleading:** No, you don't need to don a short skirt and shake pom poms, but happy families DO cheer for each other. Whether it's rooting for your high school daughter as she takes to the softball field or planning a special dinner to celebrate dad's new promotion—happy families celebrate each other's accomplishments. Celebrations don't need to be elaborate or expensive—just heartfelt.

5) **History:** Research shows that the bonds between family members are strengthened when stories of the family's history are shared. Photo albums, journals and video recordings are great ways to archive your family's stories so that they can be passed down and shared through the generations. This appreciation for one's heritage makes family members feel a sense of connection and pride in one's roots.

ALL OF THIS FAMILY BONDING IS GREAT BUT DON'T LET YOUR KIDS SUCK THE LIFE OUT OF YOU

There it is. I said it.

I love my kids more than anything in this universe and yet sometimes I feel like they are literally sucking the life right out of me. I mean, it definitely isn't as bad now that they are young adults as it was when they were toddlers (thankfully they no longer need my help to go potty) but still...I find myself giving so much of my time, energy, emotions and MONEY to my children that I often feel like I have little left over for myself.

The crazy thing is—I almost feel like this "Martyr Mom" syndrome is something that we moms wear as a badge of honor. I've been to playgroups where it felt like there was some kind of twisted *competition* going on to see which mom was the most exhausted, overextended and frazzled and then for some insane reason, *that* mom was revered as the winner because *obviously* she was the one sacrificing the most for her beloved offspring.

Hello?!? Exhausted, overextended and frazzled ARE NOT Fab**YOU**lous. Exhausted, overextended and frazzled SUCK.

Yes—being a good mom *can* voraciously consume every spare ounce of our energy and time...if we allow it to. However; we can also make the conscious choice to *not* allow motherhood to become a total immersion experience from which we emerge eighteen years later, bleary eyed, dazed and clueless as to what our own dreams and passions are. Obviously, I'm not suggesting that we *neglect* our children. I'm simply suggesting that we not neglect ourselves either. Our children grow and thrive because they receive our love and attention. Let's stop considering it *selfish* to spread a little of that love and attention to our own dreams, desires and self-care. Instead, let's consider the fact that it just might be *healthy* and *empowering* for our children to see their mothers as capable, accomplished women who value their own physical and mental health and who understand that the only way to truly care for others is to first care for one's self. Let's (as the trusty flight attendant always tells us) make sure that *our own* oxygen mask is firmly in place *before* we attend to our children, because let's face it—what good are we to our kids if we're slumped over, deprived of oxygen, rest and rejuvenation?

We must begin this quest for balance by getting smart and strategic. We must develop strategies to help us better manage our children so that they consume less of our time and energy and yet still get every bit of what they need from us. In order to help accomplish this goal, here are four FabYOUlous tips for nurturing your children *and* your dreams...

1) **Fool them with FUN:** It's no surprise that 80% of parental energy goes into things like nagging children to finish their homework, get dressed for school, clear the dishes, feed the dog etc. However; just as we can often fool our kiddos into eating their veggies when we combine them into other tasty dishes; we can also fool our kids into doing their required chores if we get a little bit creative and add some fun to the mix. For example, I used to have a terrible time getting my youngest son to cooperate in getting himself dressed for school. This all changed one day when I decided to time him to see how fast he could do it. Something about turning it into a competition suddenly spurred him into action and he got himself dressed faster than I even dreamed could be possible (I later discovered

that his speediness was due in part to the fact that he
would just skip putting on his underpants—but that's
a story for another time). Then, each consecutive
morning, I would challenge him to see if he could beat
his previous record. This simple, silly tweak turned our
grueling morning routine into something fun and filled
with laughter. It also helped to ensure that he was sent
off to school with a smile on his face while I retained a
small portion of my sanity (at least until it was
discovered that he was underpantsless, but again—a
story for another time).

Though they will never admit it, children secretly crave
management that holds them to a higher standard.
They need rules and consequences in order to
gradually build a framework for self-management.
Adding an element of fun to the mix is a great way to
ensure that this foundation for self-reliance is being
laid in a manner that is enjoyable for everyone
involved.

2) **Make your passions a regular part of the routine:** I
discovered (through a lot of trial and error) that if
there was something important to me and I made a
regular and consistent time for it in my life, my boys
eventually learned to accept it as a normal part of our
routine. Whether it is working out, writing, studying or
simply enjoying a luxurious bubble bath; consistently
scheduling time for ourselves *can* work as long as our
children's needs are met, expectations are made clear
and we are consistent both in our scheduling and our
expectations. It's crazy, but I learned that when there
was simply no other option other than to cooperate—
my boys cooperated. Maybe not at first, but with
enough consistency and reinforcement, I was able to
establish set blocks of time that were *my* time to do *my*

thing with limited interruption. Now that my boys are young adults with busy lives of their own, this is no longer an issue. When they were younger however, routines and consistency were a key component to me being able to progress on some of my most important goals and aspirations.

3) **Establish a kid-Free zone:** It used to drive me CRAZY to enter into my at-home work area (at the time it was just a corner of a room where I had my computer set up and a small bookshelf) and step on a lego or find candy bar wrappers on the floor (especially when there was a waste basket less than two feet away). So, to combat the crazies, I made a rule that no kids were to enter mom's "office" without her consent. Of course, I made exceptions for emergencies (after clearly defining what exactly constituted an emergency) but for the most part, I wanted my work area to be kid-free. In order to make this edict more palatable to my boys, I also encouraged them to have a mom-free zone (a corner of our basement that they turned into a clubhouse of sorts). They liked the idea of having an area where they could go to be boys (mind you—they were six and eight at this time so I didn't have to worry about them doing anything *too* outrageous) and I enjoyed knowing that my paperwork wouldn't be covered in chocolatey fingerprints—it was a true win-win scenario.

4) **Have easily enforceable rules:** Even though I had my "office" that was a kid-free zone, this became a more difficult space to manage as my boys got older. Often, they would need to go online for school and our only computer was in my "office". In order to maintain some semblance of order in my area, I created a list of rules that my (now older) boys needed to follow in order to make use of my space. These

rules can vary depending upon each person's preferences but I especially disliked dirty dishes and litter in my space so that became a part of my rule system. I also established limits for non-school related computer use. In order to make these rules seem more credible to my boys, I typed them up and posted them where they would see them each time they entered my space. I also made it clear what consequences would result if the rules were broken, and I was consistent with those consequences. As my boys grew into teenagers, they both had laptops of their own and rarely needed to use my computer. I know though, that to this day, they still think twice before interrupting me if they see me working in my office.

By establishing clear parameters and expectations with my children, I was able to advance my own passions and ambitions a great deal while still maintaining a loving and nurturing relationship with my boys. I don't feel as though this makes me selfish at all. Instead, I have seen the benefits that my boys have been able to reap as the result of having a happy, well rested and passionately engaged mom. I hope that they have also learned the value of following one's bliss and working to achieve important goals, so that they too will be able to continue doing so once they themselves become parents. It's a delicate dance and it doesn't always go as planned, but it *is* possible to nurture your own FabYOUlous dreams and desires while also loving and nurturing your family. Don't allow yourself to fall into the Martyr Mom trap—make self-care a priority as you learn to cultivate your own FabYOUlousness.

FRIENDS ARE THE FAMILY YOU CHOOSE

"Make new friends but keep the old. One is silver and the other gold".

I remember singing those words a hundred years ago when I was a young girl attending Girl Scout camp.

Okay—so maybe it wasn't *quite* 100 years ago, but still...it was over three decades ago and the crazy thing is—some of the girls that I attended that camp with are still, to this day, dear friends of mine. In fact, I am blessed to be able to say that my *first* best friend (before we were even old enough to understand the concept of a *best* friend) is *still* my best friend to this day (I'm looking at you Mia)!

Friendship...I can't imagine life without it. There is no better feeling than that of knowing that there are people in this world who love and accept you just the way you are. I for one would be absolutely lost without my precious "broad squad" and I give thanks for them every single day.

While I have been blessed to have some wonderful life-long friendships, there have also been times when I was faced with the prospect of having to make *new* friends. This happened when I went away to college and again when I left all of my family and friends behind to move to another state. Both of these experiences took some adjustment and forced me out of my comfort zone; however, both experiences resulted in additional friendships with more incredible women that I am blessed to have in my life.

If you are faced with a situation where you need to make new friends—or maybe you're just looking to expand your current circle of friends, follow these twelve easy tips to help you find and develop authentic, adult friendships...

1) **Talk to strangers**. Yes—I know, mama always told you *not* to talk to strangers. Well...you're no longer four years old so talking to strangers is now perfectly acceptable *and* a great way to make a new friend. If you're in line at the post office next to someone who looks fun—strike up a conversation. If you can't think of anything to talk about, talk about how *sloooow* the line at the post office is. Who knows, maybe you'll discover that you have kids the same age or that you both like to run. Even if you don't discover anything to base a potential friendship on, you've at least killed some time in line at the post office.

2) **Take a class**. It is always fun to learn new things in areas that interest us. I've taken classes on everything from knitting to web design to money management. The best thing about these classes is that I *always* walk away with a lot more than just increased knowledge—I walk away with a new friend or two as well. When I register for a class, I automatically know that I will be meeting new people with whom I already share one common interest (the class subject matter). The next step is simply showing up for the class and being friendly and approachable. I'm always amazed at the way things tend to work out—the universe just seems to have a way of bringing the right people into my orbit and from there we are able to make meaningful connections and cultivate developing friendships. I'm sure that the same will be true for you as well. If you need some ideas on where to look for interesting classes, here are a few suggestions to consider...

Williams-Sonoma: Your inner epicure will delight in Williams-Sonoma's weekly one hour technique classes. You can find a schedule of their weekly classes on their website.

Bass Pro Shops, Cabela's, REI: If you are interested in honing your outdoor adventure skills, these three stores offer a variety of classes on everything from fly-fishing and archery to kayaking and camp cooking. Check your local store for a class schedule.

Jo-Ann Fabric and Craft Stores, Michaels, Hobby Lobby: These stores all offer a wide variety of in-store sewing, crafting, cake decorating, jewelry making etc. classes. Check with your local store to see what interesting classes are coming up.

Guitar Center: Try strumming a few bars in an in-store 60-minute guitar lesson for beginners.

Home Depot, Lowes: Whether you want to learn to build a birdhouse for your backyard or a backyard for your birdhouse—these two stores offer a variety of hands on DIY classes to help you build confidence in your handy-(wo)man, craftsman skills. Check with your local store for a full listing of upcoming classes and workshops.

Your local Cooperative Extension Service or Recreation Commission: From organic gardening to beginning tap dancing, most local Extension Offices or Recreation Commissions have a wonderful selection of classes to choose from.

3) **Attend a conference**. Just like taking a class will
   expose you to new people with similar interests, so will
   attending conferences. I attended my first ever blog
   conference a few years ago and am now enjoying
   friendships with several gals that I met while at the
   conference. Even though we all live in different states,
   we are able to use social media, email and good old-
   fashioned phone calls to grow our friendships.

4) **Get physical**. Whether you truly enjoy working out or
   are just doing it because you know that you need to,
   there are plenty of other people in the same boat. Try
   joining a running group or signing up for a Pilates
   class. While it might be tough to maintain any friendly
   chit-chat while you're huffing and puffing (and
   grunting, crying, cursing etc.) there is always time to
   do a little friendly mingling before and after your
   workouts. Another twist on this suggestion is to join a
   local team for a sport that you love. Several years ago,
   I joined a co-ed softball team called the Sons of
   Pitches (I'm not kidding—that's really our name).
   When I joined, I didn't know anyone on the team
   except for my husband. Now, several years later—the
   Sons of Pitches are some of my favorite people and I
   love spending time with them—on *and* off the field.

5) **Get a dog**. Not only are dogs man's best friend—their
   owners can be pretty cool too. If you are looking to
   meet some genuinely nice people, grab your pooch (or
   borrow your friend's pooch) and head to the local dog
   park. Dog owners *love* their dogs and they love *talking
   about* their dogs. So, whether your four-legged friend is
   a Bullmastiff or a Pekapoo, as long as they are friendly
   towards other animals, grab a Frisbee and head to the
   park for some fun and friend making.

6) **Have a kid**. Okay—having a child might not be the
   best tactic if your goal is simply to make friends—

234

there are *lots* of other less painful, cheaper and less exhausting ways to make friends. *However*, if you *already have* kids, they can be a great way to connect with other fun parents and form lasting friendships. My oldest son is now in his early 20's, but when he was just a little guy (like three years old) I attended a playgroup where I met my friend Amy who also had a little boy. Amy and I bonded over all of the things that moms of boys would bond over (bugs, dirt, toy cars, poop, dinosaurs, emergency room visits etc.) Our friendship continued to develop over the years as our sons entered school, played sports, got drivers licenses, went on dates etc. Amy and I now live in separate states and yet she is still one of my closest friends and our relationship is one that I will always cherish.

7) **Carpool to work.** Not only is carpooling economical and good for the environment—it can also help you to make friends. I have a friend who used to drive an hour to Denver every day for work. She was getting fed up with the headache of battling traffic every day and the expense of constantly filling her tank with gas, so she joined a carpool service. By sharing a ride with others, my friend has now made two new close friends that she enjoys hanging out with beyond just their carpool time.

8) **Steal friends from friends.** Okay—I know that this was a BIG no-no back in sixth grade, but we're all adults now, right? Besides, I look at this more as *sharing* than stealing since everyone involved remains friends. Here's how it works—my friends are amazing people and as amazing people, they are connected to *other* amazing people. I have been blessed to meet many of my friends' friends and thereby become friends with their friends myself. There's no mean

gossip or backstabbing going on—just new friendships being forged. We connect with others because our spirits are attracted to each other, so it only makes sense that we would also be attracted to those whose spirits are also attracted to those of our friends. Of course, you'll want to be careful to avoid leaving anyone out or causing hurt feelings, but there is no reason that you can't also become friends with your friends' friends.

9) **Volunteer.** There are so many good causes out there that are in need of great volunteers. Find a cause that speaks to your heart and then commit to giving your time and talent to an organization that supports that cause. As you do so, you will meet other like-minded individuals who have the same passions as you. In my previous life, I was the Executive Director for a nonprofit breast cancer support center, and had the pleasure of watching some of our amazing volunteers form deep and lasting friendships with each other. They were drawn together by a mutual desire to make a positive difference, and through their commitment to a cause, they have forged relationships built upon shared passions and a desire to serve.

10) **Connect with your alumni association.** I live in a different state from where I attended college and yet, through my involvement with my college alumni association, I have been able to meet and form relationships with others in my area who graduated from my same university. It has been so fun to share stories of our days at good ol' *Fort Hays State University* and I now have two friends that I didn't know during our college days, but have become close to now as adults. I've experienced this same phenomenon with my sorority as well. Though my college sorority doesn't have a local chapter at the university where I

currently live, I've been able to connect with other *Alpha Gamma Delta* alumni members in my local area. We may not have attended college at the same school, but having a shared sorority sisterhood has helped us to forge fun and lasting friendships.

11) **Join a club.** What are your hobbies? Do you like to sew, read, dance or cook? Chances are, if there is an activity that you enjoy—others enjoy it too and have likely started a club for it. What better way to make friends than to seek out others who share your same passions? If you don't know of a club for your particular interest—start one! Run an ad in your local paper or on your community online message board announcing your club's formation. You can also use the power of the internet to seek out clubs via interest websites such as *Meetup.com*

12) **Be a friend.** Regardless of how many of these tips you use to make new friends, there is one tip that still supersedes them all—if you want a friend, *be* a friend. No amount of dog buying, club joining, carpooling or volunteering will help you if you aren't *friendly*. People are drawn to happy, generous, optimistic people with shared interests. If you exude those qualities and treat others with kindness and respect—you'll find yourself surrounded with fun new friends in no time.

True friendship is a priceless gift. Value it and you'll see it grow into a treasure more precious than any amount of gold or silver.

FAB FUN WITH YOUR FAB FRIENDS

They wipe our tears when our hearts are breaking and they make us laugh without even trying. In the previous chapter, we discovered ways to go about widening our circle of friends; but now that we have them—what do we do with them?

When was the last time that you spent some quality time bonding with your besties? If it has been a while, here is a list of some Fab**YOU**lous, girlfriend get-together ideas that you'll want to get on your calendar pronto so that you can celebrate the gift of Fab**YOU**lous friendships!

- **Take a hike...literally**: This is one of my favorite ways to bond with my girlfriends because I happen to live in beautiful Colorado and have the spectacular Rocky Mountains right in my backyard. There is beauty everywhere however; so whether your hike is through your metropolitan city park or along a babbling country creek, grab some friends, pack a lunch, fill your water bottle and head outdoors to discover some of the natural beauty that your region has to offer. This activity is Fab**YOU**lous on many different levels because it not only helps to connect you to your friends, it also provides a great physical workout and refreshes the spirit in a way that only fresh air and sunlight can.

- **Strike a pose:** A picture is worth a thousand words, right? Then what could lift the spirits more than a few fun photos of you and your "broad squad" hamming it up? Split the cost to hire a photographer for a couple of hours (or invite a friend who is a budding photog to join you), pick a fun location for your shots, dress in bright, happy colors and say CHEESE! Not only will you have a great time and lots of laughs—you'll end up with a frame worthy souvenir that will have you smiling every time you look at it.

- **Start your own diner's club:** Make plans to get together with your girls once a month to explore a different restaurant in your town. Take turns choosing the place and agree ahead of time that everyone will enthusiastically give the restaurant and cuisine a chance. If it weren't for my girlfriends, I never would have tried sushi and guess what...because of my girlfriends, I now know that I really, really *do not* like sushi. That's okay though because I had so much fun trying something new and laughing as I tried to gag down that raw fish that I barely remember the taste (well, that's a lie—I actually *do* remember the taste quite well—BLECH!) What I *really* remember from that night however, is the laughter (mostly at my expense, but all in good fun) and the stories that were shared over those California Rolls (the only kind of sushi that I was actually able to stomach). Japanese, Thai, Italian (now you're talking—LOVE me some pasta!), vegan, seafood etc.—the possibilities are endless and not only will this type of girl's night expand your palate; it will also help you to catch up with friends while breaking bread.

- **Book it:** Book clubs are all the rage these days and for good reason—they bring together groups of women with a common interest to exchange thoughts, drink wine and socialize. Fortunately, you don't have to have a "club" of women to enjoy these same benefits—you can do the exact same thing with just one or two other friends. Simply take turns picking books from a variety of genres and then schedule a time to get together for coffee or wine to chat about what you're reading. The books don't have to be anything deep or profound—just enjoyable. Heck, right now, my friends and I are reading *The Black Dagger Brotherhood* series by JR Ward. This is a series of books written about super sexy, bad ass vampires (none of whom "sparkle"—sorry Edward Cullen). We are most certainly *not* talking Oprah book club material here, but we are LOVING the books and even more importantly, we are loving the time that we spend together chatting about the books.

- **Get cookin':** Okay—I'll confess, this one is a stretch for me because I do not generally enjoy cooking. I have maybe seven meals that I can fix decently (not well, just decently). This however; *does not* mean that I wouldn't like to expand my meal repertoire a bit. One fun way of doing this is to form a food co-op with some friends where you all make multiple batches of one particular meal that you enjoy and then swap your meals with each other so that you end up with a week's worth of meals for your family. To make this extra fun—include the recipes on fun, printed recipe cards so that your friends will be able to replicate your dish in the future.

Another fun cooking idea is to enroll in cooking classes with your friends. In most cities, it is easy to find places to learn how to cook healthy, low-fat meals, or cuisines from different parts of the world. I personally, would probably pass on a sushi making class, but I would love to learn how to prepare some healthy, Mediterranean style meals for my family. Not only will enrolling in a cooking class provide you with an opportunity to bond with your friends—it will also help you to impress your family when you serve them something other than your "every Monday, because it's Monday, Tuna Casserole".

- **Get sporty**: To me, the only thing better than spending a day at the ballpark is spending the day at the ballpark with my favorite people. Whether you like to play or are strictly a spectator, sporting activities can provide a great avenue for "broad squad" bonding. It doesn't matter if it's cheering for your favorite driver at the racetrack or perfecting your drive on the golf course—if it is something that you enjoy, increase the fun factor even more by inviting your friends to join you.

- **Get crafty**: Do you knit, crochet or scrapbook? Do you want to *learn* to knit, crochet or scrapbook? Why not schedule a craft night with your besties and knock out some projects that you've been meaning to complete? I recently had a get together with some of my friends who were wanting to learn to crochet. I taught them the basics of crochet and got them all started on a simple project. It was great fun and now those gals are all as hooked on crochet (pardon the pun) as I am. Whether you schedule a get together that is focused on one specific type of craft (Knitty Gritty Night sounds fun!) or just allow everyone to show up with whatever particular craft project they happen to be working on—a craft gathering can be a great way to relax, share patterns, learn new techniques and get some much-needed girlfriend time.

- **Educate yourself**: Is there something that you'd like to know more about? If so—there's a good chance that a few of your friends would also like to know more about it. We're not talking about enrolling in college level advanced trigonometry classes here (unless of course that is your idea of fun, in which case...do you even have friends??) There are however, lots of fun classes out there on everything from photography to yoga to salsa dancing. There are even (depending upon what you're wanting to learn) instructors who are willing to come to your home to offer a class to you and your friends on your own turf. Some classes that I've enjoyed with friends include wine appreciation, self-defense, website design and wreath making. Seriously though...I've discovered that there are quality classes out there for almost any interest. I've taken beginning woodworking classes at Home Depot and writing classes through a local author's group. Team up with your friends to multiply the fun while expanding your knowledge base.

- **Sweat it out:** Let's face it—we all need to exercise. Some people love it, others not so much. Regardless of where you fall on the spectrum— burning calories can be far more enjoyable when you are joined by pals. I am a runner and though there are definitely times that I prefer to run alone—I also benefit from occasional group runs where we chat and laugh as we log the miles. If taking care of our physical bodies is something that we all need to do anyhow; why not join together with friends and make it a little more fun, right? In my town there are numerous fitness classes available for a variety of skill levels. So, whether you're into Yoga, Zumba, Kickboxing or Pole Dancing (yes—pole dancing for fitness is a real thing—I've tried it—it's fun) you are sure to find something that will appeal to you and some of your friends. If we're going to work out anyway, we might as well join forces with our pals and make the burn more bearable.

- **Swap it up:** Have you ever looked into your crammed, over stuffed closet and thought to yourself, "I have nothing to wear"? Of course you have...we all have. Well, why not remedy the situation by organizing a swap night with some of your friends? This is a great way to weed out items that you no longer wear while adding some new pieces (well, new to you anyhow...) to your wardrobe free of charge. Even if you and your friends all wear different sizes, you can still swap items like scarves, purses, jewelry, etc. My friends and I take part in a swap night twice a year—once in the spring and once in the fall. I've only been involved in clothing/accessory swaps but I've heard of other groups who organize swap nights for things like household goods and children's toys too. Make your swap night into a seasonal event and don't forget to donate any items that are left over to your local homeless shelter or Goodwill.

- **Show your support:** There are SO many wonderful nonprofit organizations out there that need support. What better way to have fun with your friends than to do so while also helping out a local charity? What causes are important to you? Do you have a friend who is battling breast cancer? Then, sign up for (or organize) a charity walk in her honor. Do you love animals? Enlist your friends to help you clean out kennels at the local animal shelter. Buy a block of tickets to your favorite organization's annual charity ball or spend an afternoon with your friends baking items for a fund-raising bake sale. The possibilities are endless and so are the good feelings that you and your friends will enjoy, knowing that you've made a difference.

No matter how you choose to spend your time with your gal pals—the important thing is to remember that these relationships are vital to our overall well-being. Don't fall into the trap of letting these ties fall by the wayside when life gets hectic or difficult—that is often when we need the support of our friends the most. Try to commit to spending one night a month with your friends and vary the activities to help keep everyone engaged. The more we nurture and celebrate our female friendships, the more FabYOUlous life will be.

Do My Boundaries Make Me A B!tch?

Time and energy. Two of the most valuable resources that each one of us is blessed with every day. Though it is difficult to put a price tag on these two commodities, I would have to say that their value is far greater than most realize because, it is the proper application of these two resources that allows us to create an abundance of other blessings (money, fulfillment, success, significance, etc.) in our lives.

I've been thinking about this a lot lately because I've been struggling a bit with feeling as though I am constantly running out of time and energy when it comes to the pursuit of my meaningful goals. This realization really hit home this past week when I found myself rushing off to yet another get-together that I didn't really want to go to with someone that I didn't really want to be around. Then, when I got home, I was wiped out and had no energy left to work on the big-picture goals that I have for my life. Now, please don't misunderstand me—the event that I attended wasn't anything *bad* and the person that I met there is a perfectly decent human being. It's just that, as I look back now, I can see that the reason I attended was because I felt like it was something that I *should* do (even though I really didn't want to), and how much more well served I would have been if I had spent that time either on my own, working on my goals *or* with people who truly inspired, empowered or encouraged me.

All of this just confirms something to me that I've always known but have struggled to truly act upon in my life—as crucial as solid relationships are to building a FabYOUlous life, having solid *boundaries* is just as vital.

If you ever find yourself in a similar situation of battling a lack of energy *or* feeling as though you never have enough time for the activities that bring you joy; there's a good chance that you too have allowed your personal boundaries to become weak, *or*, you haven't set solid boundaries to begin with. While these things might not *sound* like boundary issues, they are. Each one of us only has a finite amount of time and energy. When we don't set boundaries to protect that time and energy, we suffer from exhaustion, exasperation and unfulfillment. Some additional signs of weak personal boundaries include…

- Doing too many things because you feel like you *have* to, rather than because you *want* to.
- Feeling guilty when you take time for yourself or treat yourself in some way.
- Not expressing yourself for fear of what others will think.
- Putting other people's wants above your own needs.
- Saying yes to something even though everything inside of you is screaming NO!
- Never having enough time or energy for your own projects or self-care.
- Avoiding conflict at all cost.
- Staying in an unhealthy/unfulfilling relationship.
- Physical and emotional exhaustion.
- Difficulty making and sticking to decisions.
- Constantly worrying about what other people think of you.

Not having rock-solid boundaries can have a devastating effect on our relationships and on our psyche, and yet despite this; establishing boundaries can be so difficult for so many of us. Why is this? Why do we have such a difficult time when it comes to protecting ourselves from time and energy vampires? For most of us, the difficulty lies in our desire to please others and not be perceived as selfish or worse—a b*tch.

I get it, I really do. I want people to like me too. *However*, in the big scheme of things, there is really only a handful of people whose opinions *truly* matter to me. This doesn't mean that I am out to tick everyone else off—it simply means that I need to set boundaries as to how much time and energy I expend on projects and people who don't encourage me to be better or help me to further my goals. The people who *do* do this for me are people that I will gladly commit time to. They are also the people for whom I will return the favor and invest in so as to elevate *their* pursuits.

So, it is time for me to get out the figurative bricks and mortar and start putting up some boundaries again. I don't do this to be b*tchy. In fact, I fully intend to still be kind to everyone. I simply do this because I know that I am only going to be able to achieve the Fab**YOU**lous life that I've envisioned for myself *if* I stop diffusing my time and energy and instead become focused like a laser on the things that are going to move me closer to my goal. There is a quote by Brene Brown that I just love that speaks to this…

"Daring to set boundaries is about having the courage to love ourselves even when we risk disappointing others"

So, in an act of courage, and love for myself and my goals—here are the steps that I intend to take in order to fortify my boundaries and protect the limited amount of time and energy that I possess— I suggest that *you* try them too…

Building Boundaries without Being a B*tch (Unless of Course, You *Have* to)

1) **Determine exactly what things and relationships are truly worthy of an investment of time and energy.** Until we know exactly what things are definite yeses in our life, we can't know what things are no's.
2) **Understand why a boundary is necessary.** Again, this isn't about being b*tchy or a snob. It is simply a safeguard to prevent our time and energy from

becoming so diluted that we have nothing left over to support our own emotional/physical health or our goals and ambitions.

3) **Clearly define the boundary.** Setting clearly defined parameters around a boundary will help to eliminate any grey areas. I have found in my own experience, that it is better to define a more rigid and tight boundary that can later be relaxed if necessary, than it is to try to shore up a weak boundary that has been violated.

4) **Understand that there will be exceptions—but only if they meet certain criteria.** If, for example, you set a solid boundary around a two hour time frame that you are going focus on your goals, but your toddler comes running up to you with a gash on her forehead that clearly needs stitches, you will obviously need to prioritize your child's emergency. These scenarios are bound to happen on occasion, but by taking step #1 and clearly determining who and what our true priorities in life are (I'm assuming that your children fall into that category), it becomes easy to see what things/people we will occasionally relax our boundaries for. If, on the other hand, your obnoxious but friendly neighbor wants to drop by and chat about your other neighbors for two hours, you need to be willing to defend your time and stick to your determined boundary.

5) **Be kind but straightforward when establishing boundaries.** I will never advocate for meanness, but I *will* advocate for firmness. It is entirely possible to be firm but polite when protecting your boundaries. Those people who truly want the best for you will understand and respect your boundaries—those who don't respect your boundaries or who get offended by them, are simply strengthening your case for having boundaries in the first place.

6) **Don't apologize for having boundaries.** Having healthy boundaries is a *good* and *healthy* thing. Don't feel compelled to apologize for taking care of the things that are top priorities in your life. The people who love and support you won't need an apology and those who don't, don't deserve one.

7) **Enlist support.** I am so blessed by the fact that my hubby is an excellent gatekeeper when I need him to be. He helps to run interference when necessary and act as an added layer of protection when I need him to. He knows how important my goals are to me and he does his part to help support my efforts. I am committed to doing the same for him when he needs it.

8) **Address boundary violations early and firmly.** I'm a kind person, I really am. I am not however; a doormat. In my first (failed) marriage, my boundaries were routinely violated and as a result, I became incredibly resentful. I was also emotionally and physically exhausted from trying too hard to keep too many people happy. Now, when I feel as though my boundaries are being violated, I do my best to address the issue early on and to be kind but firm in my delivery. Again, the people who are truly on my team and in my inner circle, understand and do not take offense when I enforce a boundary. It is the ones who *do not* understand or who *do* take offense, that my boundaries are for in the first place.

9) **Keep it from becoming personal.** My having boundaries has nothing to do with whether or not the people for whom my boundaries are created, are nice or good people. I'm sure that (for the most part) they are. My boundaries have nothing to do with *them*— they have *everything* to do with my own aspirations, priorities, needs and desires. Establishing boundaries is not an excuse to treat people poorly or to hold myself above others. It is simply a necessary mechanism that I

must employ if I am ever to live the truly
Fab**YOU**lous life that I have envisioned for myself.

10) **Trust your gut.** As I have grown as a person and in
my career, I have become aligned with new and
different people at different times. Most of the time,
these relationships are mutually beneficial and
edifying. Sometimes however; I'll come across
someone who seems genuinely nice and is very intent
on getting close to me, but for some reason, my gut
sounds an alarm. I'm not perfect at heeding the
warnings that my intuition sends to me, but I'm
getting better at it because I have learned some hard
lessons in the past from times that I ignored that
nudge. In time, people's true motivations always reveal
themselves, but if you sense a catch in your spirit
about someone, keep your boundaries firmly in place
unless/until such time as the person truly earns their
way into your priority circle. I'm (slowly but surely)
learning that my hunches are rarely wrong, and that
those solid boundaries that I have erected, end up
saving me a lot of wasted time and energy.

While boundary setting can feel a bit uncomfortable at first for
those of us who tend to be "people pleasers" by nature; it is an
absolutely vital component to our overall well-being. If, after
reading these suggestions, you still struggle with setting solid
boundaries, you might want to check out the book *Boundaries: When
to Say Yes, How to Say No to Take Control of Your Life*, by Dr. Henry
Cloud and Dr. John Townsend. This book made a pivotal
difference in my life when I desperately needed it, and is one that I
still refer to when I start to feel my boundaries crumble.

I love the quote that says, "you are not required to set yourself on
fire to keep other people warm". I don't know who originally said
it, but it is *so* true. Burning with the fire of your passion is one
thing—*burning out* by not maintaining solid boundaries is another.
Make sure that you are burning for the right reasons and utilize
your boundaries to help in that endeavor.

"Find a purpose in life so big
that it will challenge every
capacity to be at
your best"

David O. McKay

PREPARE MENTALLY

This entire book is designed to help you discover and live your FabYOUlous purpose. This particular section of the book however, will provide some additional (and easy to implement) tips and practical inspiration as you navigate your way through the jungle of mediocrity toward your FabYOUlous desired destination.

We've already covered the importance of preparing spiritually and physically for our FabYOUlous awakening, so now it's time to kick things up a notch and begin preparing *mentally*—though, to be honest, if you're reading this book, you've already begun your mental preparation for a FabYOUlous life. Still…there are four key components that I feel lay a strong foundation as we mentally prepare ourselves for any important undertaking. These four pillars of solid mental preparation consist of…

1) **Research.** You can include reading this book in this category. Whenever we have a dream that we long to pursue, the first step that we can take to move the needle on our progress is to research exactly what our dream will require of us. I have a good friend who thought that her dream was to own a fitness studio. She loved working out and wanted to help others reach their fitness goals. As she began to research her dream however; she quickly learned that opening a studio was going to require a lot of work in areas that she *wasn't* passionate about. She didn't want to spend long hours on tasks such as bookkeeping, marketing, hiring etc. She really just wanted to work out and to

help others to live healthy lives. Thus, (based upon the research that she had conducted), my friend decided to shift her goal from owning a fitness studio to becoming a certified fitness trainer. The research that she did helped her to clarify what her *true* dream was and then strategize a plan that would help her to achieve that dream. Now, my friend is happily working as a full-time fitness trainer and loving her FabYOUlous life.

As we begin to research our goals, we may find that the research leads us to shift our desires, *or*, we may discover that the research gets us even more excited and anxious to start acting in pursuit of our dreams. One thing is certain though—doing adequate research will help us to identify the potential roadblocks and obstacles that we may encounter along the way to our FabYOUlousness and thus allow us time to strategize ways to avoid or deal with them.

2) **Get the necessary training.** When I first set out on my quest to build FabYOUlous Life Enterprises, I was pretty computer savvy, *except* in the area of website creation. This was a problem because as a start-up entrepreneur, I didn't have the budget to hire someone to build a website for me, and yet I knew that having a strong online presence was going to be critical to my success. So, I bought a few books on website design, immediately decided that I was in over my head, and then caved and signed up for a website creation class that was offered through my local recreation commission. The class was very basic but it was also cheap and it gave just enough information for me to become dangerous. I'll admit—my first website (and my second, third, fourth…) sucked, but with each progression, I learned something new and was able to

develop my newfound knowledge until I eventually had a website that I was proud of.

Chances are, if you are working toward a big FabYOUlous goal (and you *are*, otherwise why would you be reading this book?) there are going to be things (*a lot* of things) that you will need to learn along the way to your FabYOUlousness. In order to prepare yourself mentally for your journey, you need to be willing to seek out and take any necessary trainings that will help to fill any knowledge or skill gaps that you may have. Fortunately, with the popularity of YouTube and webinars, in addition to traditional learning environments, it is possible to find trainings on almost *any* subject these days.

3) **Develop relationships with mentors and teachers.** There is a quote by Wayne Paulson that I love. It reads "any two of us are smarter than any one of us". Please don't try to build your FabYOUlous life alone. No matter what goal you are striving to reach; *someone* has already reached it. Seek out those who have gone before you and learn from their wisdom. If possible, reach out to them in person—take them to coffee, chat with them on the phone, etc. Try to forge a mutually beneficial relationship with them in which you *both* benefit from your time together. This may feel like a challenge since technically, *they* are the one with the wisdom that you are hoping to gain, but at the very least, you can offer to pay for lunch or maybe bring them a small token of appreciation.

I have a good friend who happens to be a published author so guess who I sought out as I began to formulate my plan for *Finding FabYOUlous*? Yep— her. The thing is though, she wasn't really my *friend* at the time; she was just a casual acquaintance that I had met a couple of times at various networking functions. Still, she had published a book and that was something that I wanted to do, so I summoned the courage to stalk her LinkedIn profile and send her a message inviting her to lunch. I wanted her to say yes, so in my message I talked about how impressed I was with her and how much I loved her book (both true—*please* be sincere if you use this technique, people can tell when you're just sucking up for the sake of getting something from them). Fortunately, she agreed to meet me and as we chatted together, we began to discover that we had a lot of similar life experiences *and* the same twisted sense of humor. Not only did our lunch meeting result in me gaining a lot of valuable book publishing insight, it also resulted in a wonderfully fulfilling friendship. As it turns out—she was interested in becoming a better public speaker (something that I have a lot of experience with) so I was able to help guide her in that endeavor as she helped me to navigate the world of book publishing. To this day, we still regularly get together for lunch or coffee and continue to share our lives with each other.

4) **Be hungry and humble.** A FabYOUlous life requires hunger. Not the literal, my stomach is growling, I need some Cheetos kind of hunger, but rather a hunger for knowledge, wisdom and opportunities. Mental preparation means always being on the lookout for opportunities to learn something new. Whether it be in a classroom, on a webinar or on the subway, there are lessons to be learned all around us. In order to learn these lessons however; we must possess the humility to know that there is a lot that we don't know. Being mentally prepared to undertake our

journey to a Fab**YOU**lous life means that we *must* commit to being lifelong learners.

When we lay the groundwork, and combine our mental preparation with spiritual and physical preparation, we give ourselves the best possible opportunity to succeed in our quest for a Fab**YOU**lous life. These three aspects of development are what I refer to as the Training Trifecta. As we train ourselves and grow more confident and connected in these three aspects of life, our Fab**YOU**lous purpose will begin to unfold and manifest much more quickly.

☀ USE YOUR PAST TO FUEL YOUR FUTURE ☀

The past, present and future walked into a bar...it was tense

HAHAHA! My degree is in English so this is probably my all-time favorite joke. Seriously, if you don't find it funny, I just don't know what to say about that. What's *not* a joke however, is the way in which too many of us allow the trials and traumas of our past to rob us of our joy in the present *and* our dreams and aspirations for the future. We still hang our heads in shame over the mistakes we made, losers we dated (or married), opportunities we missed, things we said (or didn't say) and a myriad of other moments that we just can't seem to let go of or forget (even though *everyone* else no doubt *has* forgotten them). *Or*, maybe the mistake wasn't necessarily *ours*, but we remain held hostage by the cruel words that someone spoke to us in fourth grade or emotionally crippled because of actions that were taken against us that made us feel small and victimized. Regardless of the circumstances, the fact of the matter is that the past is, all too often, one of the biggest hindrances that we face in our efforts to create a Fab**YOU**lous future.

While there are certainly some issues from the past that need to be handled delicately with the help of a professional therapist or counselor (instances of abuse for example); many of our past traumas have a far tighter grip on our psyches than is appropriate. I should not (as a forty-something year old woman) still feel ugly or inferior because the class "mean girl" called me gross back in fourth grade (I've let this one go...really, I have...I *swear*!)

261

No matter how we might wish the contrary, the fact of the matter is that we cannot change the past. We can however, learn to *reframe* it. We can't deny the past, but we can *defy* it. We have within our possession, the ability to take the past, learn the lessons that it has to offer and *use* those lessons to fuel the fire of our Fab**YOU**lous future. The key is to keep the past in its proper perspective. I like to compare my past to the rearview mirror in my car. It's there and it can provide valuable feedback when I take a quick glance at it. However; my rearview mirror is tiny compared to the size of my car's front windshield because the action in front of me is *far* more important and deserving of my attention than anything that is behind me. I will not be able to cruise along on the highway to my Fab**YOU**lous life if I spend more time looking in my rearview mirror than I do the windshield. Instead, I'll wind up crashing and burning, stuck in some ditch, dented and deflated.

So, how then do we keep our past where it belongs (in our rearview mirror—*not* our windshield) and use it to help us create a more Fab**YOU**lous future? Try these four suggestions for starters…

1) **Change the filter.** I just love the social media platform, Instagram. I love it because it offers so many fun filters that you can use to change the appearance of your photos. I can take a hum drum photo of my cat and turn it into a veritable work of art simply by switching up the filter on the photo. This is the exact same approach that we need to take with our past. I have some pretty horrible memories of incredibly volatile fights with my ex-husband. Even though I am now happily married to an amazing man who treats me with incredible love and respect, the memories of these fights and the emotions that I felt as I was being spit on and called atrocious names still rear their ugly heads from time to time. Fortunately, I (with the help of copious amounts of therapy) have learned to switch

the filter through which I view these memories. Instead of seeing these memories as difficult, scary and damaging, I now see them through the filter of Fab**YOU**lousness. I view these memories as instances where I was becoming stronger. I see the girl in these memories as someone who was finding her voice and learning to stand up for herself. I recognize these past moments as crucial puzzle pieces that were needed in order for me to get my life together, make the break that set me free to be Fab**YOU**lous and move forward in a new direction. Were these past experiences difficult? Yes, *incredibly* so; but they were also *necessary* in order for me to become the person that I am today, and the person that I am striving to become in the future. Changing my filter has allowed me to see that.

You too can choose a different filter through which to view the circumstances of your past. Are there memories that are hard or painful? Of course there are—it's called being human. The fact that you are still here however, shows that those moments didn't destroy you. Now, flip the filter on those memories and begin to see them as moments that shaped, strengthened and taught you valuable lessons. Let them serve to empower you rather than enslave you.

2) **Look for the patterns.** Sometimes our past can hold clues as to where we need to make adjustments in our behavior. For example—do you constantly seem to find yourself in unfulfilling relationships with narcissistic jackwads? If so, you probably need to do some inner work to discover why your psyche is continuously drawn to emotionally unavailable jerks. Or…do you look back and see an ongoing cycle of emotional shopping followed by soul crushing debt? Maybe it's time to figure out what emotional void you

are constantly trying to fill with new shoes and handbags. Maybe your pattern is one of playing small when you long for so much more in life—settling for an administrative job when you *know* that you have management potential or serving on a PTA committee when you really want to be PTA president.

We *all* have negative patterns in our lives that will continue to repeat themselves unless/until we take the steps to break them. The first step to breaking these cycles is to recognize that they exist, and by glancing back in our rearview mirrors, we can begin to identify those patterns, figure out the purpose that they serve in our lives and establish new, positive behavior patterns to take their place.

3) **Stop picking at the wound.** We all know what happens when we skin our knee (say from wiping out on your son's skateboard that you really had no business being on in the first place...not that I would know anything about that). The wound bleeds like a mofo for a little while but then it eventually starts to scab over. If we allow the scab to form and exhibit enough self-control to keep from picking at it, the wound will eventually heal and we'll be no worse off than we were before the alleged skateboard show-off debacle took place.

If, however; we pick at the scab, never allowing it to harden and do its job of protecting the wounded skin beneath, we run the risk of infection, scarring and prolonged pain. The same is true when it comes to our pasts. While it may be beneficial to occasionally peel back the Band-Aid and take a quick peek at the wound (a quick glance in our rearview mirror for example), it is never helpful to pick at it and cause it to continue bleeding. Peeking at the wound will allow us to assess the rate of healing that is taking place, help us to protect the area from further injury and provide input on ways to prevent further damage. *Picking* at the wound however, does nothing but leave us open and raw. We simply cannot heal our past if we relentlessly continue to pick at it.

4) **Move on or get help.** When we change the filter on our past, identify and replace harmful patterns and allow our wounds to truly heal, we are setting ourselves up for a FabYOUlous future. By allowing the past to teach us and empower us, we are effectively using the past to fuel our futures. If, however; you are not able to reframe your past in a way that helps you to move forward, please, *please* seek out the help of a qualified therapist or counselor. Your FabYOUlousness is far too valuable to allow it to be sabotaged by the specter of past wounds or victimization. You deserve to be healed of your difficult past and there is no shame in seeking out help in this endeavor. I speak from experience here. I've overcome a lot in my life (dangerously toxic marriage, devastating eating disorder, self-sabotaging behaviors...I could go on and on) but I didn't overcome these issues alone. I had the support of family & friends *and* the professional guidance of a counselor. Seeking out professional help when you need it *does not* make you weak—it makes you smart.

15 Questions to Help You Find Your Purpose

Nothing contributes to a truly Fab**YOU**lous life more than the confidence that comes from knowing that we are doing the very thing that we were put upon this earth to do. Without a clear sense of purpose, life can be a struggle of confusion, disillusionment, and exhaustion. A life *on purpose* however, is one that is filled with energy, passion and enthusiasm.

Why are we here? What is our mission in life? The Japanese call it ikigai—one's reason for being. *We* call it one's truest expression of Fab**YOU**lousness. The good news is that, according to the Japanese, *everyone* has an ikigai. Finding it might require some soul searching and struggle—but once it's found, it can bring incredible meaning, joy and Fab**YOU**lousness to life. Dan Baker, Ph.D. and coauthor of the book, *What Happy People Know*, says "if you're not sure what your purpose is, then your purpose is to find a passion".

This entire book is focused upon helping you to find your Fab**YOU**lousness, and following the suggestions that are lined out in each of the chapters will help you to do just that. To simplify things a bit more, here are 15 questions that will help to get you into the right frame of mind and assist you in discovering your purpose. As you prepare to answer these questions, it is recommended that you find a quiet place where you will not be interrupted (see the *Find Your Place* chapter) and that you write down (don't just *think* your answers—there is power in the act of putting your thoughts on paper) the first responses that pop into your head. Give yourself less than sixty seconds per question (you don't want to fall into the trap of overthinking your answers) and most importantly...BE HONEST. Don't worry about editing or sounding silly. This exercise is for you and you alone. No one else will read your answers and there are no *wrong* answers. Finally— *enjoy* this exercise and smile as you write.

Once you have answered the questions, you will be instructed on how to translate your answers into a powerful and personal mission statement that will serve as a tool to guide you as you transition your life from drab...to FAB!

15 Questions to Guide You to Your FabYOUlous Purpose

1) What activities, events, projects, hobbies, people, etc. bring a smile to your face whenever you think of them?
2) What activities cause you to lose track of time when you are doing them?
3) Who inspires you the most? You don't have to know these individuals personally, so be willing to consider authors, leaders, musicians etc. *in addition* to individuals within your own personal sphere of connection. What qualities do these individuals possess that you find to be inspiring?
4) What activities were you naturally drawn to as a child? Do you still feel a pull towards those activities?
5) What physical, emotional, intellectual, spiritual and social attributes do you possess that make you feel great about yourself?
6) What causes do you strongly believe in, connect to and support?
7) What values do you hold to be sacred?
8) What natural skills, abilities and gifts do you possess?
9) What challenges and hardships have you overcome? How did you accomplish this?
10) What do people ask you for help with? What advice do others seek from you?
11) What new thing do you have a burning desire to try/learn/experience?

12) If you had to teach something to a large group of people, what subject matter would you want to teach and who would you want to teach it to?

13) What would you regret not fully doing, experiencing, having or being in your life?

14) Where do you find strength, comfort and inspiration during times of trouble?

15) Imagine yourself as a blissfully happy 95 year old who has lived a wonderful and blessed life. Looking back at all of the incredible things that you've achieved and acquired, and all of the meaningful relationships that you've developed—what has mattered the most to you in your life? Make a list of these items.

After you have answered these 15 questions as quickly and as honestly as possible, it is time to use your answers to help formulate your own personal mission statement. According to the late, Stephen Covey, author of *The 7 Habits of Highly Effective People*, a personal mission statement is valuable because "it forces you to think through your priorities deeply, carefully and to align your behavior with your beliefs".

A personal mission statement answers four key questions: 1.) *What* do I want to *do*? 2.) *Who* do I want to *help*? 3.) What is the *result* of my actions and 4.) what *value* will I create?

Create your personal mission statement by following these four steps...

1) Using your answers to the above 15 questions, make a list of any action oriented words that you connect with (example: give, guide, inspire, teach, write, run, organize, create, produce, travel, encourage, support, accomplish, empower etc.)

2) Based upon your answers to the 15 questions, make a list of everyone/everything that you believe you can help

269

(example: people, animals, the environment, government, causes etc.)

3) Identify your end desire. How will the *who* from your above answer benefit from the *actions* from your first answer?

4) Combine steps two and three into a short statement of purpose. This will become your personal mission statement. Make several copies of it (I suggest using a pretty font with some nice graphics on quality paper) and keep it near you at all times (I even have a small, laminated copy of mine that I keep in my wallet)

I myself, went through this process when first looking to launch Fab**YOU**lous Life Enterprises and found it to be incredibly beneficial. The purpose that I discovered and mission statement that I created at that time is the very same purpose and mission that guides me today. My Fab**YOU**lous Life mission statement is…

"to create meaningful programs, products, content and events that inspire, educate and empower women to live their most FabYOUlous lives"

What's yours?

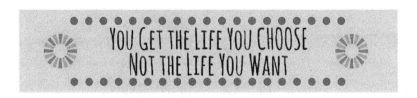

YOU GET THE LIFE YOU CHOOSE NOT THE LIFE YOU WANT

There is a song by American punk rock band, Pennywise called "You Get the Life You Choose". Don't ask me how I know this— I just do (besides, those who know me well could definitely tell you that I have always had questionable taste in music).

While some may see this song title as negative or at the very least, as a challenge (because we want the life that we *want* right?), I love the empowering notion that we get to live the life of our *choosing*. This is a message that was drilled into my head on a daily basis back when I was in treatment for Anorexia and working to put my life back together after escaping my incredibly toxic first marriage. My therapist told me *repeatedly* that our lives are the results of the choices we make. If we want better lives, we absolutely *had* to make better choices. This sounds so simple, doesn't it? Want a good life? Okay then—make good choices. Easy peasy right?

WRONG.

Despite the seeming simplicity of the whole *your choices create your life* notion, so many of us prefer to go through our lives believing that we are hapless victims of circumstance and that if our lives suck, it is because we've been dealt a bum hand; *not* because we've made some stupid choices that have landed us in a less than desirable spot. Buying into this victim mentality means that we get to pout and cry while pointing our finger at others without ever accepting any accountability for our own contribution to the situation. Unfortunately, despite the fact that this "poor me" stance might be *easier* in the short-term, it will do nothing to enhance our lives down the road.

Please don't misunderstand me on this point; I am not saying that bad things don't sometimes happen to good people—they do—unfortunately. However; even when difficult circumstances come our way, it is up to us to *choose* our response to the situation. This case is eloquently made in the bestselling book, *Man's Search for Meaning* by Viktor Frankl; an Austrian psychiatrist who survived over two and a half years in a Nazi concentration camp. While all of us will be faced with challenges from time to time, few of us will have to endure the horror of being imprisoned against our will while watching our parents, brother and pregnant wife perish. This was Frankl's experience, and yet, despite the atrocities that he was forced to deal with, Frankl was able to cope, find meaning and even move forward in life with a renewed sense of purpose.

So, if the quality of one's life truly is determined by the quality of one's *choices* (including the choice of how to react to unfavorable circumstances), doesn't it seem logical then, that we should make every effort to make consistently high-quality choices? Let the following suggestions guide you as you strive to elevate your life through the choices you make...

Live the Life You *CHOOSE*...

1) **Do a values check.** What are your most cherished values in life? Connection? Freedom? Security? Spontaneity? Once you know your values, try viewing each possible choice outcome through the values lens. Maybe the anxiety that you notice when thinking about a new job opportunity is *because* despite a significantly higher paycheck, the new job will require you to report to someone who is known to have questionable ethics, thereby challenging your closely held value of personal integrity. Taking the time to get

clear on your values *now*, will make it easier to align your choices with those values when the time comes.

2) **Think it through.** When faced with a choice, it is common to focus only upon the *immediate* outcome of the choice, i.e. "eating this entire bag of Cheetos will taste good and make me happy". Instead, make the effort to really think through the *eventual* outcome, i.e. "eating this entire bag of Cheetos will leave me feeling frustrated over the extra pounds that I've packed on and discouraged with myself because of my lack of discipline regarding my physical health". Start to make *conscious* choices by being deliberate in your analyzation of outcomes. Ask yourself 1.) what are the *probable* outcomes of this choice? 2.) what are the *possible but unlikely* outcomes of this choice? 3.) What will the outcomes be if I *don't* make this choice? 4.) what would the *ideal* outcome be? and 5.) what choice is most likely to get me to my ideal outcome?

3) **Balance your emotional feelings and rational thoughts.** Whether we realize it or not, our emotional state does have an impact upon the choices that we make. When I am feeling strong and happy, it is easier for me to make choices that will empower me and further my goals. However; when I am feeling strong and happy, I may also be more prone to overconfidence and therefore make choices that carry an unnaturally high level of risk. On the opposite end of the spectrum, it is easy to make lazy, disempowering choices when we are feeling sad or overwhelmed. Though our emotions are neither good nor bad, they *do* impact the way in which we process information. This isn't necessarily bad, it just means that we need to learn to temper our emotions with our ability to think logically about a situation. It is also crucial that we learn to tune into our emotions so that we are able to discern which emotions are directly related to the choice that we must make and which emotions are stemming

273

from some other outside influence (i.e. a disagreement with a coworker) and therefore need to be filtered in regard to our choices.

4) **Seek out advice from (qualified) others.** There is a quote by Woodrow Wilson that says, "I not only use all the brains that I have, but all I can borrow". He was SO spot on when he said this and it is something that I try to live by every day as I make choices for my life. Granted, there are some choices that are mine and mine alone to make because they are (for whatever reason) deeply personal to me. However; more often than not, I can make better, more informed choices when I seek out the advice of others who are knowledgeable in the subject matter at hand. I enlisted help from my friend Jenny who is a personal trainer and avid runner when I needed to decide on a training program for my half-marathon. I sought the advice of a website developer colleague when I needed to decide on a web hosting platform for FabYOUlousLife.com and I regularly utilize the expertise of my tech savvy, young adult sons whenever I need to upgrade my phone, decide on a new monitor for my computer or sync my wireless devices. By being willing to admit that there are a lot of things that I *don't* know, and seeking out the counsel of those who *do* know, I have been able to dramatically elevate the quality of choices in my life. There is one caveat to this however; seeking the advice and guidance of others only works *if* the person advising you actually knows something about the subject matter in question, *and* has your best interests at heart. DO NOT seek out the advice of your bitter, newly divorced, jealous co-worker if you are looking for advice on how to talk to your husband about an issue that the two of you are having; nor should you ask your friend who has filed for bankruptcy three times about a business investment that you are considering. Instead, look for individuals who have

demonstrated success in the areas connected to your choice and go to them for guidance.

5) **Listen to your hunches.** We all (whether we realize it or not) are intuitive. Intuition is simply a *knowing* that is built upon one's (often subconscious) capacity to read signals, patterns and clues based upon past experience. It is a form of unconscious reasoning that is rooted in the way our brains collect and store information. While you certainly want to employ your capacity for logical reasoning when faced with a difficult choice, it would be foolish to discount the intuitive hunches that you receive.

We are all faced with countless choices every day. Some of them are small and inconsequential (whether to wear your blue or grey socks) while others can have repercussions that impact us for years. By making it a point to become more conscious and deliberate in our choice making we can set ourselves on a positive trajectory toward our most FabYOUlous Life. Remember though, refusing to make a choice is *also* a choice that can leave you feeling stuck and powerless. Make the intention today to take back the control in your life by *choosing* to make empowering choices that reflect your goals and aspirations.

"Your destiny is determined by the choices you make. Choose now. Choose well."

~Tony Robbins~

GET OUT OF A RUT AND INTO A GROOVE

There is a huge difference between being in a rut and being in the groove and no doubt, we've all experienced both instances at one time or another—I know that I certainly have.

When I'm in the groove, I'm feeling good, things are flowing and life seems full of promise. I'm able to accomplish numerous things without even breaking a sweat and (most importantly) I'm happy.

When I'm in a rut however; it's just the opposite. When I'm in a rut, things are HARD. It's a chore to get out of bed in the morning and head to work. It's difficult to make progress on my goals (even the easy ones) and the days seem to drag on forever without much significance. In short—being in a rut SUCKS.

The worst thing about ruts is that they are sneaky and difficult to get out of. Sometimes I'm in a rut without even realizing it. I'll feel tired and bored. Nothing much excites me and I find myself watching way too much TV. I lose sight of the big, Fab**YOU**lous goals that I've set for my life and therefore, my colorful, Fab**YOU**lous life turns into an old, grainy, black & white re-run. That's the thing with ruts—they will sneak up on you and begin to suck the life out of you without you even realizing it. Often, by the time I do finally realize that I'm in a rut, I've turned my rut into a Grand Canyon sized trench that seems impossible to escape.

Believe it or not though, there is some *good* news about ruts. This good news lies in the fact that ruts are almost always caused by boredom, monotony or a lack of vision. Instead of being on top

277

of things and able to see the big picture for our Fab**YOU**lous lives, we get sucked into a routine of just going through the motions of life without really living. This might not exactly sound like good news but trust me—it is. It's good news because once we know what causes our ruts, we can come up with strategies to escape them and even more importantly, we can learn to recognize and avoid them in the first place.

The next time you find yourself in a rut, don't make the mistake of taking up residence. You DO NOT want to hang photos, pick out carpeting and set up utilities—you want to GET OUT. The longer we wallow in our ruts, the deeper the ruts will become and the harder they will be to escape. Do NOT let that happen to you. Your life is far too Fab**YOU**lous to waste even one minute at the bottom of some ugly rut.

So…the next time you find yourself feeling lethargic and unenthused about your life, it is time to take action, BUST THE RUT and GET IN THE GROOVE.

As I mentioned earlier, ruts are almost always caused by boredom, monotony or a lack of vision. Therefore, busting a rut must involve tactics to counter these triggers. We need to find ways to break out of our boredom & monotony and we need to grab back a hold of the Fab**YOU**lous vision that we have for our lives. Different tactics will work for different people, but here are a few suggestions that tend to work especially well for me.

1) **Phone a friend.** Sometimes when I'm in a rut, I tend to shut myself off from the people who care about me, the people that I have fun with and the people who see the good in me. These are the exact people that I need *in* my life when I'm in a rut. These are the people who add joy and meaning to my life. Reconnecting with them is one of the quickest ways I know to bust a rut.

2) **Change your routine.** Sometimes we can't change the big things right away but we can make small changes, and enough small changes can help us get by until we are ready to make a big change. For example, try a new restaurant for lunch, take a new route to or from work, vary your exercise routine (or start an exercise routine if you don't already have one.) Small changes like this might not seem like a big deal but they can help to break up the monotony of long days—one of the hallmarks of a rut.

3) **Try something new.** Learn to knit. Take a class on website development. Send a sexy photo to your spouse. Take a wine appreciation class (that might help you get up the courage to take the sexy photo!) Just do something new and different…something that piques your curiosity…something that tiptoes you out of your comfort zone (also referred to as a RUT). Doing something new might just be the kick start you need to revitalize your life. Let this one thing lead to another one thing and then another. Soon, you'll realize that life is Fab**YOU**lous again and your rut is far behind in the rear-view mirror.

4) **Refocus on your vision.** Remember that big, Fab**YOU**lous vision that you have for your life? The vision that got buried under the carpet that you had installed in your rut? Well, pull up that carpet and start focusing on your vision once again. Cut pictures out of magazines that remind you of that vision. Pin images on *Pinterest* that remind you of that vision. Journal about what your life will be like when your vision becomes a reality. Do whatever you have to do to reignite the passion that you have for your vision. This vision is going to be the biggest RUT BUSTER you have in your arsenal, so use it.

There are many rut busters out there. In fact, there are more rut busters than there are ruts (which is Fab**YOU**lous news). The key is to make sure that you recognize the signs of being in a rut so that you can quickly implement these rut busting techniques. Think of some rut busters that will work for you and keep them handy. Before you know it, you'll find that your life is Fab**YOU**lous again and you are out of your rut in back in the groove.

GAIN SOME PERSPECTIVE

I'll confess. As I'm sitting here typing out this chapter, I'm writing it as much for myself as for anyone. You see, I've been having one of *those* weeks. I've been feeling tired and a bit overwhelmed at all of the things that I need to get accomplished. I'm sore and worn out from the training that I'm doing for a half-marathon that I will be running next month (my first ever half marathon—lord help me!) *and* I've had a hard time remaining focused on the Fab**YOU**lous big picture goals that I have set for my life. This *blah* feeling is pretty unusual for me as I tend to be a naturally high-energy and driven individual, and I must say—I DON'T LIKE IT.

As usual though, the universe always seems to know exactly what I need and when I need it, so when I looked at my editorial calendar and saw that this week's chapter was to be on the subject of perspective, I just had to chuckle. Well played universe, well played.

Yep—a fresh perspective is *exactly* what I needed this week so I *love* the fact that my research for this chapter has helped me to gain exactly that.

If you're feeling a bit overwhelmed, stressed out or aimless, you too need a fresh perspective on your life. Follow these eight Fab**YOU**lous tips and you'll be seeing clearly again in no time.

1) **Get a detached view.** Sometimes when we are in the trenches it is hard to see a realistic view of our situation. All we see are the piles of laundry that need to be folded (wait…were these even *washed*??), the bills that need to be

paid and the work assignments that keep piling up. We feel inundated with responsibilities and rendered ineffective as a result of sheer exhaustion. It is during these times that we need to ask ourselves if this current perception of our reality is, in fact, accurate.

The best way for me to do this is to take what I call a "Queen of the Mountain" view of my life. I go somewhere quiet (even if it's just a stall in the ladies room at my office) and take a few minutes to look at my life from the perspective of someone who is high upon a mountain. I imagine this person looking at my life from a vantage point that allows her to see not just my current scenario, but the last decade or so of my life. Sure, she sees the teeny-tiny piles of laundry (that we have now determined have *not* been washed) but she *also* sees the huge victory that I experienced as I overcame a devastating Anorexia Nervosa diagnosis and escaped from a toxic marriage that was slowly killing me. She sees the successful career that I have built for myself and the sacrifices that I made in order to provide a safe and loving home for my boys. She celebrates the fact that she can see my joy as I experienced falling in love with and then marrying my husband and she delights in the life that we have created together. She sees that I'm soaking my weary body in a hot bath after having run eight miles, but she also sees the fact that I RAN EIGHT MILES. Sure, she can see that I'm tired and feeling a little overwhelmed; but she can also see that compared to where I've been—my life right now is *cake*. Best of all, she can see the direction in which I am heading in life and she can see that if I keep putting one foot in front of the other, I *will* reach the Fab**YOU**lous destination that I have envisioned for myself.

By detaching from the situation at hand and allowing myself to see my life through *her* eyes, I am always able to shift my perspective and gain a new appreciation for how far I've come in my life *and* get reinvigorated over the direction in which I am heading. Yes—I still need to tackle that laundry, but doing so no longer seems so insurmountable.

2) **Show yourself some love.** It never ceases to amaze me how something as simple as a manicure, massage or milkshake can give me a whole new outlook on life. Sometimes all I need is a little smidge of self-care to nourish my spirit and shift my perspective. I'm not suggesting a self-indulgent shopping spree that lands you deeper in debt here, but a small expression of self-love that you allow yourself to enjoy, can be just the thing that you need to pull yourself out of your tailspin and have you flying high again.

3) **Tune in.** If you've already read the *Your FabYOUlous Spirit* section of this book, you already know about the incredible benefits of meditation *and* you've read about creating your own sustainable meditation practice. Simply taking the time to get quiet and meditative can be just the thing that you need to open yourself up and receive the guidance and clarity needed in your situation. I am constantly amazed at how spending time in meditation can lead me to new insights and provide me with a renewed sense of purpose and perspective—even though I *am not* a new-age, hippie dippie wackadoo (no offense to all of my hippie dippie wackadoo friends—of whom I have *many*. I love you all!)

4) **Tune out.** This one goes hand in hand with the previous entry because in order to truly tune in to our inner guidance system, we must first learn how to tune *out* the outside interference that bombards us on a daily basis. For me, this means unplugging from social media, my phone

and other human beings and going for a run. It's hard to maintain a proper sense of perspective on life when we are constantly inundated with images of the Kardashians or caught up in the drama of Facebook politics. I know that this one can be tough if you (like me) tend to experience mini anxiety attacks whenever your phone is more than 10 feet away; but taking time to unplug and tune out, can result in countless benefits, including a restored sense of balance and a recalibrated perspective on life. Currently, I only practice this tuning out for an hour or so as I go for my evening runs; it helps, but my goal is to work myself up to an entire weekend without social media—we'll see if I can survive.

5) **Get a nature fix.** Nature is the ultimate soul soother and perspective fixer. Connecting with nature is a great way to tune out so that we can tune in. Nature has a rhythm all its own—seasons change, dawn follows dusk and the moon chases the sun across the sky. When we surround ourselves with nature, we allow ourselves to become a part of that rhythm. No matter how stressful or exhausting my week has been, it always seems less so when I'm stopped near the lake by my house watching the sun set behind the mountains in the distance. There is just something about the majesty of nature (be it a grove of trees colored with the beautiful hues of autumn or a dark, starry sky) that makes all of my problems or concerns seem far less significant than they did when I was trapped in my office with a slow internet connection and looming deadlines in my face.

6) **Lend a hand.** Nothing, and I mean *nothing* puts my life into perspective faster than coming face to face with someone who is less fortunate than I am. As an Executive Director for the American Red Cross, I see loss and devastation on an almost daily basis. Whether we are responding to a family who has lost everything in a house

fire or sending supplies and support to an area that has been wiped out by wildfires or flood waters, there is no shortage of people who are in dire need of assistance. Seeing the plights of these individuals and the odds that they are up against is such a humbling experience and *certainly* provides a huge shift in perspective. It's hard to grumble about unfolded (or unwashed??) piles of laundry when you've just met with someone who escaped rising flood waters with nothing more than the clothes on their back. If you are looking for an instant way to shift your perspective, try lending a hand to someone less fortunate than you. Donate some toiletries or paper goods to a homeless shelter, make a contribution to an organization like the Red Cross, or take a meal to a friend who is going through chemo. Reaching out to those in need is an incredibly powerful way to put your own life's challenges into proper perspective and leave you feeling abundantly blessed.

7) **Educate yourself.** Part of reformulating your perspective is educating yourself by looking deeply into a variety of sources and opposing views. Without being confrontational, ask someone with opposing political beliefs to explain to you their rationale behind their beliefs. Don't challenge them or judge them, just *listen* to them with the intention of *learning*. You can also use this "listen to learn" technique to diffuse an argument with your spouse or to gain understanding while working with a difficult co-worker. Becoming more educated might not necessarily cause you to change *your* perspective but it can help you to become a more tolerant individual as you gain a greater understanding for the perspectives of others.

8) **Change the meaning.** One very powerful lesson that I have learned in life is that experiences are only good or bad according to the way that we *choose* to define them. For example, most people would look at the period in my life

285

when I was sick and struggling with an emotionally (and sometimes physically) abusive marriage and debilitating eating disorder and call that a dark time in my life. For the longest time, I agreed with that assessment. Now however, I have learned to reframe that period of my life and view it instead as a *refining* period where I was able to break free from harmful influences, get the help that I needed and rebuild myself into a more competent, confident and resilient individual. I now know that if I *had not* gone through those difficult experiences, I never would have been free to experience the love, joy and success that makes up my current life. Yes, sometimes it takes a passage of time before we are able to add positive meaning to challenging circumstances, but doing so can radically alter our perspective and even provide comfort and meaning to otherwise difficult experiences.

By implementing several of these tips, I have already been able to feel a radical shift in my perspective and as a result have felt my stress levels abate and my sense of well-being increase. I'm sure that the same will be true for you and that you'll be feeling FabYOUlous again in no time.

Get Off the Hamster Wheel

Busyness. Why are we (and by we, I mean ME) so addicted to it?

Why do we feel like we have to constantly be busy as a way of proving our personal worth or justifying our right to exist?

We juggle careers, families, social obligations, volunteer work and a myriad of other things—all for the sake of feeling like we are "good enough" or in the hopes that others will take some kind of notice of our accomplishments. We feel as though being "busy" somehow proves just how important we are and we wear our exhaustion like it's some kind of twisted badge of honor.

Why do we do this? What exactly do we get as a result of all of this busyness?

For me, the answer is exhaustion, burn out, frustration and overwhelm.

I am blessed to be a naturally high-energy person, and yet there are still times when I find myself wiped out (sometimes even to the point of physical illness) from going a few too many rounds on the hamster wheel of life. I've learned the hard way that burning the candle at both ends simply means that you burn out a whole lot faster. Fortunately, I've also learned (out of a desperate fight for self-preservation) that there are ways to combat this insidious culture of *busyness*. The sanity saving strategy that works best for me when things get a bit too chaotic, is to step back and create space in six key areas of my life: my physical environment, my relationships, my emotional health, my thought-life, my finances and my spirituality.

By making the effort to create space in my life, I not only prevent the inevitable physical and emotional collapse that too much busyness precipitates; I also create an environment in which creativity, connection and serendipity can work together to bring about greater opportunities in my life. I am confident that the same will hold true for you.

Creating Space for FabYOUlousness

Physical Environment: Take a look around. Do your physical surroundings energize and inspire your or do they drain you? What things are you holding onto that you no longer need or that no longer serve you? Often, our outer environment is a reflection of what is going on inside of us. If our surroundings are disorganized and chaotic; there's a good chance that our inner being is experiencing the same kind of turmoil. Go through your closets and get rid of anything that you haven't worn in the past year (take your cast-offs to a thrift store or nonprofit organization so that others can benefit from your purging). Tidy up the desk in your office. Pick up the clothes on your bedroom floor. Do whatever you have to do to transform your physical space from chaos to calm. Make an effort to create your own personal oasis within your home.

By eliminating the clutter from our personal environments, we create space for positive energy and creativity. By only possessing items that we truly love and giving away the things that no longer serve us, we allow ourselves more freedom to truly enjoy our possessions while also blessing others with the things that we no longer want/use.

Relationships: Do you enjoy heartfelt connections with people who honor, love and value you? Do the people in your life lift you up and encourage your goals and aspirations or do their negative attitudes drain you of your energy and enthusiasm? Sometimes eliminating chaos in our lives means eliminating (or at least limiting) our connections to certain people.

As difficult as it may seem to create space within our relationships—it is vital for our emotional well-being and it frees us up to invest more time and energy into those relationships that are edifying and honoring to our spirits. Sometimes, we may even need to inject a little space into a relationship that is supportive and nurturing simply because we need to allow ourselves a bit more *alone* time. This is nothing to feel bad about or apologize for. Those who truly know us and love us will support our efforts to create a culture of calm as an antidote to the chaos of our busyness.

Emotional Health: How do you *feel* today? Whether we like it or not, emotions drive the majority of our thoughts and actions (this is especially true for women); therefore, it is important that we become emotionally intelligent and learn to manage our emotions so that they don't get out of control and take up too much space within our psyches. It is essential that we learn to recognize emotions for what they are—gauges of well-being and indicators of possible distress. There is nothing wrong with feeling our emotions—it is healthy to do so. The problem comes when we allow our emotions (which are not always logical or even based in reality) to spin out of control and take up more space in our lives than is necessary or healthy.

When I am consumed with *busyness*, I am at the greatest risk for losing a grip on my emotions. At times like these it is especially important for me to create space within my emotions by learning to observe them, feel them, allow them to flow through me (rather than taking up residence) and then *use* them to create new, more positive actions.

Thought Life: What do you spend your time thinking about? Are your thoughts positive and productive or do you have a negative tape that constantly runs through your mind with thoughts of lack, stress, frustration and overwhelm? The problem with an undisciplined thought life is that left unchecked, negative thoughts can blow up and squeeze out any positive thoughts that we might have. Not only that—negative thoughts also tend to be completely unproductive thoughts that rarely resolve anything and instead just perpetuate *more* negative thoughts.

Don't let unruly, negative thoughts get the best of you. T. Harv Eker, author of *Secrets of the Millionaire Mind* says that "what you focus on expands". This is why it is so crucial that we train our minds to focus on positive thoughts. We want our positive thoughts to expand so that we create space in our minds for intellectual stimulation and creative engagement.

Finances: How do you use your money? Are you making the most of your hard-earned dollars and being mindful with your resources? Or...do you have a mountain of debt that has left you feeling stuck and hopeless? Whether we like it or not, money is energy and our feelings about our money (or lack thereof) take up a lot of emotional and mental space.

If you are spending too much time and energy fretting about how you are going to pay the bills, it is time for you to take the necessary steps to create some space in this area of your life. Whether it is setting up a budget, tracking your expenses, hiring a financial planner or simply cutting back on your cable bill; creating space in this area can alleviate so much unnecessary stress and thereby open you up to more abundance and a sense of security.

Spirituality: Do you feel a connection to a Higher Power? Do you make time to practice your spirituality? Sometimes when I am experiencing a true crisis of *busyness* I tend to let my own personal spiritual practice fall by the wayside even though I know that it is precisely the thing that I need most, in order to once again create space and restore balance to my life.

Whether it's attending worship service, praying, meditating, chanting, reading scriptures, singing songs etc., it is this connection to something bigger than ourselves that can provide refreshment to our souls and cultivate an inner peace. Creating space to nurture our spirits will open us up to greater understanding and tranquility. It will also help us to hone our powers of intuition, recognize divine guidance and experience truly peaceful rest.

Once we take the steps to create some space in our hectic and chaotic lives, we will begin to understand that *busyness* is nothing but a symptom of a larger, more pervasive problem within our culture and that being *busy* doesn't necessarily mean being productive (like that hamster in the hamster wheel—always in motion but going nowhere). Creating space will allow us the time and perspective to make conscious and mindful choices about what we devote our time and energy to. It will allow us room to grow a life that is truly Fab**YOU**lous.

CULTIVATING COURAGE EVEN WHEN YOU THINK YOU CAN'T

I believe wholeheartedly that courage is the one attribute that can make the biggest difference when it comes to living our most Fab**YOU**lous lives. In fact, Winston Churchill called courage "the first human quality" because it is the one quality that guarantees all others. At the same time, however; I know from plenty of personal experience that courage can be so, so difficult to muster when faced with uncertainty and possible peril.

I distinctly remember the first time that I (as an adult) *really* pondered the notion of courage. I had made the decision to leave my dangerous marriage even though I knew that leaving would mean that I'd be fully responsible for providing a good life for my two little boys (my ex *barely* provided for them when we were married so I knew that he wouldn't pony up once we were divorced). A friend, who was helping me move into the little condo that I had rented, made a comment about how fearless I was. I remember how hearing that comment made me burst into tears and start sobbing (we're talking big, ugly, body wracking sobs here). My poor friend was beside herself trying to console me while also trying to figure out how something that was intended as a compliment could have upset me so much. When I was finally able to reign it in enough to talk, I explained to her that I most definitely was NOT *fearless*. At that particular moment in time, I feared *everything*. I was scared of being alone, I was scared of the unknown, I was terrified of not being able to financially support myself and my sons, I feared retribution from my soon-to-be ex and I was scared of being seen as a failure by my family and friends. I was the exact opposite of fearless—I was **fearful**, as in FULL OF FEAR.

That's when my sweet, and oh-so-wise friend said to me, "well in that case, you're something even better than *fearless*—you're *courageous*". She then sat me down, put her arm around me, handed me a box of tissues and explained to me that true *courage* is demonstrated in one's ability to push on *in spite* of one's fears; because let's face it—it doesn't take *courage* to do something that doesn't scare you.

Whoa.

That stopped me in mid-sniffle. I had amassed a lot of adjectives to describe myself over the years—but courageous was *never* one of them. And yet, sitting in my new little place surrounded by packing boxes with my two young sons playing in our new little (postage stamp sized) backyard; I, for the first time ever, began to see myself in a new light. Instead of the sad, beat down, broken spirited little victim that I had felt like for years; I now began to see myself as someone who was *courageous* enough to take the steps to remove my boys and myself from a sad and scary situation. I still had no clue as to how I was going to make everything work, but I was determined to press on despite my fears and uncertainties. I was (by my friend's definition) truly exhibiting *courage*.

That one courageous decision to take my life back all those years ago, has made all the difference in setting my boys and I on a solid path to FabYOUlousness. There certainly were difficult times (plenty of them), but throughout every ordeal, I forced myself to keep moving forward despite my fears. Now, I get to enjoy the benefits of living a full and FabYOUlous life of financial security, meaningful commitment to a man who is truly my partner *and* my love, career success and getting to watch my (now older, but still amazing) sons thrive in young adulthood. All of this is possible because of that one courageous decision that I made (albeit out of desperation) back when I was terrified to leave but *even more* terrified to stay.

This makes me wonder though...if courage is an attribute that has so much potential to so drastically alter our lives for the better, why is it such a struggle for so many of us?

Well, the answer to that question is simple. It is hard to be courageous because *fear* is such a powerful (though usually deceitful) force. In fact, I would dare say that fear, more than anything else, is what holds people back from making positive changes. We fear the unknown, we fear change, we fear failure, we fear pain, we fear heartbreak, we fear *so* many things and therefore we remain stuck in our "safe" little bubbles of predictability without ever experiencing the full range of our Fab**YOU**lousness. And yet, when we look at those people whom we admire and who have made significant contributions to society, we will see that they (like us) also experience fear—unlike us however; they have mastered the skill of moving *through* their fear into action. They have *learned* to be courageous.

Fortunately for all of us, courage isn't just something that you either have or you don't. Instead, courage is like a muscle—it can be developed and strengthened over time. You learned a few fear-busting techniques back in chapter 7 but here are a few more courage building strategies that you can add to your Fab**YOU**lous life toolbox. Try implementing these strategies in your own life so that the next time you *really* need to take courageous action, your courage muscle is primed and ready to go.

1) **Try something new.** Not every act of courage has to make you break out in a cold sweat. Try adding new experiences to your life that make you stretch just a bit out of your comfort zone. For me, this meant attending a blogging conference a few years ago even though Fab**YOU**lousLife.com was so new that I didn't even have

five posts on the site and I felt as though I was in completely over my head. That experience was so valuable to me though because it helped me to get my site started off on the right foot *and*, as a bonus, I met several other bloggers who have become mentors and friends.

No one likes to feel like an inexperienced newbie but the only way to become great at something is to *start* something. Yes, you'll face a learning curve and you'll screw up more times than you can count, but having the courage to start something new might just lead to your greatest breakthrough.

2) **Speak to someone you don't know.** Who knows? The woman beside you on the bus might just be an expert in the very skill that you are trying to learn—or at the very least, she might be able to tell you the best place in town for a decent calzone. Too often, we shut ourselves off from the world by burying ourselves in our smartphones thus missing the opportunity to connect with others. It takes courage (especially for those who tend to be more introverted) to strike up a conversation with a total stranger, but the benefits can be astounding. I have a good friend who met her amazing husband simply because she commented on his tattoo while they were both waiting in line at the grocery store—imagine if she had been too engrossed in Candy Crush to notice his ink.

3) **Express what is in your heart.** The word 'courage' comes from the Latin word 'cor' which means 'heart'. It makes sense then that expressing what is truly in our heart takes courage. All of us at one time or another have suppressed our feelings due to a fear of rejection or judgement. A good way to work our courage muscle however, is to start expressing ourselves more freely. Give your opinion when asked, dare to (respectfully) disagree with someone, ask the cute guy for his phone number,

stick up for someone who needs support. Yes—expressing yourself in these ways does mean that you will incur some risk and might be rejected or ridiculed; however, it also means that you are someone who has the courage to give voice to the things that matter to you. The more you learn to freely express that which is in your heart, the easier and easier it will become to do so.

4) **Analyze less, act more.** How do you enter a cold swimming pool? Do you ease yourself in slowly, inch by frigid inch or do you cannon ball yourself off the diving board? My parents have a swimming pool at their house so I've done plenty of both, and I can tell you from experience, jumping in will get you used to the cold water much more quickly than easing in will. I believe that the same is true when it comes to taking action. Obviously, it is important to assess any situation before we leap in (I've jumped into many a cold swimming pool in my lifetime but I would NEVER jump into a cold swimming pool full of hungry piranhas) but sometimes we are *too* cautious and err on the side of *over* analyzation. While there is nothing wrong with gathering data in order to determine the most prudent course of action, there does come a time when planning and analyzing become nothing more than a justification for procrastination. Flex your courage muscle by taking action on your dream rather than waiting around for perfect conditions—because the truth of the matter is, conditions will *never* be perfect.

5) **Embrace failure.** As you begin to act more courageously in your life, you will start to see your world expanding with new experiences and opportunities. You will also, however; experience more set-backs and failures. University of California, Davis professor Dean Keith Simonton explains that creative geniuses are prolific when it comes to failure—they refuse to allow their fear to stop them. They understand that failure is simply a part of the

success process rather than a defining factor of their work. In order to experience our most Fab**YOU**lous life, we must learn to be less afraid of failure because the more courageous action that we take, the more opportunity we will have to fail. On the other hand, the more courageous action that we take, the more opportunities we will have to experience success. Failure is not fatal, it is simply a learning tool on our way to success.

These five courage building steps will (if practiced on a regular basis) help to strengthen your capacity for courage so that when the time comes that you need to draw upon your courage reserves, there will be plenty there to utilize. Start exercising your courage muscle today so that it will be strong when you most need it to be. Having the courage to act in the pursuit of your dreams is one of the most surefire ways to reap the rewards of a truly Fab**YOU**lous life.

TURN YOUR JOKER INTO AN ACE
MAKE THE MOST OF THE HAND YOU'RE DEALT

"We are all faced with a series of great opportunities brilliantly disguised as impossible situations"

Charles Swindoll

If you got excited when you read the title of this chapter because you thought that you were *finally* going to get some advice on how to turn your goof of a boyfriend into a suave, debonair gentleman—I'm sorry to disappoint you. This chapter is *not* about changing your man. It *is* however, about changing your life circumstances, and let's face it—that's probably going to be a bit more impactful on your overall Fab**YOU**lousness levels.

We all know that life can be a bit of a roller coaster at times with both highs and lows. The highs are awesome—we're rockin' our job, our new boyfriend is *so dreamy* and every day is a good hair day. We are on fire and nothing can touch us.

Until it does.

Not only does it touch us—it straight up sucker punches us right in the kisser. The kisser that we are no longer using to kiss with because Mr. Dreamy left us to hook up with our best friend, which we are convinced is because we've let our hair get all frizzy and overgrown due to the fact that we can no longer afford to go to the salon because we got the axe during our company's last round of lay-offs.

Life is cake when everything is going well, but what do we do when things have gone awry? How can we turn things around and find some good in the crappy hand that we've been dealt?

One of my all-time favorite quotes is from the prolific, early twentieth century writer (and early champion of feminism), Virginia Woolf. The quote reads, "arrange whatever pieces come your way". I love this quote's matter-of-fact instruction to take whatever pieces that life throws at you and arrange them in such a way so as to make sense of them and create something positive. Now, as an English scholar who studied *way* more Woolf than any sane person should have to, I'll admit that I find it difficult to reconcile the fact that my favorite *inspirational* quote comes from a woman who tried to commit suicide at the age of 22 and later *succeeded* in that endeavor at the age of 59, but still…it's a great quote.

The ability to handle life's curve balls (and occasionally knock one out of the park) is a key component to living a truly Fab**YOU**lous life. The difference between being a *victor* and a *victim* lies within one's ability to take a bunch of crap and turn it into fertilizer. When we can use the painful and difficult trials that we experience as fuel for our personal growth, we can move through any type of hardship with grace and resilience.

When I find myself at life's poker table holding nothing but a hand full of jokers, there are three questions that I ask myself…

1) Is there something that I could've done differently to prevent this fiasco?
2) Is there anything that I can do right now to improve this situation?
3) What can I learn from this experience?

Typically, in asking these questions, I will discover that there usually isn't a whole lot that I can do with question number one. Yes, maybe I could have/should have done something different and (if that's the case) certainly, I *will* do things differently in the future—but often, difficult situations happen despite me having done all of the right things in all of the right ways. Life isn't fair and—like it or not—sometimes we end up facing hardships simply because of the "luck of the draw".

The second question is one that I can usually do a bit more with. No matter how bad an experience is or how unlucky I'm feeling, I can typically come up with a few things that I can do to improve either the situation *or* my reaction to it. If I'm facing a financial setback, I can tighten my belt, start clipping coupons or start looking for additional income opportunities. If I'm sick, I can go to my doctor, rest and take my vitamins. Even when I can't change the situation, I can meditate, journal, exercise or spend time with uplifting friends. These activities might have no impact whatsoever on my circumstances, but they most certainly will have an impact upon my state of mind *regarding* my circumstances.

The final question is the one that I can do the most with. All situations—good and bad—have so much to teach us. When we look at what's happening to us, around us or inside of us with the intention of obtaining wisdom, we will never be disappointed. The ability to gain and apply the wisdom gleaned during times of adversity is what sets us apart from those who never experience the fullness of a Fab**YOU**lous life.

In order to learn the valuable lessons found in adversity and thereby turn your joker into an ace, you'll need to develop your resiliency. Resilience (also known as grit) is the ability to bounce back from difficulties and transform adversity into opportunity. The more resilient we become, the less fearful we'll be of painful life experiences because we'll see them for what they are— opportunities to grow into the next, better version of ourselves. Here are some tips on how to facilitate that growth and more quickly turn that joker in your hand into an ace...

1) **Look for the lessons.** There is something that can be learned from virtually every situation that we encounter in life. When faced with a problem, choose to change the way

in which you view the situation. Instead of a "problem", see it as an opportunity that is strengthening you for future endeavors. This will allow you to constructively cope with the situation at hand while learning valuable lessons that will benefit you down the road.

2) **Take control of the elements over which you have power.** Granted, when faced with a negative scenario, there might not be a whole lot about the situation that you can control. However; researchers have found that optimism levels tend to be much higher in subjects who feel that they have a fair amount of control in their lives; therefore, in order to turn your joker into an ace, it is imperative that you take steps to control those things (no matter how few) that you can. At the very least, learn to control your reactions and attitudes toward what is happening. Additionally, you can take extra steps to control parts of your life that are not directly affected by the situation, i.e. self-care, personal development, relationships with friends/peers etc.

3) **Develop healthy coping skills.** We've all heard the old adage "life is 10% what happens to us and 90% how we react to what happens". Well, as cliché as it sounds—there is a lot of truth in this sentiment. Stocking your emotional toolbox with a selection of healthy coping skills that you can pull out and use when necessary is a key skill when it comes to turning your joker into an ace. A few coping mechanisms that you might want to include in your arsenal are: meditation, physical activity, staying connected to positive, upbeat friends, pursuing a range of hobbies and interests so that you are not consumed by the one difficult aspect of your life, leaning on your spirituality/faith, spending time with a beloved pet, getting an adequate amount of sleep and practicing gratitude.

4) **Change your language.** No, I don't expect you to start speaking Swahili or Hindi—I just want you to start using

the language that you *do* speak in a more beneficial way if you want to turn your negative situation around. A great deal of research has been done on the power of our words, and the result of that research shows that speaking just one negative word has the power to generate stress-producing chemicals in our brain which then manifests negative side effects throughout the rest of our body. Knowing this gives us a great advantage over those who don't understand the power of their words. This awareness allows us the opportunity to change the way that we speak about our circumstances. Try swapping the word "problem" for something neutral like "situation" or the word "mistakes" for "lessons". Another favorite phrase that I like to flip is "I have to". Instead, I try to say, "I get to". For example, instead of "I have to go for a five-mile run tomorrow morning", try, "I *get* to go for a five-mile run tomorrow morning…yay…" Okay, so maybe this strategy doesn't *always* work; still, it *does* work enough of the time that if used regularly, it can have a significant impact upon the way in which you view your situation.

5) **Stop the comparisons.** Here's a newsflash for you—no matter how rich, smart or good looking you are, there will always be someone out there who is richer, smarter and yes—even better looking. Holding your life and your accomplishments up against those of another is a bad habit that needs to be broken. One way to nip this comparison trap in the bud is to stop *idealizing* other people and start *humanizing* them instead. This simply means that you stop putting other people on a pedestal and instead understand that they (no matter how shiny and perfect they look on the outside) are human beings with flaws, fears and struggles—just like you.

6) **See the many shades of grey.** I'm not talking about the movie here (though certainly feel free to download and enjoy the movie if that's your thing—no judgement here, I

myself read the books). We are talking instead about the many, many variations that fall between black and white in life. When life is good, it isn't *all* good and when life is bad it isn't *all* bad. Don't let one rotten situation convince you that your entire life is rotten. It isn't. I promise. Yes, you may have one or two joker scenarios in your life that are stressing you out, but I *promise* you that you also have plenty of good things going for you. The more you see that things aren't just black or white, good *or* bad, the more you'll be able to keep things in perspective and keep from catastrophizing the negative. By focusing your time and attention on the *good*, you'll draw into your life *more* good to focus upon. That's how it works—every single time.

By taking the steps to develop a greater sense of resiliency, you'll find that you no longer live in a state of anxious dread, because you'll trust yourself enough to know that you can face any challenge when the chips are down and you're left holding nothing but a hand of jokers. You'll have the determination and confidence to play your hand as if it were full of aces.

THE POWER OF PURPOSEFUL PLAY

Way back in chapter two of this book, we discussed the importance of embracing your inner child and the value of adding purposeful play into your days. Well, now as we end this book, we've come full circle because we have come back to this notion play.

Unfortunately, for many of us, the concept of play is just that—a *concept*. We understand that incorporating time for leisure activities and fun into our lives is important, and yet despite this knowledge, we still have an incredibly difficult time actually *doing* it. If this is you, it is time to get over yourself and make play a priority. Here are a few suggestions to help you out...

1) **Stop "shoulding" on your play time:** Okay—we get it. You're a grown up and you have real responsibilities and commitments. Guess what...we ALL do. I am not suggesting that you shirk those important tasks or drop the ball on your obligations. I am simply suggesting that you incorporate more minutes of guilt-free play time into your day without dragging yourself down with all of the imagined things that you *should* be doing instead. Studies have shown that those who regularly incorporate scheduled play time into their daily routines are actually *more* productive than those who keep their nose to the grind-stone all day, every day; so, stop being a martyr and begin allowing your own emotional health to become a priority in your life. If a task is truly important—it *will* get done. If you allow yourself time to refresh and reinvigorate with some playtime, it will get done even *better*. Stop using

305

"busyness" as an excuse because there is always a way to make time for the things that are truly important. Your emotional well-being and enjoyment of life *are* worth *at least* the level of commitment that you give to your other tasks and responsibilities

2) **Adopt *PLAY* as a way of life:** Once we've set the intention of adding more playfulness into our days, we need to get serious about acting upon that intention. Usually, we go about living our lives, doing all of the things that we *need* to get done and then...if we have any time or energy left over, we *might* allow ourselves a little snippet of time to play. Unfortunately, this approach is (as my grandpa used to say) "bass ackwards". Instead of fitting some playtime in *if* we have a few extra minutes (because seriously—when is THAT ever the case?), we need to make an effort to schedule our pleasure and give it the same level of importance that we give to our "to do" list.

We can also find ways to add an element of play to our other less enjoyable chores. For example—I don't like to cook. I'm not particularly good at it and when I'm cooking I can always think of a bazillion other things that I'd rather be doing. However—since my family seems insistent on eating, I cook out of necessity. Reading, on the other hand, is something that I LOVE and that I could easily spend hours doing. I'd much rather read than cook but my family can't eat books, so cooking is something that I must do. Fortunately, modern technology has allowed me a way to incorporate my love of reading into my cooking time. I simply turn on the "read to me" function on my Kindle Fire and let my device read to me while I'm cooking. I've found that this simple playtime tweak has actually made my time in the kitchen something that I now look forward to...or at least *tolerate*.

3) **Play *your* way:** When it comes to play, we all have different styles. Every person was born with individual joy sparks that add fun and passion to what would otherwise be ordinary situations. My youngest son loves to strum his acoustic guitar and write his own songs, my hubby enjoys sports and lifting weights and my oldest son could spend hours tinkering on cars and planning camping expeditions. For me, playtime consists of reading, knitting, crocheting, writing, doing crossword puzzles and working on the Fab**YOU**lous Life website. I get teased sometimes because many of my play time activities tend to resemble those found in a home for the elderly—but I don't care. I know what kind of play brings me joy and that's all that matters. Don't compare *your* fun to someone else's fun. Just do what makes *you* happy. Sure—your friend's obsession with snowboarding might inspire you to try it out, but don't be discouraged if you're more of a "sit in the ski lodge, drinking hot cocoa and reading a good book" kind of person. Discover what type of play makes *you* come alive and incorporate more of *that* kind of play into your life.

4) **Slow down and simplify:** The idea of incorporating more play into your life *should* get you excited. Unfortunately; far too many people react to this concept with overwhelm instead of delight. This happens when people are so bogged down with never ending to-do lists, deadlines and obligations that adding more play into their life just sounds like one more chore that they don't have time for. Ironically, *these* people are the ones who most desperately need more play time.

If you feel like you might fall into this category, you are in serious need of simplification. To ease yourself into a more simplified way of life, try asking yourself these questions: What are your priorities? What excites you? What are your values? What drains your energy? What are you doing now that you *know* you need to stop doing? Are you watching too much TV/spending too much time online etc.? Are you spending your days the way that you *want* to be spending them? Take note of all the things that you are doing that drain your energy without feeding your spirit and see if you can eliminate or limit them. When we begin to simplify our lives, we naturally create more space in our lives for the things that bring us joy.

5) **Try some LSD:** Noooooooooo!!!! I do NOT mean the mind altering, illegal substance type of LSD—it may have helped to create some great music in the 60's but that is NOT what we're going for here. Instead, I mean the type of LSD that Steve Chandler, author of *100 Ways to Motivate Yourself*, refers to as Laughing, Singing and Dancing. One of the most energizing ways to incorporate play into our lives is to get up and get moving. I most certainly do not consider myself a good singer *or* dancer, and yet I love to do both. I am constantly getting busted by other motorists at stoplights when they look over and catch me rocking out to my favorite 80's hairband station. I also like to prance around the house to music whenever I get the chance. This (terrible) singing and dancing on my part always ends up leading to a fit of laughter—which is also good for us.

If dancing isn't your thing, that's fine—just find another form of physical movement that your body enjoys— hiking, surfing, roller skating, etc. I recently bought a bicycle (I hadn't owned one in over a decade) and have rediscovered the joy of the wind in my hair as I pedal my legs off. Not only is this type of physical activity good for our health, it's good for our psyche as well because it is just plain FUN.

6) **Simmer down:** Yes—getting physical and being loud (as outlined in the previous entry) can be a lot of fun, but so can quieter pursuits. As I mentioned earlier, I love to read, write, knit and crochet. These activities might not seem particularly "playful" but when I am doing them, I am flooded with feelings of delight and joy. It is the spirit of play that is flowing through me that matters.

   We *all* need moments of quiet play. It nourishes our spirits in a powerful way. If you find yourself constantly reaching for things that aren't good for you (sugar, caffeine, internet shopping etc.) it might be your spirit's way of reminding you that you need to spend more time in restorative play. We all have different needs and play types—some like more adventurous endeavors while others prefer quieter pursuits. Regardless of where you fall on the spectrum— quiet, mindful play is essential for emotional well-being.

7) **Go with the flow:** Making time for playful activities is an important step in creating a more playful lifestyle but don't get too hung up on the details. Maybe we *plan* to spend an hour knitting but the weather is nice and now a bike ride sounds more appealing—fine, go for a ride. Set aside time for play but don't be rigid when it comes to determining what type of play you're going to partake in. Maybe you'll feel like shooting some hoops with your daughter, maybe you'll feel like cooking a new dish for your family (yes—as hard as I find it to believe—some people actually *enjoy* cooking). Whatever playful feeling strikes you, go with it. Our bodies and spirits have an innate way of knowing what we need. If you feel a pull toward a particular playful activity, go for it. Spontaneity is good for us and allowing for some flexibility in our playful habits will help to boost the pleasure factor.

Regardless of what type of play you enjoy—be sure to make it a regular, on-going part of your life. Playfulness is one of the quickest, most direct ways to ditch the drab and find your **FAB**.

**"A playful path is the shortest
road to happiness"**

~Bernie DeKoven~

A Final Word

Whew. We made it. Thank you for taking this journey to your FabYOUlous life with me. It has been my extreme honor to walk this path with you.

If you've read the chapters and taken the steps outlined throughout the book, you are well on your way to reclaiming your FabYOUlousness and rockin' it for all to see.

Here's the thing though…the journey isn't over. Yes—you've come SO VERY far and I am so incredibly proud of you; but you still have steps to take and mountains to climb. You do, I do…we *all* do.

You see, a FabYOUlous life isn't something that you just accomplish one day and then check off your "to do" list. No, a truly FabYOUlous life is more like the north star, guiding you ever onward toward more fulfillment, more joy, more abundance and an ever-expanding sense of purpose in your life. You'll reach new heights only to discover (from your new, elevated vantage point) that there are previously unseen realms yet for you to explore.

Don't become complacent, don't get too comfortable. Stretch yourself, test your boundaries, push the limits, continue to grow.

If you find yourself feeling stuck or sidelined, go back to the chapter that addresses the issue that you are facing and work through the exercises again. Sometimes in life we have to repeat lessons in order to truly gain the wisdom that they offer.

Most importantly, as you continue on your quest and begin to enjoy the abiding fulfilment associated with your ever-expanding experience of FabYOUlousness; be willing to let your life serve as a beacon of hope to others who long to begin their own journey. Loan them this book (or better yet, buy them their own copy), offer words of encouragement, form an accountability partnership with them...do whatever you can to help them along their path. No candle ever became dimmer by lighting the wick of another. By offering your own light to those around you, you make this world an even brighter, warmer and more FabYOUlous place for all.

Thank you. I love you and I am grateful for the opportunity that I've had to cross paths with you. I don't believe in accidents but I absolutely believe in happy synchronicities; therefore, it is my belief that we were meant to travel this path together. May you be blessed with every step that you take and may your FabYOUlousness burn bright for all the world to see.

"At the center of your being, you have
the answer; you know who you are and you
know what you want"

~Lao Tzu~

"I have been a seeker and still am,
but I have stopped asking the books and
the stars. I started listening to the
teachings of my soul"

~Rumi~

Coming Soon

Finding Fab**YOU**lous Workbook & Journal

The Fab**YOU***list*: 365 Lists to Help You Ditch the Drab and Find Your FAB

For updates on these publications *and* the latest information on Fab**YOU**lous Life news and events, please visit *www.FabYOUlousLife.com* and subscribe to the mailing list

Follow the Fab...

www.Facebook.com/FabYOUlousLife

www.Instagram.com/FabYOUlous_Life

www.Pinterest.com/FabYOUlousLife

www.Twitter.com/FabYOUlousLife

#FindingFabYOUlous #FabYOUlousLife #SelfHelpwithSass

About the Author

From trainwreck to trainer, Melissa Venable has taken the ride, hit the bottom, done the work and risen from the ashes. She brings the agony *and* the inspiration from her experiences of wrestling with a life-threatening Anorexia Nervosa diagnosis and battling to escape an emotionally (and sometimes physically) abusive marriage; and delivers a message of hope, empowerment and love to women who long to rediscover and re-ignite their innate Fab**YOU**lousness.

As a coach, author and speaker, Melissa is the founder of the popular personal development website, FabYOUlousLife.com and has been featured on *Ewomen Network Radio* and in publications including *Mind+Body Magazine* and *Ladies Home Journal*. In 2015, she was honored as one of twelve *"Colorado Women of Vision"*.

For information on working with Melissa or to schedule a speaking engagement, please visit the contact tab at www.FabYOUlousLife.com